Dickens and Demolition

Edinburgh Critical Studies in Victorian Culture
Series Editor: Julian Wolfreys

Recent books in the series:

Rudyard Kipling's Fiction: Mapping Psychic Spaces
Lizzy Welby

The Decadent Image: The Poetry of Wilde, Symons and Dowson
Kostas Boyiopoulos

British India and Victorian Literary Culture
Máire ní Fhlathúin

Anthony Trollope's Late Style: Victorian Liberalism and Literary Form
Frederik Van Dam

Dark Paradise: Pacific Islands in the Nineteenth-Century British Imagination
Jenn Fuller

Twentieth-Century Victorian: Arthur Conan Doyle and the Strand Magazine, *1891–1930*
Jonathan Cranfield

The Lyric Poem and Aestheticism: Forms of Modernity
Marion Thain

Gender, Technology and the New Woman
Lena Wånggren

Self-Harm in New Woman Writing
Alexandra Gray

Suffragist Artists in Partnership: Gender, Word and Image
Lucy Ella Rose

Victorian Liberalism and Material Culture: Synergies of Thought and Place
Kevin A. Morrison

The Victorian Male Body
Joanne-Ella Parsons and Ruth Heholt

Nineteenth-Century Settler Emigration in British Literature and Art
Fariha Shaikh

The Pre-Raphaelites and Orientalism
Eleonora Sasso

The Late-Victorian Little Magazine
Koenraad Claes

Coastal Cultures of the Long Nineteenth Century
Matthew Ingleby and Matt P. M. Kerr

Dickens and Demolition: Literary Afterlives and Mid-Nineteenth-Century Urban Development
Joanna Hofer-Robinson

Artful Experiments: Ways of Knowing in Victorian Literature and Science
Philipp Erchinger

Victorian Poetry and the Poetics of the Literary Periodical
Caley Ehnes

The Victorian Actress in the Novel and on the Stage
Renata Kobetts Miller

Forthcoming volumes:

Her Father's Name: Gender, Theatricality and Spiritualism in Florence Marryat's Fiction
Tatiana Kontou

The Sculptural Body in Victorian Literature: Encrypted Sexualities
Patricia Pulham

Olive Schreiner and the Politics of Print Culture, 1883–1920
Clare Gill

Dickens's Clowns: Charles Dickens, Joseph Grimaldi and the Pantomime of Life
Johnathan Buckmaster

Victorian Auto/Biography: Problems in Genre and Subject
Amber Regis

Culture and Identity in Fin-de-Siècle Scotland: Romance, Decadence and the Celtic Revival
Michael Shaw

Gissing, Shakespeare and the Life of Writing
Thomas Ue

The Arabian Nights and Nineteenth Century British Culture
Melissa Dickson

The Aesthetics of Space in Nineteenth Century British Literature, 1851–1908
Giles Whiteley

For a complete list of titles published visit the Edinburgh Critical Studies in Victorian Culture web page at www.edinburghuniversitypress.com/series/ECVC

Also Available:
Victoriographies – A Journal of Nineteenth-Century Writing, 1790–1914, edited by Diane Piccitto and Patricia Pulham
ISSN: 2044-2416
www.eupjournals.com/vic

Dickens and Demolition

Literary Afterlives and Mid-Nineteenth-Century Urban Development

Joanna Hofer-Robinson

EDINBURGH
University Press

Edinburgh University Press is one of the leading university presses in the UK. We publish academic books and journals in our selected subject areas across the humanities and social sciences, combining cutting-edge scholarship with high editorial and production values to produce academic works of lasting importance. For more information visit our website: edinburghuniversitypress.com

Edinburgh University Press Ltd
The Tun – Holyrood Road,
12(2f) Jackson's Entry,
Edinburgh EH8 8PJ

First published in hardback by Edinburgh University Press 2018

Typeset in 11/13 Adobe Sabon by
IDSUK (DataConnection) Ltd

A CIP record for this book is available from the British Library

ISBN 978 1 4744 2098 3 (hardback)
ISBN 978 1 4744 6273 0 (paperback)
ISBN 978 1 4744 2099 0 (webready PDF)
ISBN 978 1 4744 2100 3 (epub)

Contents

List of Illustrations

Figures

Plates

Acknowledgements

As in *Oliver Twist*, the years I have spent working on this book have 'present[ed] the tragic and the comic scenes in [. . .] regular alternation' (p. 134). The completed project owes as much to the support of family and friends as it does to academic colleagues and mentors.

Dickens and Demolition developed from a PhD dissertation, supervised by Clare Pettitt, Alex Werner and, briefly, Josephine McDonagh. I am very grateful to them all for their time and advice during my four years researching and writing at King's College London. My sincere thanks also go to the Arts and Humanities Research Council (AHRC) and the Museum of London for funding this degree. The insightful comments of John Bowen and Lynda Nead during my *viva voce* examination helped me to start the process of revising the dissertation for a book, and contributed significantly to developing my academic work. After a period of juggling rewrites with various part-time jobs, the Irish Research Council's one-year Postdoctoral Fellowship then gave me time to return to the project in earnest. University College Dublin was a great environment for me to undertake this work in, but Nicholas Daly's generosity with his time and expertise was instrumental in giving it focus and direction.

Along the way I have been fortunate enough to have opportunities to discuss this project with friends and colleagues. I fear that if I try to name them all, the list would span several pages. However, special encouragement from the following people must be acknowledged: Niamh Campbell, Oskar Cox Jensen, David Evans, Elizabeth Evans, Scott Eric Hamilton, Nicola Kirkby, Beth Palmer, David Paroissien, Ruth Richardson, Frederik Van Dam, Catherine Waters, Emma Whipday and Julian Wolfreys. Finally, I must sincerely thank the staff at each of the archives I have used while researching this project, who have patiently answered my questions and given me the benefit of their advice. The archives are housed at: the British Library, Camden Local Studies and Archives Centre, Guildhall Library Archives, Huntington Library, Islington Local History Centre, London Metropolitan Archive, Museum of London, Southwark Local History Library and Archive, the Victoria and Albert Theatre and Performance Archives, and Westminster City Archives.

It remains only for me to thank my family and friends. In particular, I thank Ruth, Emma, Oskar, the Spooner family and my own – Viv, Kieran, Laura, Ella and Michael – who I have clung to through everything.

Series Editor's Preface

'Victorian' is a term that is at once indicative of a strongly determined concept and an often notoriously vague notion, emptied of all meaningful content by the many journalistic misconceptions that persist about the inhabitants and cultures of the British Isles and Victoria's Empire in the nineteenth century. As such, it has become a by-word for the assumption of various, often contradictory habits of thought, belief, behaviour and perceptions. Victorian studies and studies in nineteenth-century literature and culture have, from their institutional inception, questioned narrowness of presumption, pushed at the limits of the nominal definition, and sought to question the very grounds on which the unreflective perception of the so-called Victorian has been built; and so they continue to do. Victorian and nineteenth-century studies of literature and culture maintain a breadth and diversity of interest, of focus and inquiry, in an interrogative and intellectually open-minded and challenging manner, which are equal to the exploration and inquisitiveness of its subjects. Many of the questions asked by scholars and researchers of the innumerable productions of nineteenth-century society actively put into suspension the clichés and stereotypes of 'Victorianism', whether the approach has been sustained by historical, scientific, philosophical, empirical, ideological or theoretical concerns; indeed, it would be incorrect to assume that each of these approaches to the idea of the Victorian has been, or has remained, in the main exclusive, sealed off from the interests and engagements of other approaches. A vital interdisciplinarity has been pursued and embraced, for the most part, even as there has been contest and debate amongst Victorianists, pursued with as much fervour as the affirmative exploration between different disciplines and differing epistemologies put to work in the service of reading the nineteenth century.

Edinburgh Critical Studies in Victorian Culture aims to take up both the debates and the inventive approaches and departures from convention that studies in the nineteenth century have witnessed for the last half-century at least. Aiming to maintain a 'Victorian' (in the most positive sense of that motif) spirit of inquiry, the series' purpose is to continue and augment the cross-fertilisation of interdisciplinary approaches, and to offer, in addition, a number of timely and untimely revisions of Victorian literature, culture, history and identity. At the same time, the series will ask questions concerning what has been missed or improperly received, misread, or not read at all, in order to present a multi-faceted and heterogeneous kaleidoscope of representations. Drawing on the most provocative, thoughtful and original research, the series will seek to prod at the notion of the 'Victorian', and in so doing, principally through theoretically and epistemologically sophisticated close readings of the historicity of literature and culture in the nineteenth century, to offer the reader provocative insights into a world that is at once overly familiar, and irreducibly different, other and strange. Working from original sources, primary documents and recent interdisciplinary theoretical models, Edinburgh Critical Studies in Victorian Culture seeks not simply to push at the boundaries of research in the nineteenth century, but also to inaugurate the persistent erasure and provisional, strategic redrawing of those borders.

Julian Wolfreys

Abbreviations and a Note on Editions

Primary Texts

BH	*Bleak House*
DC	*David Copperfield*
DS	*Dombey and Son*
GE	*Great Expectations*
LD	*Little Dorrit*
OMF	*Our Mutual Friend*
OT	*Oliver Twist*

Dickens and Demolition chiefly discusses the afterlives of *Oliver Twist* that were produced between its serialised publication in 1837–9 and Dickens's death in 1870. Consequently, references to the novel will be drawn from a recent Penguin edition based on the original serial in *Bentley's Miscellany*, rather than the 1966 Clarendon edition. This is: Charles Dickens ([1838] 2009), *Oliver Twist*, ed. Philip Horne, London: Penguin Books. I feel that it is important to work from the original edition when studying appropriations of the novel dating from the time of its initial publication. References to other novels are likewise drawn from recent Penguin or Oxford World's Classics Editions.

Organisations

GBH	General Board of Health
MBW	Metropolitan Board of Works
MSA	Metropolitan Sanitary Association

Archives

BL	British Library
CLSAC	Camden Local Studies and Archives Centre
GLA	Guildhall Library Archives
ILHC	Islington Local History Centre
SLHLA	Southwark Local History Library and Archive
V&A	Victoria and Albert Museum Theatre and Performance Archives
WCA	Westminster City Archives

For my parents, Viv and Chris Robinson

Introduction

> What has become of the Saracen's Head on Snow Hill, where Mr. Squeers received his unhappy pupils, in 'Nicholas Nickleby'? Who can find the true 'Old Curiosity Shop' near Tower Hill, or Quilp's wharf, or the den of Fagin in Field Lane, or the scene of Bill Sikes' death at Jacob's Island in Bermondsey?[1]

Large-scale demolition and construction projects changed London's built environment profoundly over the course of the nineteenth century. Street layouts were altered, landmarks were removed, houses and businesses were torn down, and thousands of people were displaced. By 1894, when the *Illustrated London News* asked readers what had happened to Charles Dickens's London, the Saracen's Head and Field Lane had been cleared to make way for new infrastructure, and Jacob's Island had been redeveloped to improve its previously insanitary conditions. Dickens reinforced received ideas about the cultural and social identities of these places when he chose them as the setting for plots dealing with nefarious characters or underhand activities. For many middle-class readers, these place names would have evoked dangerous associations from Newgate novels or newspaper reports about crime or prostitution. Yet despite the wider notoriety of many slum areas, later commentators often used Dickens's characters and stories as representational devices to crystalise and convey their negative connotations, and to talk about the physical redevelopment of the cityscape.

The imaginative and the material intertwine in the *Illustrated London News*'s representation of London's modernisation in the above quotation. On the one hand, the journalist's fictional referents articulate how embedded social, cultural or historical associations are challenged by physical changes to the built environment, which destroy or alter prior landmarks or pathways. The pattern of rhetorical questions reinforces her or his disorientation in the modern city when familiar sites are removed. But, on the other hand, Dickens is evoked as a common property through which readers can envision themselves as part of a richly historical and integrated urban matrix. It allows readers to conceive London's past and present in reference to shared images of an imagined history, and – in so doing – to see themselves as part of an established community. Indeed, the utility of Dickens for constructing broader spatial or communal identities is evident in the material legacies of his fiction in London's built environment. Although real places like Field Lane, Jacob's Island and the Saracen's Head no longer exist, originally fictional sites have been constructed in London. A shop that calls itself the Old Curiosity Shop can be found on Portsmouth Street by Lincoln's Inn Fields, for instance. Alternatively, Dickens's urban legacy is visible in the streets and buildings that have been named after him and his creations. The *Illustrated London News* is right to note that there is no Quilp's Wharf adjacent to the River Thames, but there is now a street named Quilp Street nearby in Borough.[2] The commercial and emotional appeals of literary tourism are certainly motivations for reinforcing, even building, links between Dickens's fiction and London's built environment, and the journalist's comment that there is no 'true' Old Curiosity Shop emphasises that contemporaries recognised the curatorial practices of literary space-making in London. Nevertheless, Dickens's novels also provided a symbolic vocabulary through which contemporaries with a public voice could conceptualise and represent the concurrent erasure of parts of the urban scene while appearing to retain clear links to Old London.

London's modernisation was far from wholesale in the mid-nineteenth century, but this does not mean that its effects were insignificant. Even before any centralised body was established to oversee the building of city-wide infrastructural reforms, new roads, railways, docks and housing expanded the city's perimeters, and substantially reorganised or demolished central districts. In some cases, the necessity for change was obvious. Natural growth and mass inward migration from rural England and overseas meant that the metropolitan population increased rapidly during the nineteenth century, and put further pressure on already inadequate resources. Urgently needed sanitary and housing reforms drove large-scale urban developments, as well as opportunities for capital venture. Unlike the systematic rebuilding of Paris under Haussmann, London's modernisation was gradually effected by competing, rather than integrated, initiatives, planned by private speculators, the crown and various government bodies. Although commonly described as 'metropolitan improvements', the term encompassed diverse projects and processes, from the building of new housing and infrastructure, to the demolition of areas that were euphemistically labelled 'nuisances'. So, while the terminology used to conceive of such alterations implies a linear, developmental narrative, in fact it refers to piecemeal, even overlapping, construction and destruction.

Londoners inhabited a city in which progress and stasis, past and present, were visibly entwined.[3] Recent urban historians, including Lynda Nead, Billie Melman and James Vernon, have recognised that the past was paradoxically present both in the material processes of modernisation in the mid-nineteenth century and in its imaginative representation. London's heterogeneous architecture and living conditions drew the close juxtaposition of old and new buildings, infrastructure and technologies into focus. The modern city sat closely and uneasily beside older buildings and areas, and cycles of economic boom and bust meant that some new projects were mothballed and, remaining incomplete, fell into disrepair themselves. Meanwhile, as Nead has usefully shown, Victorians referred to bygone versions of the city to 'conceptualise its present [and] future', even as modernity, in its simplest form, was conceived as a break with the past.[4] *Dickens and Demolition* builds on this scholarship to argue that history was not the only frame of reference used by nineteenth-century commentators to understand and articulate London's fragmented modernisation. As the quotation from the *Illustrated London News* indicates, fiction also offered a rich store of recognisable imagery and descriptive forms through which contemporaries conceived and represented metropolitan development. Conversely, it was not only literary allusions that were employed retroactively as a species of historical documentation against which the modern city could be compared. Fiction was also repurposed to campaign for specific material alterations to the cityscape.

Dickens and Demolition argues that Dickens has a material legacy that is traceable in London's built environment. The book analyses debates surrounding large-scale urban demolitions and reforms in the mid-nineteenth century, and tracks a Dickensian vocabulary in these discussions across multiple media and fora, including written commentaries, parliamentary debates, theatre and the visual arts. In so doing, it shows that tropes and extracts from his fiction were repeatedly mobilised to articulate and negotiate contemporary anxieties about London's built environment and linked social problems. The word 'tropes' indicates the flexibility with which later users appropriated characters or imagery from Dickens's works to convey their own opinions about how and where London's built environment should be changed. For, while tropes are 'expressions that have a figurative meaning', they can effect a decisive journey away from their original context, and in so doing be used to generate differently nuanced cultural connotations.[5] In this way, other commentators used Dickens's works as a representational or rhetorical toolkit that could be mobilised in diverse ways to persuade their audience of the benefits of specific reforms. In one of Dickens's obituaries from 1870, for example, *Harper's Magazine* calls for the demolition of Field Lane to be completed. 'The wretched inhabitants can not at all understand why they should be occasionally subjects of curious inspection. They are clearly unconscious of their fame, and have never heard of "Oliver Twist".'[6] Field Lane is the site of Fagin's den, and the writer's reference to the novel reinforces its perceived criminal identity to support his argument for its destruction. This is not to say that readers credulously accepted either Dickens's descriptions or rhetorical references to his fiction as realistic accounts of contemporary metropolitan conditions. However, Dickens's fiction certainly provided a symbolic vocabulary that later users appropriated to identify, categorise and explain why specific areas should be improved.

Of course, the potential instrumentality of Dickensian tropes to spur metropolitan change was affected by broader financial and material contexts, and so I do not suggest that a direct line can be drawn between the representation of dilapidated conditions or social problems in Dickens's works and urban creative destruction. Indeed, later users often ignore the nuances of Dickens's expansive social and environmental vision. Dickens presents London as a palimpsestuous assemblage of multiple kinds of spaces and temporalities in his fiction. In *Dombey and Son* (1846–8), for instance, cutting-edge railway technology and its impact on London's built environment is anachronously portrayed through timeless fairy-tale imagery. Trains are anthropomorphised as 'tame dragon[s]' and – following its demolition – Staggs's Gardens is eerily recast as a 'vanished land', even while its destruction is envisioned as progressive urban renewal (*DS*, p. 234). By contrast, as in *Harper's Magazine*, later users tend to favour more straightforward representational modes, through which they can clearly state their reasons for campaigning for improvement. Still, the frequency with which Dickensian tropes were appropriated as a way of talking about London's modernisation in the nineteenth century signals their rhetorical effectiveness. Commentators repeatedly mined his texts for imagery through which they could consolidate, articulate and communicate opinions about London's development and associated social problems.

Throughout *Dickens and Demolition*, I trace two major trends in how mid-nineteenth-century commentators mobilise Dickensian tropes in improvement debates. First are the ways that his fiction was used to construct or define cultural and spatial identities in advance of demolitions. Alongside the demand for improved living and working conditions, it was commonly believed that social problems such as crime were environmentally determined. Later users isolate individual characters from novels as representative figures of these issues, and deploy them as a symbolic shorthand to convey (usually negative) cultural meanings. Dickens's characters are then associated with specific places, so marking these locales as 'problem' districts in need of reform. Vignettes or descriptive passages were likewise extracted from Dickens's texts to represent the social or environmental conditions of particular areas, or to support and authenticate the user's own portrayal. Gareth Stedman Jones and Anthony Wohl have already suggested that there was a link between Dickens's, and other popular writers', depictions of London's slums and actual improvements in these areas. In *Outcast London*, Stedman Jones notes that the locations of fictional tales of crime and violence accord with later demolitions, literature having highlighted them as dangerous areas.[7] Supporting Stedman Jones's analysis in *The Eternal Slum*, Wohl states that Dickens's fiction strengthened social prejudices against slum-dwellers because situating criminal characters in such places reinforced existing trends in sociological mapping.[8] Although users often mobilise Dickensian tropes for rhetorical effect, rather than interpreting his fiction as a realistic account, allusions to his works nevertheless had a generative impact on London's improvement because they were used to identify which areas should be reformed and to argue for the benefits of their demolition.

Second, I explore how later users mine Dickens's novels for images of London's past to describe changes that had already occurred or were partially complete. Fiction became part of the dialectical relations between past, present and future, through which London's modernisation was conceived and represented. Sometimes users repurpose Dickensian tropes to justify the extent of demolitions in particular areas. At other times, as in the *Illustrated London News* article, his fiction is evoked nostalgically to memorialise a bygone version of London. The literary is superimposed to implant cultural memories by constructing coherent, apparently historical images of areas of the city that had been effaced by demolitions. In 1925, George Gissing commented that Dickens 'taught people a certain way of regarding the huge city, and to this day how common it is to see London with Dickens's eyes'.[9] Such a tautology has this opinion become that, noting how a cache of Dickensian tropes still inform many public representations of Victorian London, Judith Flanders has gone so far as to suggest that 'Dickens created London as much as London created Dickens.'[10] However, considering the ways that his works were redeployed to argue for or against specific improvements, and how his fiction was used to conceptualise London's past and its modernisation, we can indeed catch glimpses of the surprising practical effects of Dickens's fiction.

Measuring how instrumental Dickensian tropes were in driving metropolitan improvements is complicated by the diverse ways in which his work was appropriated and repurposed by other people. Dickensian allusions were not stable or singular, but positioned source texts in dialectical relations with changing social, political and environmental contexts. Single characters or descriptive passages became porous complexes of different, competing agendas. For example, Bumble was multiply utilised in parliamentary speeches in the latter part of the nineteenth century. He is evoked in discussions about how to persuade the poor to attend church services in 1860, as a symbol of institutional cruelty in a debate about housing reforms for the working class in 1867, and to advocate the proper auditing of local councils in 1899.[11] Given this multiplicity, applying Foucauldian theories to such evidence or contending that Dickensian tropes are performative is inappropriate for this study.[12] The unsystematic deployment of Dickensian rhetoric indicates that its potential to drive material change in London depended on who witnessed or mobilised later allusions. Improvements were approved by known boards and individuals. Each demolition or development had to be authorised by the passing of a specific parliamentary bill and obtain financial backing before it could go ahead. This means that later users had opportunities to repurpose Dickensian tropes as targeted persuasive devices. Simultaneously, however, Dickens's writing helped more generally to stir a groundswell of public feeling, which contributed to convincing certain Londoners that improving specific places would ameliorate urban conditions, as connections linking social problems with particular slum spaces cut across both fiction and non-fiction. As Mary Hammond has rightly argued, then, cumulative or repetitive occurrences of literary tropes can still reveal 'potentially significant patterns', in spite of the diverse cultural meanings that Dickensian afterlives were used to express.[13]

Dickens and Demolition attends to the variety of ways in which Dickens's fiction was appropriated, remediated and repurposed by examining the rhetorical strategies employed by each afterlife individually, and with an awareness of its intended audience. Afterlives are linked cultural products or expressions, inspired by, but not replicating, an original source. Examining where, how and by whom Dickens's fiction was repurposed in discussions about London's improvement reveals how widely literary afterlives proliferated in high-level fora, such as parliamentary debate and the press, and how frequently such allusions were deployed by people who had the power to influence or implement urban change during Dickens's lifetime. It is part of the project of this book to suggest that tracking Dickensian tropes exposes relations of power underpinning the production of London's built environment. Juxtaposing a macro view of the socio-historical contexts of mid-nineteenth-century improvements with close analysis of non-literary texts and images, then, *Dickens and Demolition* examines how literary tropes were used to address and persuade the people who had opportunities to influence urban change, while excluding the slum-dwellers who were directly affected by the destruction of their homes and communities.

The frequently abstract and mobile ways in which later users made fiction intersect with commentaries on metropolitan development did not necessarily limit its effectiveness. Over recent decades, urban theorists have contended that cities are not stable settings for human spatial practices. Instead, they are always unfinished products of multiple, overlapping, even chaotic social processes. Henri Lefebvre, for instance, insists that space comes into existence through dialectical interactions between three conceptual models for thinking about space: spatial practice, representations of space and representational spaces, which he defines as a 'triad of the perceived, the conceived, and the lived'.[14] In other words, abstract ways of thinking about space cannot be separated from its physical forms, or how people engage with their environment in everyday life. According to Lefebvre, the production of space is the result of unruly interactions between multiple social processes, and so does not follow a coherent or totalising logic, even though it remains fundamentally politicised because of the power and capital relations embedded in social practices and relations. If we conceptualise space as a product of competing processes, the fact that Dickensian tropes were not deployed systematically in mid-nineteenth-century improvement debates is not a barrier to its rhetorical or material instrumentality. As Lefebvre puts it, '[w]e may be sure that representations of space have a practical impact, that they intervene in and modify spatial *textures* which are informed by effective knowledge and ideology'.[15] Indeed, it is in the dissimilarity between appropriations of Dickens that we can perceive the ways in which later users manipulated fiction to promote various agendas and representations of space. Tracking Dickensian tropes in improvement debates thus reveals traces of the competing social processes that shape urban space. Their variety gives textual form to opposing pressures and interests that contributed to forming London's built environment.

Today, it is easiest to locate the material afterlives of Dickens's fiction in the preservation of historic buildings, or in retrospective reimaginings of the built environment for literary tourists. The heritage industry has responded to Dickens's enduring popularity by repurposing sites connected to his biography. For instance, his former home on Doughty Street in London has been transformed into the Charles Dickens Museum. Additionally, connections to his life and œuvre have contributed significantly to campaigns to protect historic buildings. Ruth Richardson's recent efforts to save the Cleveland Street workhouse from redevelopment were materially assisted by her discovery of its association with Dickens.[16] Still further material afterlives are locatable in the byways and buildings that have been named after the author and his characters. There are several Dickensian street names near to where the Marshalsea Prison was previously located in Borough, for example, including Weller Street and Little Dorrit Park. The names pay tribute to this area's significance to Dickens's biography, but also evoke a sense of historical continuity that is mediated by the author and his works.[17] Noting similar reuses of Walter Scott's fiction, Ann Rigney contends that fictional soubriquets are 'a way of implanting a sense of history' in urban environments and 'flagging a collective affiliation to an imagined history'.[18] However, *Dickens and Demolition* is not a tourist book that maps literary London; nor does it chart how Dickensian spaces have been curated in the city. Instead, drawing on memory studies scholarship, which insists that forgetting is equally as important as remembering, this book will propose that Dickensian afterlives are traceable in what is missing, as well as what remains.

By locating Dickens's material legacy in areas of London that have been demolished, as well as those that have been preserved, this book emphasises how imaginative worlds linger in physical spaces in unexpected, practical ways. In so doing, *Dickens and Demolition* extends the parameters of what we conceive as literary afterlives. This is already a broad field. In addition to how fiction is embedded in the physical world through streets signs and heritage sites, afterlives can take the form of various cultural products and experiences. Dickens's life and works have inspired a plethora of theatrical, film, television and digital adaptations.[19] There is a veritable industry of 'Dickens tourism', including guided walks, dedicated museums and major exhibits. Artists and businesses have traded on his popularity, and 'Dickensiana' ranges from fine art paintings, such as Robert William Buss's unfinished *Dickens's Dream*, to the detailed Pickwickian handkerchief held in the Museum of London's collections,[20] to Charles Dickens board games.[21] There are also, of course, whole library stacks dedicated to the 'posthumous repackaging' of Dickens's novels in new editions, and the critical books that this study joins.[22] In addition to such material traces, Dickensian allusions have been absorbed into common parlance. Dickens's obituaries note that, even during his lifetime, his writing had come to '[mingle] with our daily converse and our daily life, where he finds admittance with more freedom than Shakespeare, and with greater facility than Solomon'.[23] Sentimental though this assertion certainly is, it is indicative of how Dickens's popularity causes his afterlives to multiply and diversify. It supports David Brewer's claim that readers' tendency to expand imaginatively on the lives of fictional characters reveals widely held assumptions that novels are 'the common [imaginative] property of all'.[24] Consequently, Dickensian afterlives are characteristically miscellaneous, and continue to diversify as more and more people produce and consume them.

Criticism that 'seek[s] to understand what ideological needs [literary afterlives] serve' by tracing the 'cultural history' or 'social life of texts' has been influenced by scholarship on cultural memory.[25] Cultural memory is a 'heuristic tool with which to describe how stories about the past emerge as common points of reference and, in the process, help to define collective identities'.[26] However, while literary afterlives, such as naming streets after fictional characters, can contribute to implanting a sense of shared history or cultural heritage, the different ways that texts are reimagined in multiple media means that literary afterlives simultaneously reveal that these cultural memories are far from stable. Drawing on recent memory studies scholarship, which conceptualises memory through dynamic, multiple and ongoing processes 'of remembrance and forgetting',[27] emphasises the 'active role' played by media 'in shaping our understanding of the past',[28] and insists on the 'transcultural' mobility of memory,[29] current critical works on literary afterlives have taken a broad historical and geographical scope. Ann Rigney's, Mary Hammond's and Juliet John's important works – *The Afterlives of Walter Scott*, *Charles Dickens's Great Expectations: A Cultural Life* and *Dickens and Mass Culture*, respectively – all trace the international proliferation of fictional afterlives, and stress their 'portability' across various media and contexts.[30] Or, to use Paul Davis's term, they examine afterlives as porous and changeable 'culture-texts', which are continuously reimagined and updated.[31] *Dickens and Demolition* joins these studies in exploring how literary afterlives have been consciously mobilised by later users to convey specific socio-political meanings. Yet, while I acknowledge Dickens's longstanding international significance and the importance of transcultural research,[32] my narrower focus on how Dickensian afterlives were deployed to comment on London's improvement in the mid-nineteenth century reveals specific material and human consequences of literary appropriation.

For the former inhabitants of slum areas, demolition meant displacement. Tenants were given scant, if any, compensation, and little appropriate housing was built to accommodate the people who were forced from their homes. Contrary to Dickens's humanitarian ideals and reputation as a social reformer, afterlives of his fiction in mid-nineteenth-century improvement campaigns were, in fact, used to rationalise the unjust treatment of the poor. This paradox is brought into focus with hindsight; at the time, however, improvements were frequently conceived as beneficial to both the poor and the wealthy. Aside from removing dilapidated and insanitary housing, slum clearances were also seen by many wealthier contemporaries as a way of combating urban social problems. Not only were slums perceived to be refuges for criminals, but also it was feared that their overcrowded living conditions brought members of the respectable poor into companionship with dangerous people. The dispersal of slum communities was presented as a measure to make the city safer and to protect law-abiding people from being drawn into illegal activities. Given the inadequate supply of affordable housing for the poor, in reality slum-dwellers were forced to pack even more closely into remaining tenements when their homes were demolished, and at higher rents driven by increased demand. Appropriations of Dickensian tropes to argue for the benefits of proposed demolitions, or to justify why prior slum clearances were necessary, thereby implicate afterlives of his novels in facilitating forms of social injustice that we now perceive as opposite to Dickens's broadly humanitarian ethos. Conversely, Dickens's own approach to metropolitan improvements in his work is predictably difficult to categorise.

Dickens's fiction and journalism are replete with descriptions of various forms of urban development, through which he examines its potential to ameliorate and to exacerbate social problems. Particularly in his advocacy of sanitary reform, Dickens joins his contemporaries in viewing certain demolitions as necessary interventions.

Nevertheless, he also notes that improvements frequently failed to deliver the progress promised by developers. In 'On Duty with Inspector Field' (1851), for instance, Dickens angrily complains that 'we make our New Oxford Streets, and our other new streets, never heeding, never asking, where the wretches whom we clear out, crowd'.[33] Yet despite observing the injustice of mass displacement, Dickens's ire is tempered by his awareness that slum conditions were awful, caused untold suffering and could not remain unchecked. 'How many, who amidst this compound of sickening smells, these heaps of filth, these tumbling houses, with all their vile contents, animate and inanimate, slimily overflowing into the black road, would believe that they breathe *this* air?'[34] The description evokes contemporary theories that disease was spread by contaminated air known as miasma, and so emphasises that destruction of insanitary areas is needed to ensure good public health. Demolition is not the real evil in this article. Instead, the poor are portrayed as subjugated by bureaucratic muddle – 'Red Tape' – that delays the amelioration of these sites, or the building of suitable accommodation for the displaced.[35] Dickens draws attention to the human consequences of different kinds of improvements, as well as the human imperatives that allowed demolitions to be conceived as essential changes. In this, 'On Duty with Inspector Field' reveals his nuanced engagement with London's chaotic, sometimes unsuccessful modernisation in the mid-nineteenth century.

In a recent *Dickens Quarterly* article, Trey Philpotts likewise argues that Dickens responds dynamically to London's improvement because it

> forces two of [his] most cherished ideas into direct and dramatic conflict. On the one hand, we have his deep sympathy for the plight of the poor, and the imaginative engagement with their dispossession, and, on the other, his abiding faith in technological and civic improvement.[36]

By examining Dickens's journalism and his description of railway building in *Dombey and Son*, Philpotts usefully demonstrates that these texts answer evolving contemporary attitudes to various forms of urban improvement, as well as reacting to specific projects. None the less, as Chapters 4 and 5 of this book discuss, Dickens also repurposed his fiction selectively to comment on, or drive, metropolitan change. Similarly to other appropriators, Dickens recognised that tropes, descriptions or characters from his fiction could be redeployed as rhetorical or representational tools, and used them to reinforce his arguments for the urgency of specific reforms or philanthropic projects. Moreover, he attempted to direct how other people interpreted intersections between his writing and contemporary urban problems: for instance, by reframing early works with new paratextual material that highlighted how his older writing could be applied to updated cultural contexts. Despite Dickens's participation in mid-nineteenth-century improvement debates, and his efforts to influence how his works were used to comment on contemporary reforms, however, Dickensian afterlives remained multivalent and messy.

Dickens's novels were brought into dialogue with numerous and ongoing processes of de- and refamiliarisation when later users plundered and variously interpreted his fiction to serve different agendas. It is because of this alternation between recognisability and difference that David Bolter and Richard Grusin's concept of remediation has been useful to the development of this study. Remediation is a way of theorising transmediality, which, though inspired by the development of new digital media, has its genealogy in earlier forms of intermedial exchange: for example, in the adaptation of texts for the visual arts, or the realisation of fine art paintings as dramatic *tableaux*.[37] The reason that remediation is significant to this book is because Bolter and Grusin insist that our experiences of transmediality are predicated on 'oscillation' between immediacy (the suspension of disbelief) and hypermediacy (an awareness of media) – otherwise the interactions between audience immersion, the progenitor and its new versions.[38] Bolter and Grusin's concept is pertinent to examining the different ways in which Dickens was appropriated and revised for multiple media because it shows how apparently derivative cultural products can be referential to the original, as well as being new. In this sense, Dickensian afterlives can powerfully convey topical or political inflections because remediation permits familiar and novel points of reference to be evoked simultaneously. In other words, the imaginative associations that specific references to Dickens's works evoke – such as criminality or violence, when mentioning Bill Sikes – are juxtaposed with the afterlife's new context to illuminate nuanced cultural meanings.

Prior studies of literary afterlives have similarly drawn on remediation as an appropriately broad term to denote, rather than to delimit, the various and surprising ways in which literary texts are fragmented and reformed, reimagined and transplanted into new contexts and media. Hammond, for instance, sees remediation as a concept through which critics can

> consider the cultural (including industry-motivated) uses to which [novels] ha[ve] been put without [being] shackl[ed] either to technological determinism or to fidelity criticism, which has tended to judge all adaptations

> through the lens of their likeness to an ('the') original text [and] to think about the cultural event [. . .] not as an immutable work of art to be kept behind glass and admired from a distance, [. . .] but as an Ali Baba's cave of treasures which can be [. . .] plundered at will.[39]

Like literary afterlives themselves, the concept of remediation remains dynamically open to refiguration, and so allows literature's ephemeral or allusive traces to be analysed through a logical terminology. It rightly shows that it is not always easy to distinguish absolutely between different genres of afterlives, such as adaptations or appropriations. Nevertheless, working from critical texts such as Gérard Genette's *Palimpsests* and Julie Sanders's *Adaptation and Appropriation*, *Dickens and Demolition* employs a differentiated terminology where possible to explore the diverse social and ideological work that afterlives perform, and how the cultural meanings they can convey alter over time and between media. For example, between the 1840s and 1860s, illustrators for *Punch* appropriated the character of Fagin individually from *Oliver Twist* (1837–9) for multiple political cartoons. Even though the subjects of their satires were as dissimilar as the 1848 French Revolution and the 1867 Reform Bill, each evoke Fagin's characterisation in the novel to convey and reinforce offensive anti-Semitic stereotypes.[40] These xenophobic overtones were later somewhat neutralised by Ron Moody's performance in Carol Reed's 1968 film of Lionel Bart's musical adaptation *Oliver!*,[41] yet alongside the lapse of over one hundred years, another reason why the character's Jewishness is re-presented differently in the later afterlife is because Reed's film is in a different mode to *Punch*, as well as a different style. Adaptations differ from the selective appropriation of a single passage or character because they exhibit a sustained engagement with their source narrative. Unlike plagiarisms, adaptations of literary works require the text to be moved into a different medium, meaning that the story must be revised at the same time that it is remediated. Consequently, adaptations allow opportunities for substantial and internally coherent adjustments to the whole, such as Moody's amusing interpretation of Fagin. Recent adaptation theory thereby stresses that adaptation is an essentially ongoing process of textual renewal. Still, the mobility and flexibility of appropriations are, as Sanders explains, even 'less straightforward', as 'appropriation frequently affects a more decisive journey away from the informing source into a wholly new cultural product and domain', even when it preserves well-known aspects of its original.[42] Denoting the selective repurposing of textual elements, such as characters or imagery, the parameters of users' engagement with the source in appropriations shift each time to produce polymodal afterlives. The variegated terminology I use in *Dickens and Demolition* thus seeks to indicate how Dickens's works were multiply repurposed in relation to London's improvement, and the many media and fora in which the city's social and environmental conditions were discussed.

For readers who are unfamiliar with the historical contexts underpinning London's improvement in the mid-nineteenth century, Chapter 1 offers an account of the processes and problems of improvement during Dickens's lifetime. Addressing the fragmentation of the built environment and the diversity of actors and institutions who commented on and influenced metropolitan developments, it suggests that the haphazard nature of improvement in the mid-nineteenth century dovetailed generatively with Dickens's style and popularity, and that this enabled his works to be used effectively to promote urban change. Conversely, returning to focus specifically on Dickensian afterlives, Chapter 2 considers early theatrical adaptations of *Oliver Twist*. Analysis of dialectical relations between the text, the *mise en scène* and theatrical ephemera reveals that, even before the novel was complete, it was already being reimagined by other users to promote a variety of agendas and mediate different images of the city. These findings are taken up in the final three chapters, which present case studies exploring how Dickensian afterlives variously intersect with representations of, or campaigns for, the demolition or development of specific places: Field Lane, Columbia Square and Jacob's Island. Each of these chapters emphasises the diversity of Dickensian afterlives and of the actors involved in the improvement of these sites, including government representatives, journalists, philanthropists and Dickens himself. Despite Dickens's direct interventions in the Columbia Square and Jacob's Island developments, however, the case studies reveal that the manner in which Dickens's work was mobilised by other people was often very different to how he self-consciously constructed his fiction as an agent of reform. Therefore, *Dickens and Demolition* argues that Dickens's fiction was used to negotiate manifold interactions between the physical and the symbolic, and sees Dickensian afterlives as traces of the social processes that shape urban space.

Dickensian afterlives still proliferate in debates about London's built environment today. Does the public not often hear politicians and commentators labelling unsuitable or unhealthy living conditions 'Dickensian', despite the mutability of that term?[43] Therefore, one of the difficulties in critically examining Dickensian afterlives in improvement debates is how to avoid stating the self-evident – *of course* Dickens has been used to talk about London! Another challenge is to avoid making claims that are beyond the power of ephemeral archival evidence to measure empirically. Nevertheless, the sources presented in this book – gleaned from a combination of digital and material archives – prove that literary referents were repeatedly redeployed as persuasive tools and used to shape representations of the city. It is in the frequency of such literary allusions that *Dickens and Demolition* establishes its claims. Even though archives can never provide a full record, the quantity of surviving afterlives testifies to how prolific these descriptive or rhetorical techniques were, both during the execution of specific improvements and for a long time after these projects were complete.

Locating Dickens's material legacy in places that have been substantially destroyed or rebuilt enables us to perceive the impact his works have had on how London's cityscape and history have been conceived, for, where demolished sites that have been (and still are) commonly associated with, and represented through, his works – like Field Lane and Jacob's Island – Dickensian simulacra have come to stand for their cultural history. It is difficult to find traces of the actual people who lived in these areas but Dickensian afterlives survive in abundance. Therefore, despite Dickens's reputation as *the* champion of the urban poor, Dickensian afterlives implicate his work first in displacing members of London's poor population, and then in obscuring these people from view, as living memories are replaced by literary characters and imagery.[44] It is easy to see different ways in which Dickens haunts London's cityscape, but his is not the 'Shadow' he imagined would 'go into any place' to expose its inner workings.[45] Instead, Dickensian afterlives contribute to constructing both imaginative and material versions of London by erasing or supplanting what or who was there before.

Notes

1. Anon. (1894), 'The Last of Doctor's Commons', *Illustrated London News*, 2898, 2 Nov., p. 555.
2. Situated close to the previous site of the Marshalsea prison, where Dickens's father was imprisoned for debt during Dickens's childhood, the name Quilp Street responds to both his fiction and his biography.

3. Billie Melman summarises that 'Improvement and the demolition of places and remnant of an ever-present past made up what recent historians of urbanism have recognized as a distinctly British form of modernization, at its most characteristic in London' (p. 94).
4. Nead, *Victorian Babylon*, p. 5.
5. Erll, *Memory in Culture*, p. 96.
6. Thomas Bucklin Wells (1870), 'Footprints of Charles Dickens', *Harper's Magazine*, 41, New York: Harper and Brothers, pp. 610–16, p. 612.
7. 'It is noticeable that the street clearance of the 1840s and 1850s included nearly all the quarters embellished with surreal horror by literary imagination' (Stedman Jones, *Outcast London*, p. 180).
8. 'In a period when the extent of overcrowding among "respectable" working men was unknown, and attention was drawn by Dickens and journalists to the great, notorious criminal rookeries of St Giles, or Jacob's Island in Bermondsey, it was readily assumed that where slums existed they were the haunts of the morally depraved only and the inevitable consequence of grave personal failings' (Wohl, p. 8).
9. George Gissing, '*Oliver Twist*', in Dickens, *Oliver Twist: Norton Critical Edition*, pp. 421–5, p. 424.
10. Flanders, p. 12.
11. *Hansard*, 3rd ser., vol. 186 (12 Apr. 1867), c. 1639; *Hansard*, 3rd ser., vol. 160 (22 Aug. 1860), c. 1700; *Hansard*, 4th ser., vol. 67 (23 Feb. 1899), c. 404.
12. Examining allusions to Dickens's works as a 'performative' practice is inappropriate because the cultural meanings they conveyed were so flexible and often addressed a specific group. Nevertheless, performativity theorists draw attention to 'the role of witness in constituting the space of the speech-act', which usefully emphasises that the degree to which Dickensian afterlives contributed to arguments for specific material change depended on where they were articulated, and to whom they were addressed (Andrew Parker and Eve Kosofsky Sedgwick, 'Introduction: Performativity and Performance', in Parker and Sedgwick (eds), pp. 1–18, p. 11).
13. Hammond, p. 65.
14. Lefebvre, p. 39.
15. Ibid., p. 42. Italics in original.
16. When Richardson joined the campaign to save the workhouse in 2010, English Heritage had already recommended that the building should be listed, yet this had been refused by the government minister responsible at that time. Richardson explains that '[a] ministerial decision cannot be appealed without "*substantive*" new evidence and [at first] we had nothing to add' ('At the Workhouse on Cleveland St', *Spitalfields Life* (para 7 of 17). Italics in original). Richardson's discovery of the connection between the workhouse and Dickens's biography was a game-changer. 'We knew that we now had something of inestimable value with which to defend the Workhouse' (*Dickens and the*

Workhouse, p. 25). Indeed, a second petition saw part of the building receive Grade II listed status because of the association. However, a Certificate of Immunity was not issued for the rest of the site and, at the time of writing, the site is again under threat of redevelopment.

17. Dickens's father was imprisoned in the Marshalsea in Dickens's boyhood, during which time Charles was forced to live separately from his parents and work in Warren's Blacking Factory. Dickens remembered this period throughout his life as one of acute childhood suffering.
18. Rigney, p. 1.
19. For instance, the *Dickens: Dark London* app produced by the Museum of London in 2011, or Dickens's guest appearance as a character in the computer game *Assassin's Creed.*
20. London, Museum of London, 94.164. *The Pickwickians* (c. 1839–45), commemorative handkerchief.
21. For instance, Oliver Twister and The Dickens Game.
22. Hammond, p. 54.
23. Anon. (1870), 'Saturday Morning, June 11', *Glasgow Herald*, 9498, 11 Jun., p. 4.
24. Brewer, p. 2.
25. Hammond, pp. 2–3; Rigney, p. 19.
26. Rigney, p. 17.
27. Astrid Erll and Ann Rigney, 'Introduction: Cultural Memory and its Dynamics', in Erll and Rigney (eds), *Mediation, Remediation, and the Dynamics of Cultural Memory*, pp. 1–14, p. 2.
28. Ibid., p. 3.
29. Erll, 'Travelling Memory', p. 15.
30. John, *Dickens and Mass Culture*, p. 17.
31. Paul Davis, p. 4.
32. There is scope for further research into how transcultural Dickensian afterlives have been associated with the construction of built space. In his article for *Harper's Magazine* in 1870, for instance, Thomas Bucklin Wells suggests that Dickens's *American Notes* 'was the first thing that led to the improvements of a region which had become almost impassable – which have ended in the railway [built in Northern Virginia]' (p. 612).
33. Dickens, 'On Duty with Inspector Field', p. 267.
34. Ibid., p. 265.
35. Ibid., p. 265.
36. Philpotts, 'Dickens, the Metropolis and the Railway', p. 339.
37. See Meisel.
38. Bolter and Grusin, p. 19.
39. Hammond, p. 11.
40. Anon. (1846), 'The Royal Fagin of France Instructing His Boys', *Punch*, 3 Oct., p. 138; Anon. (1847), 'The Fagin of France After Condemnation', *Punch*, 2 Oct., p. 124; Anon. (1867), 'Fagin's Political School', *Punch*, 9 Nov., p. 188.

41. Sharon Aronofsky Weltman has argued that Moody's portrayal has contributed significantly to a cultural reassessment of Fagin, which has resulted in the iconography of the musical's advertising posters and logo being developed to reinforce the character's central role in the adaptation. The part has since become a star vehicle (p. 378).
42. Julie Sanders, p. 26.
43. During a debate about a housing bill in the House of Commons in 2004, for instance, 'Dickensian' was used three times by two different speakers. The word's adjectival connotations are taken to be self-evident, and it is applied to discuss legislation passed twenty years after Dickens's death, the Housing and Working Classes Act of 1890 (*Hansard*, vol. 416 (12 Jan. 2004), c. 591). In press reports, too, 'Dickensian' is a commonly used adjective. For instance, a recent *Guardian* headline repurposed the word for an international context, proclaiming that 'Dhaka's Dickensian workhouses should shame us all' (Elliott). Nevertheless, 'Dickensian' is not a stable term. At the British Association for Victorian Studies conference in 2016, Holly Furneaux chaired a round table that explored how the word can imply varied descriptive meanings and be encoded with gendered or national connotations.
44. I will explore this in more detail in Chapter 5.
45. Dickens, '*To* John Forster [7 October 1849]', *Letters, Volume Five*, pp. 621–3, p. 622.

Chapter 1

Charles Dickens and Metropolitan Improvements

London was a very different city at the end of the nineteenth century from what it had been at the start. Suburban expansion pushed the city's perimeter outward in every direction. Dilapidated inner-city areas were cleared to make way for new housing, commercial buildings and infrastructure. Monumental architecture was built to reflect, and help to construct, London's identity as the capital of an empire. Even the colours of the city changed. Alongside the century's eclectic use of architectural styles, building materials were updated and Londoners saw street scenes alter 'from brown brick to brawn and red, then to red; from Portland stone to granite or Mansfield or to red or buff terracotta'.[1] The streets were also much busier, as the metropolitan population was swollen by mass inward migration from rural England and overseas, as well as natural growth. In the term commonly used by nineteenth-century commentators and developers, London was improving. However, progress was slow. Large-scale demolitions, supposed to make room for new construction, in fact created sites that resembled wastelands in the heart of the city. Owing to delays, obstructions from local government, or the mothballing of partially complete projects, these liminal spaces occupied central districts for long periods. For example, the whole of the Farringdon Street area was cleared in the mid-1830s and remained undeveloped for more than thirty years, becoming known as 'Farringdon Waste'.[2] Connoting both a barren, alienating space and the mismanagement of resources, the name preserves derisive popular responses to metropolitan improvements that coexisted with the positive claims of their backers. Still, calls for better living conditions and infrastructural development in the mid-nineteenth century resulted in more demolition. Figure 1.1 gives a snapshot of further destruction near to Farringdon in the 1860s. Henry Flather's photograph depicts railway navvies building the underground Metropolitan District railway line,

Figure 1.1 '"Dipping" under Blackfriars Bridge: c. 1869' (Source: © Museum of London. IN37543).

using the 'cut-and-cover' method, which dug up roads so that tracks could be laid below street level. It was taken from the west side of Blackfriars Bridge, looking north-east towards St Paul's Cathedral, which can be seen in the background.[3] The photograph thus gives a perspective on how, in the mid-nineteenth century, monumental architecture, and the technological advances represented by railway construction, sat uneasily beside vast and visible disordered spaces, and by remaining slums, which were often made more noticeable by the destruction of other buildings that had previously masked them from view. Contrary to teleological narratives of improvement, the effects of this creative destruction on London's built environment were multiple and uneven.

The cultural phenomenon called Charles Dickens coincided with this period of extensive development in London, and contemporaries quickly recognised that his novels provided imaginative resources for conceptualising and representing the city's modernisation. In 1858, Walter Bagehot famously commented that the form and style of Dickens's novels were

> especially suited to the delineation of city life. Everything is there, and everything is disconnected. [. . .] he does not care to piece them together. On the contrary, each scene, to his mind, is a separate scene, each street a separate street.[4]

Bagehot suggests that Dickens's novels mirror the diversity and fragmentation of Victorian London. For, in addition to Dickens's metropolitan subject matter, the multitude of characters that people their pages, and their episodic form, evoke overcrowded and often incoherent urban spaces. As this chapter will go on to explore, it is because of Dickens's style, as well as his London focus, that contemporaries frequently repurposed tropes or passages from his fiction to enable their own representations of the city. Conversely, the disorderliness praised by Bagehot was often lost in these later appropriations. Unlike Leo Mellor's argument in *Reading the Ruins* – which contends that fragmentary forms in modernist literature gave readers the imaginative resources to understand London's war-torn cityscape after the Blitz – mid-nineteenth-century users of Dickens treated his novels as a store of widely known imagery that could be superimposed on to the urban environment in order to represent the city as a known space, rather than to express its physical disorder or unpredictability.

Dickensian afterlives provide one means for other people to bridge an affective gap between portraying London effectively, and the vastness and complexity of its human and built environment. In other words, Dickensian afterlives make London 'legible'.[5] Kevin Lynch introduces the concept of urban legibility in *The Image of the City*, and stresses its importance to the everyday spatial practices of individuals, as well as to city planners.

> Just as this printed page, if it is legible, can be visually grasped as a related pattern of recognisable symbols, so a legible city would be one whose districts or landmarks or pathways are easily identifiable and are easily grouped into an over-all pattern.[6]

Legibility allows individuals to navigate the city. It facilitates interactions between people: for instance, by enabling separate parties to find their way to, and identify, pre-arranged meeting points. But legibility also responds to 'the need for identity and structure in our perceptual world'.[7] Therefore, Lynch's concept has both practical and emotional applications, for, in addition to finding one's way around the city, legibility allows individuals to perceive their spatial practices as embedded in an interconnected matrix. Through this, we can more fully realise the terrain because we can conceive our relation to other people and between different places. Claiming that Dickensian afterlives make London legible is not equivalent to stating that people try to plot London cartographically in reference to Dickens's fiction, though many maps of Dickens's London have been produced for literary tourists over the past two centuries. Rather, literary allusions and descriptive passages provide a toolkit of widely 'recognisable symbols' that can be used to 'identif[y]', categorise and explain the social or environmental conditions of specific urban areas.[8]

Dickens and Demolition argues that contemporaries with public voices mobilised tropes, extracts and characters from Dickens's fiction to persuade their audiences of the benefits of improving specific places in London. This chapter, however, focuses on why Dickens's writing was particularly apposite for appropriation in mid-nineteenth-century discussions about London's improvement in public fora, such as press commentaries and parliamentary debates. Further, it asks why contexts of urban development at this time allowed Dickensian afterlives to enter generatively into processes of spatial production. It is hoped that this chapter will provide an introduction to contexts of London's improvement during Dickens's early career for readers who are unfamiliar with how dramatically the city changed, despite bewildering systems of governance and obstructions from vested interests. In particular, it focuses on the period between Dickens's first publications in the 1830s and the establishment of the Metropolitan Board of Works (MBW) in 1855. As the next section will go on to explore, these decades differ from other phases of urban development in the city. Building on the many fine histories of London in the nineteenth century that are already available,[9] I draw attention to London's fragmented administrative structures and culture of *laissez-faire* speculation to show how a multiplicity of interests competing to develop in the period contributed to the haphazard modernisation of the city. Significant to the argument of this book is the fact that heterogeneous interactions between competing interests allowed unlikely actors to influence contemporary urban change. Administrative practices were less formalised prior to the centralisation of improvements under the MBW. This opened opportunities for individuals to intervene in processes of urban development – as members of parliamentary or local government boards, businessmen, philanthropists, commentators or campaigners. In addition to London's material disarray, this miscellany of actors and processes meant that the ability to construct and convey coherent images of the city and its redevelopment was a valuable skill.

Dickens's career dovetailed with this administrative and physical disorder. But more than simply overlapping with these contexts, his unique style, popularity and London focus allowed contemporaries to repurpose his works as representational or rhetorical tools to debate metropolitan improvement, or to represent current urban change clearly. In so doing, users mobilised Dickensian afterlives to enable discussion about large and complex social problems, to make their critiques more pointed and memorable, or to make the built environment or contexts of its improvement legible.

London Improvements

London was never laid out according to a coherent plan. Even after the Great Fire of 1666, Christopher Wren's idea to redesign the street plan in *étoile* formations was disregarded in favour of individualistic development. Metropolitan alterations continued to be haphazard and *laissez-faire* for much of the nineteenth century. In *London in the Nineteenth Century*, Jerry White distinguishes different stages in London's development, based on who planned and funded large-scale improvements. He states that, during the Georgian period, private venture led functional developments like dock expansion, while the crown initiated new streets and monumental architecture.[10] Arguing that public feeling was against such grandiose projects, White suggests that in 1830, on the death of George IV, 'the reign of the retrencher and the tightwad – who had agitated from the wings for many years – began'.[11] In other words, local government took on a more formative role and prioritised budgetary control above aesthetic embellishment in municipal architecture.[12] Still, more widely, post-Georgian developments were eclectic and often elaborate in style.[13] This diversity was partly due to the fact that there was no unified London authority until the London County Council was established in 1888. Officially, 'London' referred only to the City of London, the area administrated by the Corporation.[14] Meanwhile the crown and private speculators continued to develop other areas of the city. The nineteenth-century capital is best understood as a series of distinct, if connected, localities, administered separately by different bodies.

One of the reasons why development was protracted and piecemeal in London is that developers were required to negotiate with numerous actors before and during processes of construction. Multiple land laws had built up over the course of centuries to ensure continuity of ownership by landed dynasties, charities and religious bodies.[15] Private and public developers faced the daunting task of ascertaining who owned the land and negotiating its purchase, as well as providing businesses with compensation for lost trade. Various government bodies also had to be consulted before any new development could go ahead. Developers had to secure the support of central government, as parliament had to pass a specific bill to approve each improvement, but improvers also required authorisation at a local level. Particularly in the first half of the nineteenth century, a plethora of local administrative bodies operated simultaneously. As James Vernon explains,

> New systems and jurisdictions were layered on top of, and did not replace, older ones. By 1835 a single locality could come under the multiple jurisdictions of the parochial church vestry, the manorial court leet, justices of the peace, the country quarter sessions, the town council, and the poor law union.[16]

This heterogeneity of competing interests and coexisting administrative bodies meant that improvements were often localised in the first half of the nineteenth century, as spanning parish boundaries created further difficulties and opportunities for obstruction.

As is still the case today, there were wide discrepancies in living conditions between different areas. Civic improvements, such as sewerage networks and some new roads, were planned and implemented by local vestries, and so were confined to parish boundaries. The vestries who regulated sanitation and poor relief varied in effectiveness, but they also had different amounts of money at their disposal, having to fund these local initiatives through the collection of poor rates. The process of implementing civic improvements changed when the MBW was established in 1855. While the advent of centralised administrative procedures in the mid-nineteenth century did not prevent individuals from influencing the course of urban development, it did levy certain controls on previously fragmented and heterogeneous procedures. The MBW had the power to override parish borders, the authority of their vestries, and the claims of hereditary land ownership through compulsory purchase. However, while the MBW made significant changes to London's cityscape, their remit remained far from comprehensive and local disparities remained.

Periodising London's improvement in the nineteenth century into three phases, as White does, superimposes a systematic order on to processes that were actually overlapping, even chaotic. It erroneously implies that London's development was experienced as a linear progression. Instead, we should remember Lynch's assertion that in a city '[n]othing is experienced by itself, but always in relation to its surroundings, the sequences of events leading up to it, the memory of past experiences'.[17] This is powerfully illustrated in Flather's series of sixty-four photographs documenting the construction of the Metropolitan District

Figure 1.2 'Construction of the Metropolitan District Railway' (Source: © Museum of London. IN37487).

Railway. In Figure 1.2, for example, up-to-date railway technology (the steam-powered crane in the centre of the image), Georgian-style buildings, and the subterranean strata that were playgrounds for antiquarians are juxtaposed. Spaces above and below street level, signifying different time zones – from the city's Roman past to its modern present – are visible simultaneously. Creative destruction exposed the built environment's palimpsestuous layers to view, even while improvements were conceived as forward progress. Demolitions thus created material disorder akin to the 'rubble-heap' that Walter Benjamin's Angel of History contemplates in horror, rather than a linear historical narrative.[18] Nevertheless, White's periodisation helpfully draws attention to shifts in procedure. Through this, we can see that widespread material disarray created a demand for legible representation simultaneously with a time when *laissez-faire* development and fragmented administrative structures permitted unlikely actors to influence debates about the city's improvement. The impact such actors had on the built environment was sometimes considerable for, while improvements were erratic, the scale of projects could be vast.

Flather's photographs illustrate that improvements created material disarray in the centre and peripheries of London. Spanning large areas, these demolitions created vast and visible liminal spaces, which were hard for Londoners to avoid. In this image, the trench being dug so that tracks can be laid below street level nearly reaches the doorways of surrounding houses and shops, and can be crossed only by wooden planks thrown across the cutting as walkways. Meanwhile the properties just outside of the frame on the left-hand side are ominously propped up with wooden struts, as though threatening to fall into the crevasse at any moment.

Housing

London's rapid population growth in the first half of the nineteenth century made the demand for housing acute. In the 1840s alone, famine in Ireland, European revolutions and rural poverty in Britain meant that London's populace was swollen by an influx of around 250,000 migrants in addition to natural growth.[19] Attempts to accommodate large inflows of people were effected in part by the expansion of London's suburbs, although this was patently inadequate. A comparison between maps produced in 1836 and 1847 reveals the extent of suburban expansion in the mid-nineteenth century (Plates 1 and 2). On the 1836 map, north London extends to Islington, yet developments to the north of the New Road (later Euston Road) are still sporadic. On the south side of the Thames, development is less expansive, and the open spaces of Lambeth and Walworth indicate that these districts are not yet densely inhabited. The 1847 map, on the other hand, captures a version of London that has increased in size and density in every direction. Both the population and the city continued to expand with unprecedented speed during the 1850s and 1860s. Natural growth and migration into London increased over subsequent decades. Census returns reveal that between 1851 and 1871, London's population had grown by 892,024 people, making the city's populace around 3,254,260 in 1871, the year after Dickens's death.[20] The map in Plate 3 depicts London in 1876, and shows that new building had continued to widen London's perimeters, and pack further developments tightly into the central districts throughout the middle decades of the century. However, supply still did not keep pace with demand, and overcrowding in working-class dwellings exacerbated the poor sanitary conditions in many areas of the city.

One reason why suburban expansion failed to address the housing crisis adequately was that it was accompanied by the mass demolition of central London slums. Slum clearances aimed to upgrade living conditions by rehousing slum residents in modern suburbs, but these improvements in fact resulted in mass displacement, as little appropriate accommodation was built to replace the housing that was destroyed. Between 1851 and 1871, the number of inhabited houses was reduced from 14,580 to 9,415 in the City alone, mostly to make way for new roads and railways.[21] Although, as the maps demonstrate, London's East End was gradually extended to accommodate working-class families, this new housing was not always suitable, as many poorer people living in central locations subsisted on casual labour. Casual labourers had to reside close to their workplace because securing employment on any given day depended on arriving early in the morning to be on hand to do whatever work was required. Walking for miles on the off-chance of being hired simply was not practical. Even where transport infrastructure was sufficiently advanced to carry labourers across suburbia's sprawling topography, railway travel was prohibitively expensive until workmen's fares were introduced in 1860.[22] People were forced out of their homes, only to be compelled by necessity to pack even tighter into the already overcrowded neighbouring tenements that remained, and at higher rents driven by increased demand.[23]

Slum tenants were usually displaced without any provision for alternative accommodation or financial compensation in the first half of the nineteenth century.[24] Practices began to change in 1853, when a bill was passed requiring Demolition Statements to be submitted prior to any new development. These gave details about the number of people under threat and how they might be assisted; nevertheless, any restrictions imposed through this new protocol remained easy for developers to overcome.[25] In fact, slum clearance was often seen as beneficial for both their inhabitants and wealthier members of society. In addition to the desire to remove insanitary and unfit living conditions, slum clearances were impelled by widely held beliefs that social problems were environmentally determined. As Gareth Stedman Jones explains in *Outcast London*, slums were regarded with fear because their labyrinthine road networks made them difficult to access and police.[26] Slums were also associated with outbreaks of epidemic disease that threatened the whole city. According to contemporary theories about the spread of disease through contaminated air, slums were dangerous because their densely inhabited and confined courts prevented healthy ventilation. Consequently, the promise that a development would eradicate existing slum conditions was often used as a tactic by private venture capitalists to garner parliamentary support for their endeavours in this period.[27]

The frequent failure of improvements to better the lives of London's populace is explored in *David Copperfield* (1849–50). David and Mr Peggotty discover a mothballed housing development when they follow Martha to the banks of the Thames. Forestalled before its completion, the 'carcases of houses, inauspiciously begun and never finished, [rot] away' (*DC*, p. 685). Dickens's description emphasises that environmental amelioration is not guaranteed by improvements, and that unsuccessful capitalist speculation worsens already insanitary conditions in certain districts. In this scene by the Thames, 'the ground [is] cumbered with rusty iron monsters of steam-boilers, wheels, cranks, pipes, furnaces, paddles, anchors, diving-bells, windmill-sails, and I know not what strange objects, accumulated by some speculator' (*DC*, pp. 685–6). The site is left disordered and uninhabitable. However, Dickens goes on to reveal that London's modernisation remained uneven, even when improvements were successfully implemented.

Disjointed development meant that new streets were built in close proximity to remaining slums, where conditions further degenerated as a result of increased overcrowding. Consequently, modern housing could fail to attract or retain wealthier tenants. Stuccoed town houses replaced dilapidated slums, but these improvements were impermanent and large dwellings were partitioned into tenements or communal dwellings. Sometimes the housing cycle was completed within a single generation.[28] In *David Copperfield*, Martha's lodgings in Golden Square represent the end of a housing cycle. '[T]he houses were once fair dwellings in the occupation of single families, but have, and had, long degenerated into poor lodgings let off in rooms' (*DC*, p. 721). Dickens picks up on widespread contemporary beliefs in the environmental determination of social problems when he metaphorically aligns Martha's lodgings with her 'fall' into prostitution: 'she beckoned me to follow her up the common staircase, which was like a tributary channel to the street' (*DC*, p. 721). The house evokes Martha's physical vulnerability as a prostitute, as it is overcrowded and permeable to intrusion from outside elements or persons. Dickens thus represents such improvements as superficial. The social problems or illegal activities that demolition and new building were supposed to address continue to be practised in the sites that replaced slum housing. Thus Dickens emphasises that urban space is produced by multiple, dialectical interactions between human spatial practices and urban planners.

Infrastructure

Infrastructural development profoundly altered London's suburban and central districts in the first half of the nineteenth century. Railway building began to carve paths through the dense urban fabric as early as the 1830s, when the Greenwich and Blackwall line was built. Although parliament generally resisted petitions from developers to extend tracks into central London up to the 1850s, the pace of railway construction accelerated in the 1840s and demolished vast areas in the course of its progress. The London and South Western Railway, for instance, affected over 2,000 properties, of which 700 were demolished, when the line from Nine Elms was extended to Waterloo on the south bank of the Thames in the mid-1840s.[29] Dickens describes one such railway clearance in *Dombey and Son* (1846–8). The scene is likened to a 'great earthquake', which has 'rent the whole neighbourhood to its centre' (*DS*, p. 68). The destruction makes the built environment illegible, and 'wholly change[s] the law and custom of the neighbourhood' (*DS*, p. 68). The effect is disorientating and Susan Nipper gets lost when she tries to return to this Camden locale later in the novel, only to find that 'There was no such place as Staggs's Gardens. It had vanished from the earth' (*DS*, p. 233). *Dombey and Son* follows contemporary progress narratives, which conceive demolition as part of a creative process of urban amelioration. A more prosperous and genteel area takes the place of Staggs's Gardens, and the former residents largely benefit from the railway: 'the master chimney-sweeper, whilom incredulous at Staggs's Gardens [. . .] now lived in a stuccoed house three stories high' (*DS*, p. 233). Nevertheless, the destruction itself is portrayed as chaotic, meaning that subsequent progress is presented as a happy accident, rather than a logical and planned conclusion.

Although civic improvements tended to be localised until the MBW was established in 1855, private venture spurred large-scale construction and destruction. Other big infrastructural developments could be found down river, where dock building created vast topographic changes. In 1799, the West India Dock Company were granted a licence to build docks in the Isle of Dogs between Limehouse and Blackwall, and dock expansion continued for much of the nineteenth century. Both railways and docks needed huge warehouses to store the goods being imported and exported, as well as the materials required during their construction. Railway, dock and commercial developments were driven by private investment but the state still played a role in developing infrastructure. Street improvements were carried out by both private capitalists (as in the case of Great Dover Street) and public bodies (Her Majesty's Office of Works).[30] New roadways demolished and reorganised large areas in the inner city prior to 1855. For example, the arterial Cannon Street, Commercial Street, Farringdon Road, New Oxford Street and Victoria Street were all built between 1830 and 1856.[31] These improvements were designed to ease traffic congestion, modernise the street scene and facilitate communication and trade between different areas. Moreover, they were conceived as socially beneficial because they effaced dilapidated buildings and ameliorated public health. Lynda Nead has already explained that 'motion and circulation were the two guiding principles of mid-nineteenth-century modernisers'.[32] The new, wide, straight streets cross-sectioning the prior street plan were the spatial opposite of 'Old London', which was imagined as dark, insanitary and labyrinthine. The MBW's more integrated approach to urban planning from 1855 on thus built on substantial, if unsystematic, improvements begun in the first half of the century.

Even though the MBW's remit consolidated previously disparate spaces, bodies and processes, their projects were first experienced as large and far-reaching demolitions. In undertaking topographic reforms, the MBW carved existing neighbourhoods into segments (as in the formation of Garrick Street in 1861, to improve access to Covent Garden) and erased others entirely (like Middle Row, Holborn, in 1867).[33] Nevertheless, Dickens saw the MBW's wider jurisdiction and focus on sanitation as a significant step forwards from the old system of 'Vestrylization':[34] in other words, the localised administration of improvements, which he believed stood in the way of social and urban progress because their priority was to protect vested interests.[35] The MBW's most significant achievements include the embankment of the River Thames and Joseph Bazalgette's mass sewerage network. Conversely, the demolitions carried out by the MBW initially exacerbated the material disorder caused by other developments, particularly because these coincided with a frenzied period of railway construction into central London (both above and below street level), which reached its peak in the mid-1860s.[36] The high proportion of railwaymen serving as MPs in this period no doubt made it easier for private railway capitalists to have new bills passed to authorise their endeavours, even despite objections from high-profile philanthropists such as Lord Shaftsbury, who drew attention to the damaging effects that demolishing densely inhabited areas had on the poor.

Monumental architecture

The construction of monumental architecture affected the street scene in many areas of London, as both public and private developers invested in grandeur. In general terms, crown- and state-funded developments were built around Westminster, including Trafalgar Square (1829–41), the National Gallery (1832–8), the Houses of

Parliament (1840–60, rebuilt after a fire in 1834) and Nelson's Column (1845). In the West End, subscription-based charities or clubs, and private individuals, built Italianate gentlemen's club-houses and Gothic churches, generally speaking between the 1830s and 1850s.[37] Then, between the 1850s and 1870s, a variety of grandiose facades 'dedicated to the building-owner's sense of status' were constructed by commercial interests in the City.[38] Finally, grand hotels and termini were built in numerous areas to service metropolitan railway lines, of which Paddington was the first (1852–3).[39] In *The Image of the City*, Lynch argues that landmarks play a key role in helping individuals to navigate urban space. One can assume that new monumental architecture had a significant impact on Londoners' engagement with the city, yet it was experienced differently by various social groups. Monumental architecture is utterly irrelevant to Jo, the crossing sweeper in *Bleak House* (1852–3), even though he registers its commanding physical presence. When Jo looks up at the dome of St Paul's Cathedral, its cross is simply 'the crowning confusion of the great, confused city; so golden, so high up, so far out of his reach' (*BH*, p. 315). Jo is moved on between various sites in the novel, and so comes to see many of the same localities as other characters; however, his abjection acutely emphasises the coexistence of contrasting viewpoints on the same sites. Denied the education to interpret the symbols that might help him to understand his environment, like written text or religious iconography, Jo is rendered figuratively 'stone blind and dumb' (*BH*, p. 257). Jo's inability to perceive the symbolic significance of St Paul's thus underscores the social and spatial disconnect that Dickens explores in the novel. Grandiose buildings did not necessarily create a sense of nationalistic pride or identity. Moreover, as monumental buildings were constructed in a variety of styles in this period, there was never a unified British architecture. Although, in part, such edifices were erected to assert national, social or commercial status, the eclecticism of Victorian building contributed to the cumulative diversification in the street scene – altered by improvements, and increasingly crowded.

People

Planners' faith in metropolitan improvements to drive both social and environmental reform was reinforced by widely held beliefs in progress.[40] Thomas Macaulay captured a contemporary mood in his *History of England* (1848) when he wrote that 'the history of our country during the last hundred and sixty years is eminently the history of physical, of moral, and of intellectual improvement'.[41] Nor did such assertions of Britain's advancement appear unsubstantiated. An abundance of statistical studies, such as the decennial census begun in 1801, offered opportunities for contemporaries to measure the population and its wealth, education, living conditions and even (supposedly) moral values to an unprecedented extent.[42] Twelve years prior to the publication of Macaulay's influential *History*, G. R. Porter's *Progress of the Nation* similarly stated that 'this country and [particularly] the present generation, [have] made the greatest advances in civilization that can be found recorded in the annals of mankind'.[43] He contended that this was proven by objective numerical data:

> the materials which can be brought in aid of a labour of this kind, and which relate to the occurrences of the present century, are vastly superior in amount and value to those that are to be collected from existing records of earlier date.[44]

The obsessive way in which Victorians attempted to quantify and qualify London through statistical analysis and mapping was a process through which contemporaries attempted to comprehend the city's overwhelming vastness and diversity. Public servants used these apparently neutral measures to apply to metropolitan reforms Jeremy Bentham's Utilitarian principle of ensuring the greatest happiness for the greatest number.[45] However, the limited success of improvements in ameliorating the lives of the displaced is a testament to the fact that it was actually very difficult to count, monitor or control London's working-class population, particularly those who had been unhoused by demolitions.

Improvements were planned and funded by commercial or moneyed interests, and reflect the values and cultural assumptions of wealthier classes. Ideas about the immorality, criminality and potential political subversiveness of the poor underwrote the perceived social role of metropolitan developments. In a study originally published in 1850, for example, the social explorer and preacher, the Reverend Thomas Beames, argued that ameliorating the living conditions in rookeries was a preventative measure against future revolutions: 'when rebellion recruits her forces she is fed by the denizens of these retreats'.[46] Beames's anxieties were fuelled by the outbreak of multiple European revolutions in 1848. Still, he was not alone in believing that close and overcrowded living conditions enabled seditious individuals to 'meet, discuss, harangue, plot, combine – wait their time', as well as to lead members of the 'respectable' poor astray.[47] How effective breaking up slum communities actually was as a strategy for control cannot now be discerned. Nevertheless, frequent claims that demolitions would facilitate social stability and improve public morality expose how influential an area's perceived cultural identity could be in determining which places were targeted for demolition.

Strategies for the *embourgeoisement* of London and its populace were incorporated into the planning of certain metropolitan improvements from at least the 1830s. A report penned by Percy J. Edwards, Clerk of the Improvements Committee at the London County Council, reveals that government representatives expected two-way observation between slum-dwellers and their wealthier neighbours to result in the poor becoming more respectable:

> The Select Committee of 1838 [. . .] called attention in its report to the fact that there were districts in London through which no great thoroughfares passed, and which were wholly occupied by a dense population composed of the lowest class of persons who being entirely secluded from the observation and influence of better educated neighbours, exhibited a state of moral degradation deeply to be deplored. It was suggested that this lamentable state of affairs would be remedied whenever the great streams of public intercourse could be made to pass through the districts in question. It was also justly contended that the moral condition of these poorer occupants would necessarily be improved by communication with more respectable inhabitants [. . .][48]

Edwards indicates that the committee conceived improvements as one way of reinforcing social discipline. Such measures were seen to be effective because slum-dwellers knew that they were being observed, but also because the poor could watch and learn from the behaviour of wealthier people. Conversely, this kind of spatial policing was not straightforward. Breaking up slum communities even heightened contemporary anxieties about potential disorder, as demolitions made slum populations even more difficult to monitor and, when slum housing was cleared, its 'former inmates' were 'dispersed into quarters once tenanted by the more decent among the poor'.[49] Moreover, cutting new streets through slum districts only made the dilapidation and insanitary conditions of these areas newly visible. Horrified reactions to such sights published in the press emphasise that, instead of facilitating integration, improvements reinforced impressions of slums and slum-dwellers as Other to more prosperous factions of society.

Slum-dwellers were the social group most severely affected by demolitions and least able to dispute them. Unlike the social progress promised by improvement narratives, mass displacement in fact created an unquantifiable, mobile population, who found shelter and subsistence by any means left available to them. Demolished sites were not ruins, despite the fact that both are visually characterised by voids rather than solids. As Julia Hell and Andreas Schonle put it, '[t]he ruin is a ruin precisely because it seems to have lost its function or meaning in the present, while retaining a suggestive, unstable semantic potential'.[50] Conversely, the demolished spaces left by improvements did not cease to be included in the everyday spatial practices of certain factions of society, some of whom were compelled by necessity to continue to reside in these areas. Journalists repeatedly comment on the 'strange places' that the poor inhabit, including '[a]rches, coal cellars, in unfinished roads, on flags made warm by the ovens of sugar and bread bakers, in unfinished houses'.[51] Reginald Wilfer walks through one such 'tract of suburban Sahara' on his daily commute to the City in *Our Mutual Friend* (1864–5) (*OMF*, p. 33). Like the journalists who reported on how the poor used demolished spaces, Dickens reveals that this 'desert' is not a barren, unproductive wasteland, located paradoxically adjacent to London's economic centre. Various forms of labour are carried out on the site: 'tiles and bricks were burnt, bones were boiled, carpets were beat, rubbish was shot, dogs were fought, and dust was heaped by contractors' (*OMF*, p. 33). Instead of effacing disorder from the city, metropolitan improvements in fact produced spaces for miscellaneous accumulation and shady dealings; even though demolitions were seen to play a social role, then, London's population remained difficult to control.

Discipline was not the only motive behind slum clearance. Although some prominent individuals (including Lord Derby and Lord Shaftsbury) drew attention to the social problems caused by mass displacement, Lord Granville did not voice a unique opinion when, speaking in parliament in 1861, he stated that 'some of [London's] districts [. . .] [a]re of so disreputable a character that it would be doing the lower classes a service to destroy the existing houses'.[52] Addressing a parliament dominated by railwaymen MPs desirous to further their interests, Granville's speech probably reveals his financial and political acumen. None the less, his remarks built on long-held beliefs that slum clearance was socially ameliorative for *both* the poor and the wealthy. Slums were the spatial antithesis to the light and airy boulevards that symbolised improved urban space, and demolition was a means of removing these physical obstructions to the free movement of people, goods and healthy air around the city, as well as eliminating terrible housing conditions. Inadequate (or non-existent) sanitation and overcrowding made slums breeding grounds for disease. Living in these areas was dangerous for their inhabitants, and periodic epidemics threatened the wider city. Autocratic though improvements certainly were, therefore, discourses of social control and philanthropy coexisted in the planning and execution of these developments.

Dickens

What was it about Dickens that made contemporaries plunder his writing for representational or rhetorical tools to discuss London's modernisation? As we have seen, concurrently with his career, Londoners were faced with a disordered built environment, teeming with a diverse, mobile and ever-growing population, and subject to competing plans for its material alteration. Part modern, part antiquated and – in some places – in transition between the two, Dickens's varied representations of London and Londoners across his œuvre pay tribute to the city's ineffability. Conversely, later users generally appropriate tropes, descriptions and characters to construct legible representations by which the city and its inhabitants can be identified as a known space or community. In 1866, for instance, 'A Peer' wrote to the *Pall Mall Gazette* to express his negative opinion of Reform League demonstrators in Hyde Park:

> I wish to testify emphatically to the fact that I and my companion, so far as we could see, failed to see anything resembling a real body of working men in Tuesday's crowd. I saw Bill Sikes and Nancy and the flash Toby Crackit in every variety and stage of growth, and nothing but them.[53]

Dickens's characters are mobilised as representative figures, through which the unknowable mass that is the urban crowd can be understood and categorised. This section will suggest that the form, style and content of Dickens's novels make his works suited to such appropriation. However, the aptness of such practices in mid-nineteenth-century improvement debates also depended on Dickens's authorial persona and popularity.

Contemporaries with a public voice were able to use Dickensian afterlives to convey social and environmental connotations because they trusted their audiences to recognise the cultural meanings embedded in this store of imagery. Without Dickens's extraordinary popularity and the mass dissemination of his works, the significance of allusions to and extracts from his fiction would not have been perceived and these devices would have been ineffectual. This familiarity was secured partly by the popularity of the original serials, but also by audiences' knowledge of the illustrations and various remediations of the novels. As Juliet John argues in *Dickens and Mass Culture*, Dickens rapidly became a cultural phenomenon. After his immense success with *Pickwick Papers* (1836–7), Dickens's fiction regularly inspired theatrical adaptations, material culture and visual representations. Dickens played a part in cannily 'permitt[ing] and perpetuat[ing]' his popular appeal:[54] for example, by authorising certain theatrical adaptations of his novels instead of others 'like a royal patent'.[55] Opportunities for Dickens to address a broad public were made possible because his career coincided with technological developments that allowed his fiction, and visual representations of his narratives and characters, to reach a vast audience. Matthew Buckley explains:

> It was in just those years that the economies of scale provided by the new process of stereotyping created something like a mass print audience. While serial novels used the new opportunities to reach a much larger readership, the primary expansion of the print audience – and indeed the creation of an audience for illustrated serial novels – was driven by the sudden availability of, and enthusiasm for, inexpensive images. Print shops, whose audiences had been expanding continually over the preceding century, boomed.[56]

As David Brewer summarises succinctly, '[w]ith greater scale come greater returns'.[57] The commercial success of Dickensian prints, adaptations and objects inspired still further remediations, as other businesses (theatres, print shops and so on) sought to capitalise on Dickens's popularity. While the production of afterlives was encouraged by the widespread dissemination of his novels, then, these remediations also reinforced his prominence in popular culture.

Richard Altick was right to question the extent to which Dickens appealed to a mass public.[58] Nevertheless, Altick's sense that Dickens's readership among the working classes may have been less extensive than sentimental testimonies lead us to suppose is irrelevant to the effectiveness of Dickensian afterlives in discussions of metropolitan improvements. Later users who appropriated Dickens to argue for metropolitan demolitions did not address the working classes when they repurposed his novels. As has already been stated, improvements were planned and funded by commercial or moneyed interests, and reflect the values and assumptions of wealthier classes. Therefore, the cultural meanings embedded in Dickensian afterlives had to be recognisable only to the social groups driving London's redevelopment. For example, according to Philip Horne, *Bentley's Miscellany* targeted a middle-class, educated and mostly male readership at the time when *Oliver Twist* was first serialised in the periodical (1837–9).[59] This target readership corresponds with the social groups driving metropolitan improvement in broad terms. The wealthy and middle classes are similarly the audiences that later users usually address in press commentaries arguing for the benefits of specific demolitions, or in parliamentary debates. While the mass dissemination of Dickens's works and its multiple remediations certainly increases the likelihood that contemporaries would understand the cultural connotations conveyed in Dickensian afterlives, the social groups who were responsible for urban improvement were also, generally speaking, his majority readership.

The form of Dickens's novels also permits later users to recontextualise selected tropes, characters or passages, without reducing their power to convey specific meanings. Originally published as serials, Dickens's plots often develop in haphazard and disjointed ways rather than as smooth, linear narratives. The earlier novels are particularly episodic. In *Nicholas Nickleby* (1838–9), for instance, Nicholas's experiences at Dotheboys Hall are disconnected from his time as an actor in Mr Crummles's company. Yet even in the more intricately plotted later works, passages or chapters can be enjoyed as individual incidents because the novels' serial publication and multi-plot form necessitate that smaller narrative arcs are embedded within the larger, overarching structure to allow readers to enjoy and follow disparate plotlines across monthly instalments. For example, Dickens presents society as an interconnected matrix in *Little Dorrit* (1855–7). Mr Merdle's illicit financial manœuvres have an impact on characters from across the social spectrum portrayed in the novel, ruining Panks, Clennam and Merdle himself. Nevertheless, the comic turns of Mr F's Aunt do not require a broader context to be humorous or coherent vignettes. Indeed, as Mary Hammond has argued, extracting and separately reprinting selected passages, characters or tropes from longer works in fact highlight 'flashes of humour' or fine descriptions, which could otherwise 'be lost [in a] novel's broader landscape'.[60] Memorable, easily identifiable characters and readily isolatable episodes thus provide 'detachable snapshots'.[61] Even when these are 'remediat[ed] [. . .] out of context such practices do not by any means dilute [their] power'.[62] Later users could thus appropriate from Dickens selectively, without affecting the coherence of their representation or the clarity of their argument.

Writing in an episodic form suited to selective appropriation combines with Dickens's London focus to make his writing apposite to representing and discussing the city's modernisation. This is evident, as one such appropriative technique was extracting passages wholesale for republication in new contexts. Descriptions were re-presented as coherent portrayals of specific areas of the city. Alternatively, users refer to the novels as rhetorical yardsticks to conceptualise the extent to which districts have been altered by demolitions. An obituary in *Harper's Magazine* comments, for instance, that '[o]n the day after Dickens's funeral I still saw the street signs, "Little Saffron Hill," and "Field Lane;" but what a change has come over the place since the author made it the scene of his thrilling story!'[63] These sites are associated with the criminal underworld depicted in *Oliver Twist*, and *Harper's Magazine*'s allusions signal their prior degeneration. The obituary thereby recalls Dickens's novel to explain the changes made in London over the course of three decades, but simultaneously reinforces Dickens's significance to the area's perceived cultural history. Users also repurposed his fiction to articulate the necessity of demolishing specific areas. Given that improvements were often conceived as means of facilitating social and environmental amelioration, extracts or allusions that clearly detail horrific conditions enable users to consolidate and convey adverse perceptions of specific areas and emphasise the urgency of reform.

Investing real locales with imaginative associations localises large and complex social problems in certain sites, and so permits advocates of improvements to conceive the demolition of certain places as attacks on urban 'nuisances'. One example of how Dickensian afterlives were mobilised in attempts to influence how the social identity of particular places was perceived among the reading public is found in an article discussing contemporary criminal practices in *Lloyd's Weekly Newspaper* in 1868. The article's focus is on how changes in fashion have altered which items are valuable to pickpockets. The journalist refers to *Oliver Twist* to communicate her or his representation of contemporary crime: 'handkerchiefs were valuable prizes to the sharks of Field-lane and Saffron-hill. Master Bates and the Artful Dodger made something for themselves out of such plunder, and their kind old patron Mr. Fagin, made much more, and got hanged.'[64] The article suggests that the social identity of these major locations for trafficking stolen goods has changed simultaneously with a cultural shift in the objects valued by thieves. Indeed, the writer's comment that Fagin has been hung indicates how the passage of time has altered where criminal hubs are located, and what dangers threaten London's populace. However, even though the *Lloyd's* article states that the kind of pickpocketing represented in *Oliver Twist* is no longer as prevalent as it was in the 1830s, the writer indicates that Field Lane and Saffron Hill still house a criminal population. Illegal activities are specifically localised in these sites because of their explicit association with nefarious characters, who serve as representative figures of the district's broader social identity. As Chapter 3 will explore more fully, Dickens's characters were used to distinguish Field Lane as a threatening place before its demolition was decided, as well as during the process of its redevelopment between 1848 and the 1870s. Dickensian afterlives were thus mapped on to the built environment as one way of curating legible representations of dynamic spaces and consolidating the perceived social identities of slum areas.

The style of Dickens's representation of London further contributes to allowing users to repurpose his works as effective rhetorical tools to drive contemporary reform. Dickens's reputation for communicating realistic representations of dreadful conditions without offending sensitive readers meant that his fiction could be redeployed with minimal risk of affronting influential individuals with distasteful content when users addressed their arguments to middle- and high-level public fora. Moreover, given Dickens's own standing as a social reformer, references to his works may have made the audience more receptive to the user's case. A review published in the *Illustrated London News* in 1844 is typical in its assessment that:

> Mr. Dickens' works [. . .] contain a larger number of faithful pictures and records of the middle and lower classes of England of the present period, than can be found in any other modern works; and that while they communicate very varied, and frequently very squalid and hideous knowledge concerning the lower, and the most depraved classes, and without the least compromise of the true state of men and things, the author nevertheless manages so skilfully that they may be read from beginning to end without a single offence to true and unaffected delicacy. Moreover, they tend on the whole to bring the poor into the fairest position for obtaining the sympathy of the rich and powerful, by displaying the goodness and fortitude often found amidst want and wretchedness, together with the intervals of joyousness and comic humour.[65]

The review asserts Dickens's apparently realistic representation of contemporary urban conditions alongside the 'true' cultural values of privileged social groups, so Dickens's style is aligned with the supposed sympathies of his imagined readership. This is used to bolster the author's reputation as a reformer and avows that his novels are fit to provoke well-informed and considerate material change. Dickens certainly believed that his fiction and social campaigning were intimately related. For him, literature was an appropriate and effective medium for social comment and for stimulating public action.[66] Indeed, in the *Harper's Magazine* obituary, the writer states that Dickens successfully made social interventions because his popularity gave the causes he supported a prominent platform in the public consciousness:

> when we consider the new interest in the poor he has awakened, the wrongs he has brought to light, the measures which would never have been passed had he not written, we can not help feeling that he really represented this whole people before that highest legislature – Public Opinion.[67]

Of course, not everyone shared this high opinion. Walter Bagehot, Harriet Martineau and Anthony Trollope are among the most famous to have critiqued Dickens's representations of pet causes. Nevertheless, for many, Dickens could be invoked without offence because he was a cultural sign for both faithful representations of urban conditions and contemporary reform.

Dickens's style, and the form and content of his novels, contributed to making his work apposite for appropriation in discussions of mid-nineteenth-century improvements, but his engagement with the contemporary city is often very different to how his fiction was used to comment on urban developments. Dickens's London both embraces physical spaces of the mid-nineteenth-century city and, to use Henri Lefebvre's terms in *The Production of Space*, simultaneously departs from received spatial practices or representations of space. On the one hand, his narratives are mapped on to real places, and his descriptions of specific areas respond to popular perceptions of their social and environmental conditions among wealthier social groups. As Chapters 3 and 5 will explore further, Dickens situated criminal characters in slums that already had notorious reputations. However, Dickens also unsettled some readers' expectations – of both his writing and urban social types and spaces. For example, responding to criticisms of Nancy in his 1841 preface to *Oliver Twist*, Dickens asserted that 'it is a contradiction, an anomaly, an apparent impossibility, but it is a Truth. I am glad to have had it doubted, for in that circumstance I find a sufficient assurance that it needed to be told.'[68] In this, Dickens indicates that his writing challenges readers' London imaginaries, in which London is perceived as a repository of imaginative or moral connotations. The preface implies that his representation is objective. Conversely, the fact that Dickens often juxtaposes imagined locations with actual places in his novels proves that he did reimagine the city.

In fact, there is no one version of the city in his novels. As Jay Clayton states in *Charles Dickens in Cyberspace*, 'Dickens's London has always been a simulacrum, an image more real than reality.'[69] Even the term 'Dickens's London' is an illusion. While, today, 'Dickensian' or 'Dickens's London' evokes connotations of social inequality and dark and dilapidated spaces, his works do not present a definitive representation.[70] In *Little Dorrit*, for instance, Arthur states that '[i]t is always painful [. . .] to hear [Amy] call [the Marshalsea] home' because he perceives her residence there as evidence of her victimisation (*LD*, p. 280). She does not feel subjugated by her childhood experiences but exclaims fervently, 'it is home!' (*LD*, p. 281). The difference in their perspectives shows how Dickens's portrayal resists singular representations of place. Instead, multiple versions of London exist simultaneously, as the cityscape is mapped and remapped as a variable, individuated topography. The space responds flexibly to the demands of the narrative or Dickens's broader social vision, yet his dynamic representation of the city also engages with its material improvement.

Dickens recognises the imaginative and psychological significance of urban development in his representations of improvements. In *Great Expectations* (1860–1), the older Pip-narrator remarks that new developments have changed how London looked in between the novel's 1820s setting and his current perspective:

> Alterations have been made in that part of the Temple since that time, and it has not now so lonely a character as it had then, nor is it so exposed to the river. We lived at the top of the last house, and the wind rushing up the river shook the house that night, like discharges of cannon, or breakings of a sea. (*GE*, pp. 287–8)

Readers are told that they would no longer recognise Temple, which has been rendered unfamiliar, but also that remnants of the old city remain hidden behind the new buildings shielding Pip's old lodgings from view. In a novel concerned with both the materiality and insubstantiality of the objects and spaces underpinning social ranks and identities, Pip's off-hand remarks about Temple's alterations show that even the built environment is far from solid. Nevertheless, the casual tone of his observations signals that urban developments were not always perceived as cataclysmic shocks, of the kind that Dickens describes in *Dombey and Son*. Unlike the large-scale demolitions that accompanied railway building, the improvements in Temple have been constructed around, or bolted on to, existing buildings. Not only are material traces of its history locatable behind modern facades, but imaginatively too, the versions of London that are evoked in the past tense of the narrative and the present tense of the narrator's perspective are constructed dialogically. In accordance with Billie Melman's argument in *The Culture of History*, both 'the experience and representations of improvement drew on the past, [as] mid-Victorian reformers, writers, and artists constantly made analogies with history, while seeking to sever from it the cities they experienced and imagined'.[71] Dickens's differentiated representations of urban development reveal his nuanced engagement with the material conditions of the contemporary city. However, he simultaneously explores the imaginative suggestiveness of metropolitan alterations for narrative effect.

Heavy rain lashes Pip's windows on the night of Magwitch's return, described in the above quotation. The scene is desolate, and Pip feels so lonely that he 'might have fancied [him]self in a storm-beaten light-house' (*GE*, p. 288). But it is not only the weather that evokes a foreboding tone and emphasises Pip's feelings of physical and emotional alienation. The London of the 1820s haunts the present-day city, and its uncanny effect gives material expression to Pip's sense of alienation and loss of identity. Caught between contemporary materiality and memory, the visible and the obscure, Pip's reference to Temple's improvement creates an unsettling mood. As Jeremy Tambling suggests in *Going Astray*, the changing built environment conjures a disorientating sense of impermanence that exacerbates Pip's anxieties about his personal destruction.[72] Invoking the double potential of improvements both to create and to destroy, Pip's off-hand comment about Temple's physical alteration certainly heightens the tension of his reunion with Magwitch.

Later users who mobilised Dickensian afterlives to comment on mid-nineteenth-century modernisations or linked social problems do not tend to note the narrative work that improvements perform in the novels. Instead, Dickensian afterlives fragment and change their source texts. Multiple and unpredictable, they proliferate chaotically in popular culture and diversify how the public encounter Dickens's characters or narratives.[73] Users recontextualise their sources with impunity. For example, a poem published in *Punch* in 1867 evokes both *Bleak House* and *Oliver Twist* to argue that charitable works should target local causes, and that these should ideally be led by private individuals, rather than government.

> To say nothing of Borrio-boo-loo-gah, and Polynesian missions,
> And defending Southern Africa from COLENSO'S heretical scissions?
> While there's Mozambique Arabs to save, it must leave City Arabs to roam,
> For the COUTTS and PEABODY charity, that tamely begins at home.
> Has not BUMBLE got his hands full, in battling for vested rights,
> And in fighting Centralisation's and Local Self-Government's fights;
> And in keeping down the paupers and economising the rates,
> And in pooh-poohing ERNEST HART and the papers' sensational prates?[74]

Punch's satire coincides with a time when levels of state intervention were being revised. Criticising the amount of money being spent on international philanthropy, the journal follows Dickens's advocacy of domestic charity in *Bleak House* by evoking Mrs Jellyby's and Mrs Pardiggle's pet projects as shorthand for distant, supposedly misguided projects. Conversely, Dickens's specific engagement with the New Poor Law in *Oliver Twist* is eschewed to suit the poem's topical context, updated from the 1830s to the 1860s. Bumble is transformed into a general symbol for institutional malpractice and uncharitable attitudes to poor relief, in contrast to the philanthropic works of named wealthy individuals. Dickens's nuanced or imaginative engagement with contemporary social or environmental reform is thereby removed when users plunder the texts for portable terminologies and passages, through which to articulate their own agendas.

The characteristics that made Dickens's novels apposite sources for representational or rhetorical devices are particularly evident in his early works. Consequently, although Chapters 4 and 5 discuss Dickens's interest and involvement in reform and his fiction from the 1840s and 1850s, *Dickens and Demolition* chiefly focuses on the afterlives of *Oliver Twist*. Drawing on social stereotypes and generic character types from popular theatre helped Dickens to create characters who were already fully invested with complex cultural meanings recognisable and relevant to his original readers.[75] Nevertheless, the fact that the novel's characters and situations are still among the best known in Dickens's œuvre is a testament to the vividness of his portrayal. *Oliver Twist*'s mass popularity among Dickens's contemporaries is evidenced by the fact that at least seventeen adaptations of the text appeared on stages across Britain and in the United States of America before the novel had completed its serial publication. By 1870, well over one hundred plays of the novel had been performed internationally.[76] Moreover, the text's appeal to a mass audience was reinforced by the popularity of its illustrations, which could also be bought separately. The fact that *Oliver Twist* was illustrated by George Cruikshank, an already famous and respected artist, almost guaranteed an audience for prints of these images. As I will discuss in Chapter 2, even though the original publication of *Oliver Twist* was accompanied by a degree of notoriety, as the novel was caught up in wider anxieties about the negative social impact of Newgate fiction, objections to its content were met by equally strong arguments for its sensitivity. Indeed, Dickens's obituaries in 1870 indicate that his earlier novels were generally more popular with contemporary readers than his later works.[77]

The representation of London in *Oliver Twist* dovetails generatively with current thinking about the social and environmental role of urban improvements. London is subdivided as a moral topography in *Oliver Twist*. The city is portrayed as an assemblage of juxtapositional, rather than integrated, spaces. For instance, the slums of Field Lane and Jacob's Island – represented melodramatically as dangerous, criminal localities – are entirely separate from the 'islands of good' occupied by Brownlow and the Maylies.[78] Even despite the physical proximity of some of these areas – Field Lane is approximately one mile from Brownlow's house in Pentonville – the spaces could not be more different. In its juxtapositional representation of slum areas as Other to middle-class London, *Oliver Twist* picks up on arguments for metropolitan improvement that presented social problems as environmentally determined. Demolishing Field Lane and Jacob's Island could be envisioned as assaults on urban criminality because these slum areas were conceived as isolated localities, which had nothing in common with modernised areas of the city.

Of course, Dickens's representations of these middle-class and criminal areas are not as disconnected as they appear to be at first glance. Although his descriptions of the slums' physical dilapidation signals their Otherness to the novel's middle-class topographies, the movement of characters between these spaces reveals that the separation of criminal and respectable areas is only imaginative. Oliver is not the only character to move between London's different zones in the novel. Although Fagin wishes to '[avoid] as much as possible all the main streets' and is, by contrast, 'in his proper element' in Field Lane, all of the other members of the gang travel widely (*OT*, p. 204). Dodger and Charley Bates roam the streets to pick pockets, Sikes covers huge distances to break into middle-class houses, and Nancy walks the streets to pick up clients,[79] assuming a disguise that allows her to spy on Oliver even after he is adopted by Brownlow. Moving in the other direction, Monks enters Field Lane to plot Oliver's downfall. Characters' mobility between different types of spaces shows that social problems were not contained by slums, even though the sites chiefly associated with urban crime and disease remain consistent in the novel, and are implicated in the production of these behaviours.[80] Different representational modes are thereby present in the same text, as the apparent order of the narrator's *paysage moralisé* is undercut by individuals' spatial practices. None the less, the ability to distinguish between London districts and categorise them into 'good' or 'bad' areas was important to metropolitan improvers, particularly in the first half of the century when demolitions were usually localised. Despite the unsettling mobility of his characters, Dickens still imaginatively maps the city as an assemblage of discrete parts with defined social identities. As improvements attacked the social problems associated with these areas, evocation of Dickens's juxtapositional topography allowed developers and their advocates to conceive improvements as measurable forward progress.

Conclusion

Dickensian afterlives are a means of constructing and communicating public images of London or its populace. Individuals read urban spaces in different ways – navigating streets in relation to personally significant landmarks like a favourite coffee shop, for instance. Nevertheless, as Lynch stresses, personal maps must still '[approximate] the public image' to have a functional value.[81] Obvious examples of 'public' images are cartographic maps, which detail the relation between streets and significant buildings. However, as vast demolitions disrupted both personal and public images of the cityscape, improvers and individuals needed to find new ways to comprehend their environment. Dickensian afterlives provided one such resource. As D. A. Miller explores in his Foucauldian reading, novels construct an imaginative space that can be experienced as simultaneously private to the reader and shared with other members of the reading public. Later users employ this simultaneously shared and internalised vocabulary to discuss the changing built environment, identify particular places in the cityscape or communicate ideas about these sites. Audiences were encouraged to interpret the cityscape in relation to these common public, albeit fictional, images.

Later users frequently justify their appropriation of Dickens's fiction and assert its suitability to urban commentary by presenting him as a writer with specialist, first-hand knowledge of London. Sometimes writers refrain from describing places or urban social types, and instead refer readers to specific literary works in which they have been 'so well described by Dickens'.[82] Particularly prior to the foundation of the MBW in 1855, Dickensian afterlives were tools through which the city could be imagined and understood at a time when both the built environment and processes governing its redevelopment defied easy comprehension. Conversely, the legibility Dickensian afterlives appeared to facilitate was complicated by the flexible remediation of Dickens's works to suit many different agendas and interests. Therefore, constructing public images through fiction was not a counter to the unpredictability of the city, but a further complication. Dickensian afterlives did not offer stable or unified images of London, even though they were rhetorically presented as legible representative devices.

Despite frequent assertions that Dickens's novels provide reliable accounts of London conditions, in fact later users mobilised his fiction to present curated images of the city, and manipulate how both the space and the original text are re-presented in new contexts. Dickensian afterlives carry a huge variety of political inflections and were used to promote multiple causes, and to advocate different positions in debates about how and where the city should be improved. Although Dickensian afterlives are unpredictable, it is in the gap between their supposed legibility, users' selective fragmentation of the texts and the dissimilarity of different afterlives to each other that we see their rhetorical force. Despite each of these caveats, Dickensian afterlives proliferate in discussions about London's improvement and in representations of the city throughout the nineteenth century. As Chapters 3 and 5 examine, patterns of negative Dickensian imagery can be discerned in representations of specific slum areas and so, given the belief that urban improvements were an effective means of addressing social problems, practices of mobilising fictional referents as a way of conceiving and representing degraded conditions implicate his works in driving demolitions in certain areas. It is partly because of the heterogeneity of actors involved in modernising the cityscape, and the disorder of the built environment, that Dickensian afterlives were able to contribute effectively to processes of material change in the mid-nineteenth century.

Notes

1. John Summerson, 'London, the Artifact', in Dyos and Wolff (eds), pp. 311–32, p. 326.
2. Stedman Jones, *Outcast London*, p. 167.
3. *Museum of London Collections Online.*
4. Bagehot, p. 174.
5. Lynch, p. 3.
6. Ibid., p. 3.
7. Ibid., p. 10.
8. Ibid., p. 3.
9. Particularly: Nead, *Victorian Babylon*; Porter, *London: A Social History*; Stedman Jones, *Outcast London*; White, *London in the Nineteenth Century*.
10. The most famous examples of crown-led Regency developments are John Nash's Regent's Park and Regent Street. Nevertheless, these are unlike the typically fragmented approach to urban planning in the nineteenth century, as they required the implementation of large-scale, integrated plans. Still, as Steve Humphries and Gavin Weightman have noted, Nash's enterprise was 'typical in that it was modified for economic reasons, and was never finished' (p. 11).
11. White, p. 28.
12. 'The "beauty of the metropolis" as an object of public policy died with George IV and would hardly be resurrected in the nineteenth century. Almost every metropolitan improvement begun after 1830 would suffer in some way from lack of care in design and appearance' (ibid., p. 28).
13. John Summerson states that 'from 1837 to 1857' new building was 'characterised mainly by ornate Italian stucco streets, stone-built Italian club-houses, and Gothic churches' (Summerson, 'London, the Artifact', p. 312).
14. Porter, p. 13.
15. Mandler, 'Demolition', p. 5. Mandler's research is forthcoming in a developed, revised version.
16. Vernon, p. 52.
17. Lynch, p. 1.
18. Benjamin, 'On the Concept of History' (para IX of XVIII).
19. H. J. Dyos and D. A. Reeder, 'Slums and Suburbs', in Dyos and Wolff (eds), pp. 359–88, p. 362.

20. Nead, *Victorian Babylon*, p. 14.
21. White, p. 47.
22. Jack Simmons, 'The Power of the Railway', in Dyos and Wolff (eds), *The Victorian City: Images and Realities*, pp. 277–310, pp. 297–8.
23. Dyos and Reeder, 'Slums and Suburbs', pp. 364–5.
24. Ibid., pp. 365–7.
25. 'The Demolition Statements arose out of the concerns of Lord Shaftsbury about the impact of metropolitan railway building on the labouring classes. From 1853, a new Standing Order in all Private Bills involving the destruction of thirty or more dwellings stipulated that a return should be made of the actual number under threat, including the number of occupants. The proponents of Bills were also required to set out what measures they envisaged to assist the persons displaced. Over the years from 1853 to 1901, these statements record the forced removal of a total of 76,000 people' (Freeman, p. 135).
26. Stedman Jones, *Outcast London*, p. 180.
27. White, p. 29.
28. Dyos and Reeder have argued that 'it was sometimes possible to run through the whole gamut from meadow to slum in a single generation, or even less' ('Slums and Suburbs', p. 364).
29. Freeman, p. 128.
30. White, p. 21. James Vernon has also argued that military and state imperatives drove the construction of Britain's road network more widely in the eighteenth and early nineteenth centuries (pp. 27–30).
31. Wohl, p. 26.
32. Nead, *Victorian Babylon*, p. 163.
33. A Select Committee had recommended Middle Row's demolition in 1837 (Gomme, pp. 161–2; also *UCL Bloomsbury Project*).
34. Dickens, *Speeches*, p. 130.
35. The MBW's larger remit did not mean that vested interests were not protected; see note Ch. 5, n. 15.
36. Freeman, p. 128.
37. Summerson, 'London, the Artifact', p. 312.
38. Ibid., p. 315.
39. Ibid., p. 324.
40. G. R. Porter's *Progress of the Nation* measured Britain's progress against eight 'general heads of inquiry'. These are: Population; Production; Interchange; Public revenue and expenditure; Consumption; Accumulation; Moral progress ('exhibiting the state of the kingdom in regard to crime, its amount, prevention, and punishment; the progress of education, and the advancement of literature and the fine arts'); and Extent and condition of our Colonies and foreign dependencies (p. 4).
41. Macaulay, p. 14.
42. Mary Carpenter's *Reformatory Schools, for the Children of the Perishing and Dangerous Classes, and for Juvenile Offenders*, for instance,

includes a statistical table detailing the 'Religious Knowledge of Prisoners', which she measures by questions such as 'Knowing the Saviour's name, and able to repeat the Lord's Prayer, more or less imperfectly'. Carpenter seeks to establish the morality of prisoners by comparing these results with questions about whether prisoners have 'read, or heard read, books about Dick Turpin, and Jack Sheppard' (p. 23). Carpenter's investigations are discussed in Chapter 4.

43. Porter, *Progress of the Nation*, p. 1.
44. Ibid., p. 3.
45. Nead, *Victorian Babylon*, p. 13.
46. Beames, p. 67.
47. Ibid., p. 66.
48. Edwards, p. 10.
49. Anon. (1858), 'London, Thursday, Dec. 2', *Daily News*, 3916, 2 Dec., p. 4.
50. Julia Hell and Andreas Schonle, 'Introduction', in Hell and Schonle (eds), pp. 1–16, p. 6.
51. Anon. (1864), 'The Houseless Poor', *Ragged School Union Magazine*, 16: 189, Sep., 193–6, p. 193.
52. Earl Granville (1861), qtd in 'Imperial Parliament', *Morning Post*, 27208, 1 Mar., p. 2.
53. A Peer (1866), 'Correspondence', *Pall Mall Gazette*, 456, 26 Jul., pp. 2–3, p. 3.
54. Hammond, p. 30.
55. Cohen, 'How Dickens Co-opted the British Theatrical Adaptation Industry in 1844: Part I', p. 133.
56. Buckley, p. 432.
57. Brewer, p. 14.
58. Altick, 'Varieties of Readers' Response'. Nevertheless, Juliet John has argued that '[t]he *image* of a universal Dickens [. . .] is an important part of the story of Dickens's popular success', regardless of whether this can be substantiated by a numerical record of actual readers (John, *Dickens and Mass Culture*, p. 6).
59. Philip Horne (2009), 'A Note on the Text', in Dickens, *Oliver Twist*, ed. Philip Horne, pp. l–liii, p. lii.
60. Hammond, pp. 29–30.
61. Ibid., p. 42.
62. Ibid., p. 29.
63. Bucklin Wells, p. 611.
64. Anon. (1868), 'The Pickpocket of the Period', *Lloyd's Weekly Newspaper*, 1343, 16 Aug., p. 6.
65. Anon. (1844), 'Literature', *Illustrated London News*, 99, [23 Mar.?], p. 186.
66. Please refer to Chapters 4 and 5 for further analysis of Dickens's interventions in contemporary reforms.

67. Bucklin Wells, p. 612.
68. Charles Dickens, 'The Author's Introduction to the Third Edition (1841)', in *Oliver Twist*, ed. Philip Horne, pp. 456–60, p. 460.
69. Clayton, p. 159.
70. Recently, 'Dickensian' has been used as a signifier of social inequality and an outdated built environment in numerous reports of the Grenfell Tower disaster: for example, by O'Neill and by Tucker.
71. Melman, p. 94.
72. See Jeremy Tambling, 'Chapter Nine, Traumatic London: *Great Expectations*', in Tambling, *Going Astray*, pp. 187–211.
73. Within his lifetime, other recontextualisations of Dickens's work include using Dickensian afterlives to examine urban criminality, famine in Ireland and the Reform Act of 1867, to name but a few examples. (See, for example, W. C. Taylor (1840), 'The Moral Economy of Large Towns', *Bentley's Miscellany,* 7, Jan., 470–8, p. 473; Lord Morpeth (1846), qtd in 'Irish Gratitude to Lord Morpeth', *Leeds Mercury*, 5848, 3 Jan., p. 7; and Anon. (1867), 'Fagin's Political School', *Punch*, 9 Nov., p. 188.)
74. Anon. (1867), 'Coutts and Peabody', *Punch*, 27 Jul., p. 33.
75. Lane Jr., p. 95.
76. Bolton, p. 105.
77. Hammond, p. 49.
78. J. Hillis Miller, *Victorian Subjects*, p. 44.
79. Mid-century studies of prostitution, which linked sex work to the transmission of infectious disease, emphasised how individual interactions exposed the connectedness of apparently distinct communities and spaces: for instance, in William Acton's *Prostitution, Considered in its Moral, Social, and Sanitary Aspects, In London and Other Large Cities* (1857). *Oliver Twist* precedes these studies and Dickens does not represent Nancy's work directly, yet she is still the figure who most forcefully disturbs the novel's juxtapositional topography.
80. See Chapter 3.
81. Lynch, p. 46.
82. Anon. (1881), 'The Ridicule of Missionary Effort', *Dundee Courier and Argus*, 8687, 23 May, p. 3.

Chapter 2

Sets and the City: Staging London and *Oliver Twist*

London playhouses competed to be the first to adapt from Charles Dickens's works. There were at least two adaptations of *Oliver Twist* (1837–9) on stage before Dickens had even completed the novel. The earliest known version was produced at the St James's Theatre in March 1838, where, only a month before, Dickens's own play, *The Strange Gentleman*, was performed.[1] This anonymous dramatisation was a failure and the run lasted only one night.[2] Then, on 21 May, *Oliver Twist, or, The Parish Boy's Progress. A Domestic Drama, in Three Acts* by C. Z. Barnett opened at the Pavilion Theatre with a little more success, running for a week.[3] Although these productions did not have long runs, the demand for dramatisations of *Oliver Twist* is indicated by the flurry of adaptations produced immediately after Dickens published the complete novel on 9 November 1838, which ran simultaneously in different theatres for the rest of the year.[4] Only ten days after the novel hit bookstalls, George Almar's dramatisation was opened at the Surrey Theatre. Hot on its heels were productions at Sadler's Wells and at the City of London Theatre, which both opened on 3 December.[5] Before the end of the year *Oliver Twist* reached provincial houses, and by January 1839 it was being performed in the USA.[6]

Even though the plays were produced at a similar moment, the differences between these early dramatisations of *Oliver Twist* reveal how the same text was mobilised in different contexts and to serve different interests. The dynamic re-presentation of *Oliver Twist* in early theatrical adaptations is thereby indicative of the malleability of Dickensian afterlives in nineteenth-century improvement debates. Similarly to rhetorical appropriations of his works, Dickens's *Oliver Twist* is fragmented and revised by processes of adaptation. Even as multiple theatres traded on the writer's fame by proclaiming the name 'BOZ' on playbills, unauthorised adaptation meant that Dickens lost control of his text.[7] Playwrights irreverently reworked the novel in multiple directions to suit a theatre's preferred genre, or altered it in length to fit the bill on different nights.[8] *Oliver Twist* appeared as both a major and a minor feature on playbills. For instance, in addition to the longer adaptations listed above, individual characters or incidents were extracted from the narrative as short interludes. One example is *Bumble's Courtship. From Dickens's 'Oliver Twist.' A Comic Interlude, in One Act*, by Frank E. Emson.[9] Further variations were created as dramatists, actors, stage managers, artists and musicians incorporated their own cultural or political opinions into their adaptations. Fagin's final words before his execution in the Sadler's Wells version pointedly draw attention to popular anti-Semitism: for instance, 'Say I've gone to sleep, they'll believe <u>you</u> – You're not a Jew.'[10] Fagin's statement asks the audience to reflect on how their own judgement is affected by social prejudices, but also indicates how adaptations adjust the text to engage in metatheatrical dialogue for social and political comment.[11] Adaptations are thus one example of how Dickensian afterlives were used to negotiate various contemporary socio-political contexts in London.

Just as social groups or current issues were diversely portrayed in coexisting productions, the book's urban setting was staged differently in each of these early adaptations. Playbills and reviews indicate that representing London on stage commanded a significant interest for nineteenth-century playgoers, and that the stagecraft helped theatre managers to distinguish their dramatisation from similar offerings at other theatres. The Sadler's Wells version emphasised that theatre's close proximity to the real places where the criminal scenes took place in their set design by building *tableaux architecturaux*. As I will go on to examine, adapting *Oliver Twist* as a so-called 'local' drama was supposed to create a stirring affect, as audiences were encouraged to associate nearby locales with heightened melodramatic action. Sadler's Wells constructed a representation of place that was intensely localised and, perhaps, recognisable to certain members of the audience. However, the adaptation running concurrently at the Surrey Theatre could not employ this dramatic effect. The Surrey was located further from the novel's main criminal settings in and around Field Lane.[12] Instead of stressing the audience's exciting closeness to the action, therefore, scenes of London's underworld are advertised on playbills as an opportunity for armchair tourism. The different advertising strategies for these productions indicate that each theatre's representation of London responded dynamically to their target audience, the conditions of the city and the playhouse's location.

In building distinctive representations of London, each adaptation effects multiple remediations between the physical and the symbolic. First, the perceived socio-cultural identities of real spaces and social groups are implicit in how Dickens's London is portrayed on stage. Part of the reason that certain locales are foregrounded instead of others is because they were already tantalisingly disreputable. Individuals' experiences of the real sites may have caused them to challenge melodramatically reimagined scenes. Nevertheless, adaptations of *Oliver Twist* evoke the existing criminal reputations of specific London places for dramatic effect when they remediate notorious locations, just as Dickens does in the novel. Second, the presumed social identities of a theatre's target audience contribute to the way in which specific urban places are interpreted and portrayed. Theatres stage differing presentations of the same locales because the productions are encoded with assumptions about patrons' backgrounds and urban experience. A single site could thus evoke alternatively nuanced cultural and symbolic resonances, depending on how the play addresses the audience. Third, London places are materially remediated as stage sets but, melodramatically reimagined to suit the drama, these actual places are transformed on stage into symbolic spaces, even while they are recreated physically as *mise en scène*. Finally, the specific cultural or moral connotations carried by the action and setting are overlaid with symbolically coded dramatic forms. Dramatisations are collaborative productions. In addition to the playwright's adaptation of the text, theatre managers, actors, musicians, artists and technicians all play a role in bringing Dickens's novel to life on stage. Audiences responded to the plot and characters at the same time as familiar theatrical and musical tropes, and the stylised performances of actors, who commonly used a gestural vocabulary to convey emotion.[13] Representations of London on stage were thereby constructed by the dialectical interaction of various material and imaginative properties.

This chapter draws on Jacky Bratton's concept of intertheatricality to explore how non-diegetic theatrical properties and performance techniques contribute to constructing meaning on stage. Denying the primacy of the text, an intertheatrical method examines play scripts alongside 'systems of the stage – scenery, costume, lighting and so forth – but also genres, conventions and, very importantly, memory'.[14] In nineteenth-century London, a vibrant theatrical scene and a choice of many different theatres facilitated the development of metatheatrical dramatic practices, which referred to other entertainments, or contemporary literary and visual arts. For instance, just as Dickens's original readers encountered the text as a multi-media product of text and image, so George Cruikshank's illustrations were embedded in early stagings of *Oliver Twist*. The scripts for the adaptations performed at both the Surrey Theatre and Sadler's Wells include stage directions that sets should be arranged '*according to the etching of the history*'.[15] Further, they indicate that performances included realisations of Cruikshank's engravings, in which the actors froze to create *tableaux* of the famous images. Productions also engaged with topical, political and social contexts. In the Pavilion's dramatisation, Dickens's critique of the New Poor Law is emphasised by a song performed by a chorus of paupers, who proclaim that 'none can know what the poor endure. / But the poor themselves – the wretched poor. [. . .] And they owe it all to the Poor Law Bill!'[16] Taking cues from Bratton's methodology, this chapter examines how theatrical representations of London were both produced and contested by the productions' self-conscious engagement with multiple material, symbolic and social contexts.

Problems face researchers who adopt an intertheatrical methodology. The ephemerality of many of the material properties of nineteenth-century theatre and the illusiveness of performance itself mean that much of the available evidence base is textual. Analyses of available sources can thereby appear to prioritise the text in a way that is inappropriate to how the audience would have experienced the drama. Sources documenting theatrical scenery are particularly scarce. Partly because of the problem of storing huge stage equipment, especially as the trend for spectacular built-out scenery gathered pace around the mid-nineteenth century, partly because sets suffered wear and tear, particularly if they were taken on tours of the provinces or overseas, and partly because practices of stage husbandry meant that older scenery was thriftily painted over for new productions, scenery simply was not saved. Moreover, written descriptions usually offer insufficient detail to develop a sense of what the set really looked like. Play scripts, for example, do not always contain detailed directions.[17] Other accounts are found in reviews and playbills, yet, as Sos Eltis rightly cautions, there are 'significant difference[s] between public utterance and private views'.[18] And, likewise, the pictorial records given in toy theatre sheets or drawings supposedly taken in the theatre cannot be taken at face value.[19] Even when images relate to the same performance event, these sources record different impressions. Conversely, such variations may also indicate how scenic representations of London responded dynamically to the demands of different dramas.

This chapter tracks multiple ways in which *Oliver Twist* and the physical city were adapted for the stage. It argues that London was a flexible frame through which the audience's reception of Dickens's work was mediated in early dramatisations, but also that *Oliver Twist* was imaginatively mapped on to London's built environment.

In staging alternative versions of the city, theatres presented differently nuanced portrayals of its inhabitants and social problems. Comingling and overlapping the imaginative and the material, the literary and the topographic, the fictional and the topical, and making these disparate elements visible simultaneously, dramatisations of *Oliver Twist* realised interactions between actual, imagined and symbolic spaces. However, these dialectical relations were not contained by theatrical performances. The final section of this chapter examines debates about the impact that adaptations of *Oliver Twist* were seen to have on life in London. Analysis of the dramas, and public reactions to them, thus reveals how contemporaries interrogated interactions between imaginative representation and the built environment, and questioned what legacies these Dickensian afterlives would leave to the city.

London and its Theatres

When *Oliver Twist* first appeared on stage in 1838, London's theatres were still split into patent and minor houses.[20] The 1737 Theatre Regulation Act granted a royal patent to only two London theatres, Covent Garden and Drury Lane. This meant that only these two theatres had the right to perform 'legitimate' drama (comedy and tragedy), which relied solely on spoken dialogue.[21] Until the patent system was repealed under the 1843 Theatre Act, the juxtaposition of acting with other modes of performance, such as music and dance, was both an aesthetic and a legal matter for minor theatres. Forbidden from staging 'straight' drama, other less 'respectable' genres developed in minor houses, including melodrama, burlesque and extravaganza. These genres achieved phenomenal popularity and were subsequently adopted by the patent theatres.[22] Jane Moody has thus rightly observed that the opposition between patent and minor theatres was not straightforward. In *Illegitimate Theatre in London*, she notes the circulation of actors, audiences and creative influences between legitimate and illegitimate theatre, and the fact that minor houses adopted numerous performance tactics to contravene the restrictions imposed on them by law.[23] Nevertheless, the division between patent and minor was still in place, at least nominally, when adaptations of *Oliver Twist* first appeared on programmes, and managers risked having their performance licences revoked if they were caught performing so-called legitimate drama.[24] All of the adaptations of *Oliver Twist* produced for the London stage in the 1830s were performed at minor playhouses (see Figure 2.1).[25] Therefore, legal pressures affected the

Play	Playwright	Theatre	Date of first performance	Length of run
Oliver Twist. Burletta. 4 Acts.	Anon. [Gilbert Abbot À Beckett; possibly J. S. Coyne and possibly even Dickens]	St James's Theatre, London	27 Mar.	1 night
Oliver Twist; or the Parish Boy's Progress. Domestic Burletta. 3 Acts.	Anon. [C. Z. Barnett]	Pavilion Theatre, London	21 May	1 week (to 26 May)
Oliver Twist. Or, That Parish Boy's Progress. A Domestic Drama [A Serio-Comic Burletta]. 3 [or 4?] Acts.	Anon. [George Almar]	Surrey Theatre, London	19 Nov.	19–24, 26 Nov.; 3–8, 10–15, 26–31 Dec. (35th performance = 31 Dec.) Into 1839 (86 performances)
Boz's Oliver Twist; or, The Parish Boy's Progress	Thomas Greenwood [R. Honner?]	Sadler's Wells Theatre, London	3 Dec.	Into 1839
Oliver Twist; or, The Workhouse Boy. Burletta. 4 Acts.	Edward Stirling	City of London Theatre, London	3 Dec.	Also performed 17 Dec.
Oliver Twist; or, The Parish Boy's Progress	Anon.	Theatre, Sheffield	27 Dec.	Also performed 29 Dec. (5th performance = 7 Jan. 1839)

Figure 2.1 Table detailing dramatisations of *Oliver Twist* staged in 1838. Information from Philip H. Bolton's *Dickens Dramatized*, pp. 109–13.

early adaptations, as productions were obliged to intersperse the dramatic action with songs, music or dance.

Nineteenth-century dramatic genres are reasonably fluid and unrestrictive, but London playhouses still built reputations for specialising in certain genres or appealing to particular social groups.[26] Reviews of versions of *Oliver Twist* in *Figaro in London* comment on, or allude to, the sociability of a night at these playhouses in addition to the dramatic fare. While *Figaro* encourages its readers to frequent Sadler's Wells, where '[t]riumphant success still attends this Theatre, which, under its present management, is daily becoming a more favourite place of entertainment', it warns against the 'drunken low players' at the Surrey, 'where any thing [*sic*] vulgar suits the appetites of the intellectual visitors, who mostly retire between the pieces to Chester's ham and beef and sausage shop, for a blow out'.[27] The extent to which the makeup of the audience was perceived to have an impact on the dramatic experience is further evidenced in the snobbish assertions made by the *Court Magazine and Monthly Critic* in August 1837:

> The two great theatres are closed; ditto the Olympic; ditto St. James's; so that, setting aside the bourgeois theatres on the Surrey side of the water, which no decent families visit, and Sadler's Wells, which is a day and a half's journey from any reasonable part of the metropolis, we have only four theatres open [. . .][28]

In fact, differently priced tickets meant that people from across a potentially broad social spectrum often enjoyed the same entertainment, even if they were separated into different areas of the auditorium according to their level of disposable income. It is difficult to reconstruct or categorise the Surrey's audience in the 1830s, for example.

> In 1843 a survey carried out for the [theatrical regulator, the] Lord Chamberlain's Office had described the Surrey audience as 'sometimes nobility and gentry, tradespeople, mechanics in the gallery, 4 women to 1 man in pit, the husbands, brothers being in the gallery to save expense'.[29]

George Almar's adaptation of *Oliver Twist* for this theatre, in 1838, responds to the likelihood that the audience will be mixed. As I will explore further on, he avoids alienating less wealthy patrons by representing poverty sympathetically, but simultaneously caters to bourgeois tastes by presenting the slums as sites of titillating excitement. Almar's style and the reviews thus reinforce the view that adaptations of *Oliver Twist* were prepared by the company, and anticipated by individuals, with certain preconceptions about these theatres' audiences in mind.

Theatres were social spaces. In part, this was because audiences spoke back to the players. Jerome K. Jerome's memoir of his brief period as an actor records that 'A Surrey-side Saturday-night audience are generally inclined to be cheerful, and, if the fun on the stage doesn't satisfy them, they rely on their own resources.'[30] Another form of sociability was in the conversations that carried on during performances. The noisiness of talk during theatrical productions is evoked in the watercolour 'Sadler's Wells Theatre' (1809) (Plate 4).[31] None of the people in the foreground of the scene appear particularly interested by the on-stage spectacle. Men and women sit and speak in intimate attitudes, while others are turning their backs to the performance, apparently to gossip with their neighbours. Contrary to Jerome's reminiscences of boisterous working-class audiences, the image implies that these members of the audience were in fact more likely to pay attention to the performance, as the indistinct figures in the cheaper gallery seats face towards the stage, while the well-dressed figures below look in all other directions. The image thereby suggests that the impact that audiences' social class was perceived to have on the dramatic experience varied between playhouses, and even within a single theatre. The importance of the audience to how dramas were conceived and received suggests that Dickensian adaptations were constructed in dialogue with the contemporary city. Still, as the image indicates, there were always multiple interactions between London's real and perceived social spaces before and during performances.

Setting the Scene

London-based dramas attracted crowds to theatres from at least the 1820s, and throughout the rest of the nineteenth century. Heidi Holder finds 'the beginnings of this trend [in] the enormous success of the dramatic adaptations of Pierce Egan's *Life in London*, better known as *Tom and Jerry*, following its serial publication in 1820–1'.[32] Tracking metropolitan themes in dramas from 1830 to 1898, Michael Booth has also shown that 'London and the life of London became one of the dominant themes in the drama of the day.'[33] Nevertheless, popular representational modes altered over time. Broadly speaking, earlier productions followed *Tom and Jerry*'s lead and portrayed the city as a site of comical revelry and outrageous pursuits.[34] By the latter decades of the nineteenth century, however, many London dramas were coloured by the social concerns brought prominently to the fore by investigative journalism.[35] In the late 1830s, adaptations of *Oliver Twist* picked up on contemporary vogues in popular and literary cultures, such as Newgate fiction. The novel's concern with London's underworld was one of its major draws for dramatists, theatre managers and audiences. Even when early adaptations intervene in social debates about the New Poor Law, like the novel, all the plays rapidly abandon the workhouse and head for London.

Aside from offering exciting plot possibilities, a London setting also responded to contradictory audience demands for verisimilitude and escapism.[36] Urban dramas could be spectacular. Booth has gone so far as to suggest that theatrical spectacles were developed in response to the growing monumentality of the metropolitan scene, which also made it an attractive subject for visual artists.

> The fact that many of these same monuments appeared repeatedly on the canvas of scene painters is evidence that the new architectural environment was too significant and too much a source of pleasure to be left outside the theatre. Conditioned to mass, grandeur, and elaborate ornamentation in the buildings about them, it is not surprising that the public responded enthusiastically to the same sort of thing translated into the values of theatrical production.[37]

Audiences' fascination with seeing London on stage was reinforced by its popular appeal in other impressive visual entertainments: for example, the panorama paintings displayed for paying audiences from the late eighteenth to mid-nineteenth century.[38] Variations of these large-scale scenic entertainments were appropriated by theatrical scene painters. Conversely, not all representations of London foregrounded its monumentality, as is evidenced in the enduring influence of William Hogarth's prints on later artists. Matthew Buckley has noted that a 'distinguishing feature of [the] new visual culture in the 1830s [was] a nearly obsessive fascination, among a greatly expanded audience, with the realistic representation of its own urban experience and milieu'.[39] In other words, the public wanted to see representations of everyday life in the city as well as its grandeur. Theatre managers thus capitalised on broader trends in popular culture and patrons' recognition of the thrills of metropolitan modernity. With these coexisting possibilities for spectacle and gritty detail, staging London dialectically responded to both the material city and its portrayal in various creative media.

As the century progressed, scenery became more spectacular, but also more detailed and realistic. Developments in stage techniques, like the use of limelight or box-sets, meant that designs moved on from the 'selective and aesthetic, almost suggestive representation' of a setting provided by sliding flats, to 'built out, [and] three-dimensional' scenery.[40] Spectacle and verisimilitude were not necessarily in conflict. Stage realism manifested both in representations of the quotidian and in elaborate reconstructions of the historical past, or recognisable landmarks.[41] These modes were still in their infancy in the 1830s, as it was not until performance runs began to lengthen in the 1850s and 1860s that the construction of elaborate sets for new productions became tenable for most theatres.[42] Still, early examples of scenery that anticipates these later trends represent London. In 1835, Lord Byron's poem *Manfred* was transformed into a Christmas burlesque, *Man-fred*, at the Strand Theatre, which recast the Count as a chimney sweep and the Jungfrau as a pile of broken gas pipes in central London.[43] An engraving of 'The Political Man Fred' in *Figaro in London* depicts this scene (Figure 2.2). Rooftops are silhouetted in the

Figure 2.2 'The Political Man Fred' (Source: © The British Library Board. P.P.5264.b).

background but the pipes appear as a three-dimensional construction in the foreground. Man-fred stands atop the pipes disconsolately.[44] *Figaro*'s decision to publish an engraving of this scene, rather than any other, suggests that metropolitan improvements were of interest to theatregoers and readers alike. Building on Booth's argument about the appeal of London's monumentality, this illustration, depicting a staging of urban development, suggests that representation of the city on stage was also a source of contemporary interest. Staging the modern metropolis permitted dramatisations to engage with current social and spatial contexts. London scenes in *Oliver Twist* thus allowed theatres opportunities to engage with popular theatrical genres and entertainments in multiple media and topical contexts, and to capitalise on the appeal of the novel.

London, Crime and *Oliver Twist*

Reviews of early adaptations of *Oliver Twist* in the press focus on their representations of urban criminality. Crime is embedded in *Oliver Twist*'s London scenes. This allowed commentators to use these adaptations as a means of talking about the dangers of the contemporary city. As Chapter 1 notes, fears that the social and political balance of the capital would be unsettled by the urban 'masses' being mobilised in rebellion was one of the reasons why slum demolitions were conceived as needed interventions. Overcrowded living conditions were sites of anxiety because, some contemporaries presumed, close-knit criminal communities would be formed as a result of the poor's tight proximity and inability to separate themselves from contact with nefarious people. Particularly in the wake of the 1832 Reform Act – which, by addressing the fact that urban centres were sparsely represented in parliament, had gone some way to relocating political power from inherited estates to cities – *Oliver Twist* provided a focal point for examining the growing, and potentially troubling, potency of urban populations. However, the different ways in which productions portray the city and engage with the issue of urban crime reveal that Dickens's text was dynamically adapted to serve different interests, and to promote various interpretations of life in London.

Oliver Twist *at the St James's Theatre, March 1838*

The first production of *Oliver Twist* was staged in London's West End. Indeed, the St James's Theatre was then the most westerly major playhouse.[45] Documenting the variety of challenging entertainments available in this district of theatreland, Bratton's *The Making of the West End Stage* has shown that the St James's position in an affluent area did not entail conservative programming. Indeed, the three plays that Dickens wrote for the St James's immediately prior to this production of *Oliver Twist* all use innuendo and suggestions of extra-marital relations to generate humour and titillate the audience. Nevertheless, the theatre's physical distance from the criminal scenes influenced their representation of London. As in the novel, the city is presented as a juxtapositional topography, clearly separated into criminal and middle-class spaces.

The thrilling, perhaps risqué, nature of the entertainment offered by on-stage criminality is indicated by the dramatist's decision to focus on the novel's London scenes. This adaptation does not set any scenes in the workhouse. Still, the St James's *paysage moralisé* draws more rigid lines between good and evil than Dickens. Unlike the novel, which, by detailing Fagin's tactics of manipulation and abuse, indicates that Oliver could have been tempted into a life of crime, in the St James's production his innate moral goodness is unassailable from the outset. Neither naivety nor privation threatens Oliver's unswerving rejection of crime. Straightaway he tells Fagin 'I don't like it – I'd rather go,' but is pressured into remaining with the gang by Charley and Dodger.[46] Nancy's role is also curtailed. She does not appear on stage again after recapturing Oliver and so is never given the opportunity to offer him protection. Despite her moral ambiguity in the text, she does not trouble the ethical division between the 'good' middle-class and criminal characters in this drama. The St James's adaptation does not present any pointed critique of the status quo. Even Bumble is somewhat redeemed. Although he remains a comically cowardly figure throughout, an implied attraction between him and Mrs Bedwin suggests that he was played more sympathetically in this production than in Dickens's text.[47] The middle class are the ethical centre of the drama, and aside from Oliver – who is, after all, middle class by birth – being poor equates to being criminal.

Differences between the plot and characterisation in this adaptation and Dickens's novel are only to be expected, given that it was produced when just ten of the monthly instalments were available – otherwise, the first of the novel's three volumes. At this point, readers were suffering the agony of a cliffhanger ending. Would Oliver survive being shot during the attempted burglary of the Maylie house? The St James's adaptation responds to readers' longing to know what would happen to Oliver next. The drama follows the serial reasonably faithfully until the final scene. Indeed, the script rehearses the major plot points in a functional manner, without pausing to embellish the dialogue with sentimental or comical soliloquies. The final scene is the longest in the piece, indicating that the adapter presumed the audience's interest would be focused on how the story would conclude. Answering desires for resolution, rather than deciding to take Oliver's narrative in a new direction, the dramatist anticipates Dickens's ending, based on what the serial has so far set up as the likeliest outcome. In the drama's concluding scene, Fagin and Sikes take Oliver to rob Brownlow's house, where all of the major middle-class characters have gathered. Oliver saves the day by alerting them to the danger, but Brownlow and Grimwig decide to admit Sikes and Fagin into the house, heroically proclaiming that they will fight them off. The scene climaxes when Sikes and Fagin try to make off with their loot and 'are met by Policemen &c Sikes fires Policemen knocks away his hand and Fagin falls. Mr Brownlow Grimwig Mrs Bedwin & Bumble Enter – the two first armed'.[48] Oliver is adopted by Brownlow, and Bumble earnestly hopes that 'he may never see a Poor house as long as he remains'.[49] Oliver's middle-class status is assured and the criminals are punished.

Urban spaces are portrayed as threatening in the St James's adaptation. On both occasions that a 'mob' is introduced on stage, the urban crowd acts as a cover for criminal activities: first, when Brownlow is pickpocketed, and then when Sikes and Nancy abduct Oliver. The streets are presented as potentially dangerous because the staging implies that criminals are hidden in busy public places. This association between crowds and potential misrule probably responds to anxieties about the fact that in 1841 there was only one police officer for every 900 inhabitants in London.[50] Despite this, London's criminal underworld does not pose a significant threat to middle-class spaces in this drama. Although the streets in which the poor and the wealthy come into contact are unruly, the middle-class characters find sanctuary in domestic spaces. Even in the final scene, Brownlow and Grimwig *decide* to let Sikes and Fagin into their home, and so automatically place the criminals at a disadvantage. The reassuringly timely arrival of policemen, and Brownlow and Grimwig's heroism, resolve the tension created earlier in the drama by the threatening spectacle of urban crowds. At the end of the play, then, the implied separation between middle-class and criminal spaces allows the wealthier characters and the forces of law and order to achieve a certain control over the city's unpredictable criminal population.

Oliver Twist *at the Pavilion Theatre, May 1838*

The next known dramatisation of *Oliver Twist* was produced in London's East End. A minor theatre only in name, the Pavilion was the leading East End playhouse until Hoxton's Britannia opened in 1841.[51] It was one of the largest theatres in London,[52] and Jim Davis and Victor Emeljanow note that it 'mirrored the patent theatres in its magnificence and aspirations', though its repertoire indicates that it catered to local people working in nearby maritime industries.[53] C. Z. Barnett's adaptation of *Oliver Twist* for this theatre is calculated to appeal to a mixed demographic. Like the St James's version, Barnett's anticipated Dickens's ending, yet, unlike the earlier production, in doing so he revised the text substantially. Barnett's predicted ending is ludicrously dissimilar from the novel: audiences nightly witnessed Oliver shoot and kill Monks.

Barnett's adaptation places the criminal characters at the centre of the drama from the outset. The first scene is set in the Three Cripples pub, rather than the workhouse, and depicts Monks hatching his plan to destroy Oliver with Fagin and the gang. This scheme impels the rest of the dramatic action, so that the coincidental or surprise encounters in Dickens's narrative are reimagined as deliberately engineered criminal machinations. In Act II, scene i, for instance, Dodger identifies Oliver prior to their introduction, and picks him up on the way to London on purpose. The centrality of the criminals to the dramatic action is further reinforced because Barnett uses the opening conceit to connect disparate episodes in Dickens's narrative. In Act I, scene ii, London criminals enter the workhouse, Sikes posing as the chimney sweep who wishes to apprentice Oliver. In this, similarly to the St James's dramatist, Barnett recognises the appeal of London's underworld to theatregoers. However, criminality and the city are presented very differently in the Pavilion's production. Unlike the previous adaptation, the poor are not indistinguishable from criminals.

Barnett's differentiation between various social groups among the urban poor is revealed in his critique of the New Poor Law. Like Dickens, Barnett presents the New Poor Law as a system of victimisation. Asserting this stance early on, the second scene opens with a chorus of paupers singing that 'The Poor Law Bill! / [Is] The poor man's bane! / It bringeth him ill, / And it bringeth him pain!'[54] Elaine Hadley convincingly argues in *Melodramatic Tactics* that the melodramatic mode informed how anti-Poor Law narratives were presented on stage.[55] She contends that melodrama's typical *dénouement*, in which the true relations between characters are revealed, provided an ideal counter-narrative to the New Poor Law's impersonal administration of welfare, and contrasted with the social alienation resulting from increased urbanisation and a loss of community. Nevertheless, Hadley stresses that the messages couched in this mode were not consistent, as the anti-Poor Law movement included people who advocated a return to an older structure of society, as well as those who agitated for further reforms that moved beyond both the ineffective parish system and the cruelty of the new law. Barnett's adaptation of *Oliver Twist* is written in the former vein. Bumble, who represents the old laws, is transformed into a hero. In Act III, scene iv, he overhears Monks and Fagin plotting Oliver's abduction and decides to alert Brownlow and save Oliver, before returning to marry Mrs Corney. Barnett's backward-facing approach is also revealed by the way that he revises the familial and social relationships between the characters.

Prior to the New Poor Law, parishes were sometimes imagined as extended families, in which members of the community knew each other personally, and the poor benefited from the benevolent, paternalistic aid of wealthier parishioners.[56] Barnett's critique of the New Poor Law is expressed in his emphasis on the importance of family relationships. Monks's evil characterisation is signalled by his betrayal of familial ties. He is cast as Brownlow's ungrateful nephew, who, disappointed when he could not marry his cousin Harriet Brownlow (she having already married a military man in secret), decides to ruin her in revenge. In the final scene, Monks recounts how he repeatedly deceived both Harriet and Brownlow to '[poison] the old man's mind against his child', and in so doing caused Oliver's mother's death.[57] Criminal though Monks's earlier actions obviously were, the significance of his betrayal is reinforced by the fact that Barnett recasts Oliver as Harriet's legitimate child, and so connects Oliver to Brownlow's family by blood and legal ties. Propagating the idea that the family is society's ideal model, the adaptation's happy conclusion is in the reunion of the legitimate family. This allows Oliver to take his place as Brownlow's heir, and implies a continuation of beneficial economic and emotional relations between these characters. However, Monks's malevolence is also enforced by his betrayal of illegitimate ties. Monks, rather than Fagin, is responsible for Nancy's 'fall' into prostitution. She is presented as the abandoned victim of Monks's seduction. Nancy is represented sympathetically, particularly when she tries to help Oliver. Her characterisation further demonises Monks but it also implies a critique of the New Poor Law's 'bastardy clause', which did not hold men to account for deserting unmarried mothers.

Barnett builds on the social concerns expressed in the novel and on stage conventions to adapt *Oliver Twist* as a conduit for his own Poor Law critique. Barnett is less faithful to Dickens's plot than the St James's dramatist. Conversely, his representation of the fluid interactions between criminal and middle-class characters and plots shows that there is no straightforward separation of middle-class and criminal spaces and social groups. In changing the relationships between the characters, Barnett adjusted how London was represented. The city is not a socially and morally divided topography; instead it is a liminal stage on which melodramatic criminal plots and opportunities for redemption are played out.

Oliver Twist *at the Surrey Theatre, November 1838*

George Almar was the first to adapt from the full novel. His *Oliver Twist. A Serio-Comic Burletta, In Three Acts* is famous among Dickensians both because it achieved an almost definitive status among nineteenth-century dramatisations of the novel, and because it was supposedly hated by Dickens. John Forster's biography relates that 'in the middle of the first scene [Dickens] laid himself down upon the floor in a corner of the box and never rose from it until the drop-scene fell'.[58]

Almar's *Oliver Twist* was also criticised by early reviewers for its fidelity to the novel. The *Literary Gazette* complains that the drama is unsuccessful because the adapter has 'attempted too much. It is impossible to bring all the circumstances of a narrative in three volumes into action in three acts, and within three hours.'[59] The reviewer makes a fair point. Almar's script certainly draws heavily on the novel, even preserving some sections of dialogue word for word. None the less, his adaptation became so popular that other playwrights revised subsequent versions of *Oliver Twist* from his script, rather than returning to Dickens's text. This led to '[v]ariant versions' of Almar's drama and its international dissemination: it was later performed in the USA.[60]

One of the reasons why Almar's adaptation may have 'attempted too much' is because it originally catered to an audience drawn from a mixture of backgrounds: 'David Osbaldiston, who became manager in 1831, gave evidence to the 1832 Select Committee on Dramatic Literature that all social classes were represented at the [Surrey] theatre.'[61] Even considering that Osbaldiston's statement would have been calculated to achieve the most favourable reception from the parliamentary committee, it is likely that the Surrey attracted diverse patrons. In 1837, the *Court Magazine* described the Surrey as 'bourgeois', yet its programme frequently featured nautical melodramas to appeal to the inhabitants of its surrounding riverside districts and passing sailors.[62] The Surrey's production of *Oliver Twist* signals that it was conceived for a mixed urban audience, as it gives nuanced portrayals of social class and crime, and does not equate poverty with criminality. For example, it recognises hierarchies within the social groups broadly conceived as working-class. Almar's script follows Dickens's novel in showing that the charity boy Noah Claypole considers himself 's'perior' to Oliver, 'whom everyone despises' as a 'verk'us' orphan.[63] Seeking to address a diverse public meant that the Surrey embedded various representations of London in their production, which competed and overlapped.

Examining Almar's script alongside available archival evidence indicates that the Surrey's production did not perform a representation of London that was socially and morally segregated. In the Pavilion's dramatisation, Monks is cast as the centripetal force of evil, and his movement between middle-class and criminal spaces unsettles the spatial and social divisions that the St James's adaptation implies. In Almar's version, however, evil is not localised around a single character, social problem or space. Oliver is threatened by diverse dangers – from institutionalised cruelties to melodramatic villains – which denies any easy division between 'good' and 'bad' people and places. Almar excites the audience's sympathy for Nancy from the outset, for instance, even though she is involved in criminal plots. Playing down her culpability in creating the 'respectable servant-maid' disguise to recapture Oliver from Brownlow, Almar presents the manœuvre as entirely Fagin's idea.[64] Nancy is already dressed in this costume when she first appears on stage, and so the audience does not witness her complicity in assuming a different identity. Not only does the costume she wears on her first entrance provide visual cues that link her to 'respectable' society, but also Almar invents further details about her back story to heighten the audience's compassionate engagement with her struggle between competing loyalties: 'I had a brother about his age that look'd like him in his coffin.'[65] The *Literary Gazette*'s reviewer did not think much to the Surrey's sympathetic portrayal:

> The only female of interest is Nance, in which Miss Martin displayed considerable talent. Why she dressed like a pretty lady's maid, with roses in her hair, &c., instead of the character, – the dweller in a ruffian's dirty garret and the debased street-walker, we cannot tell. It helped marvellously to destroy the illusion of the scene.[66]

For this reviewer, the Surrey's representation did not match her or his expectations about the character or the city. Apparently anticipating a more marked distinction between middle-class and criminal spaces, the review indicates a disappointed desire to see a melodramatically divided version of London on stage.

Available evidence suggests that the Surrey's *Oliver Twist* employed a combination of stage flats and three-dimensional built-out scenery to represent London. The script includes references to '*cast-iron cannon-shaped posts practicable attached to the wing*' and '*[i]n flat the entrance door, with steps to descend from it*'.[67] Meanwhile, an engraving of the Jacob's Island scene depicts characters mounting the set (see Figure 2.4 later). One reviewer, although less impressed by the production overall, praised its set design, stating that 'some very striking scenic effects are produced'.[68] Conversely, even though the Surrey did not present a *paysage moralisé*, various and competing representations of place in the Surrey's adaptation and its related ephemera indicate that verisimilitude was less important than the suggestion that titillating or horrifying scenes had material counterparts. Like Dickens's text, this play purveys pleasures generated by narrative, image and the imaginative appeal of London's underworld, and so constructs a portrayal of the city in which actual and symbolic spaces dialectically intersect.

The playbills for the Surrey's *Oliver Twist* imply that various representations of space were overlaid in the dramatisation (Figure 2.3). The playbill promises both verisimilitude and fiction, stating that

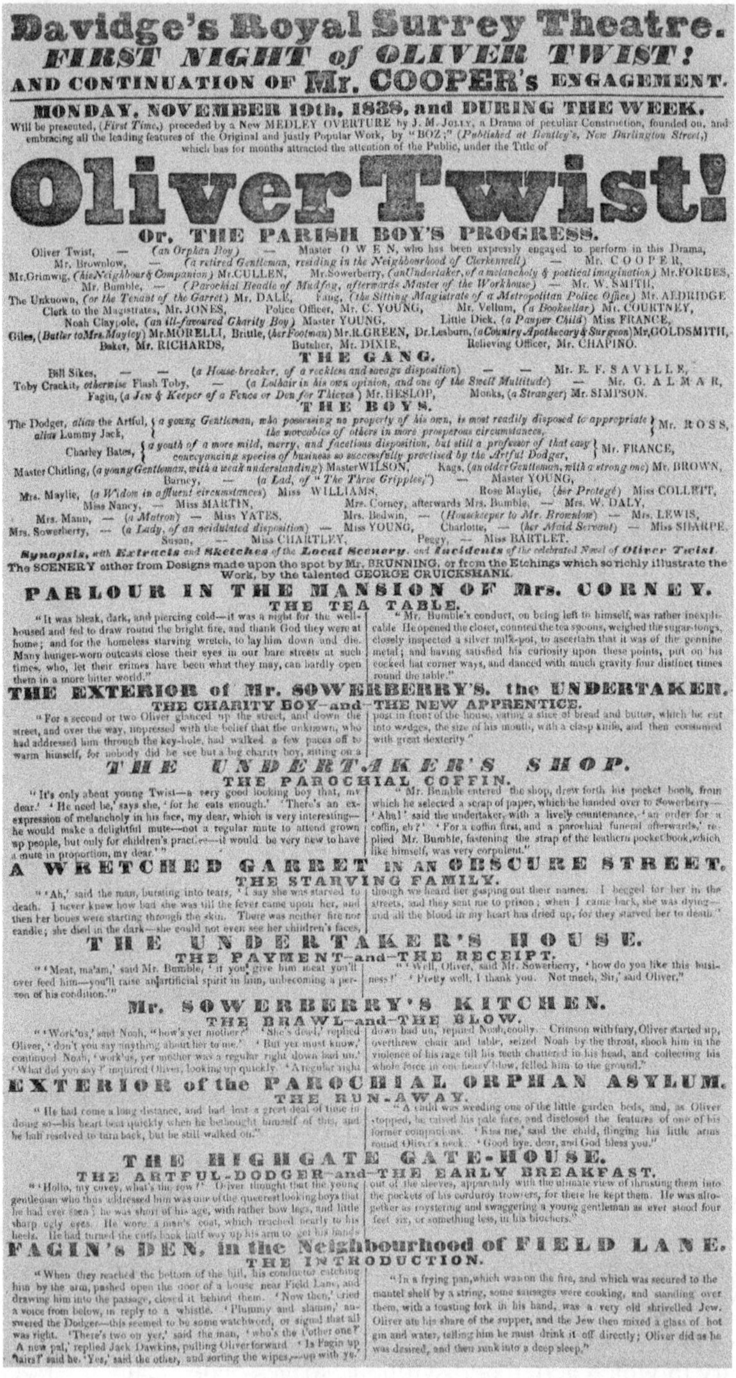

Davidge's Royal Surrey Theatre.

FIRST NIGHT of OLIVER TWIST!

AND CONTINUATION OF Mr. COOPER's ENGAGEMENT.

MONDAY, NOVEMBER 19th, 1838, and DURING THE WEEK.

Will be presented, (*First Time*,) preceded by a New MEDLEY OVERTURE by J. M. Jolly, a Drama of peculiar Construction, founded on, and embracing all the leading features of the Original and justly Popular Work, by "BOZ;" (*Published at Bentley's, New Burlington Street*,) which has for months attracted the attention of the Public, under the Title of

Oliver Twist!

Or, THE PARISH BOY'S PROGRESS.

Oliver Twist, — (*an Orphan Boy*) — Master OWEN, who has been expressly engaged to perform in this Drama,
Mr. Brownlow, — (*a retired Gentleman, residing in the Neighbourhood of Clerkenwell*) — Mr. COOPER,
Mr. Grimwig, (*his Neighbour & Companion*) Mr. CULLEN, Mr. Sowerberry, (*an Undertaker, of a melancholy & poetical imagination*) Mr. FORBES,
Mr. Bumble, — (*Parochial Beadle of Mudfog, afterwards Master of the Workhouse*) — Mr. W. SMITH,
The Unknown, (*or the Tenant of the Garret*) Mr. DALE, Fang, (*the Sitting Magistrate of a Metropolitan Police Office*) Mr. AEDRIDGE
Clerk to the Magistrates, Mr. JONES, Police Officer, Mr. C. YOUNG, Mr. Vellum, (*a Bookseller*) Mr. COURTNEY,
Noah Claypole, (*an ill-favoured Charity Boy*) Master YOUNG, Little Dick, (*a Pauper Child*) Miss FRANCE,
Giles, (*Butler to Mrs. Maylcy*) Mr. MORELLI, Brittle, (*her Footman*) Mr. R. GREEN, Dr. Lesburn, (*a Country Apothecary & Surgeon*) Mr. GOLDSMITH,
Baker, Mr. RICHARDS, Butcher, Mr. DIXIE, Relieving Officer, Mr. CHAPINO.

THE GANG.

Bill Sikes, — — (*a House-breaker, of a reckless and savage disposition*) — — Mr. E. F. SAVILLE,
Toby Crackit, *otherwise* Flash Toby, — (*a Lolhair in his own opinion, and one of the Swell Multitude*) — Mr. G. ALMAR,
Fagin, (*a Jew & Keeper of a Fence or Den for Thieves*) Mr. HESLOP, Monks, (*a Stranger*) Mr. SIMPSON.

THE BOYS.

The Dodger, *alias* the Artful, *alias* Lummy Jack, { *a young Gentleman, who possessing no property of his own, is most readily disposed to appropriate the moveables of others in more prosperous circumstances,* } Mr. ROSS,
Charley Bates, { *a youth of a more mild, merry, and facetious disposition, but still a professor of that easy conveyancing species of business so successfully practised by the Artful Dodger,* } Mr. FRANCE,
Master Chitling, (*a young Gentleman, with a weak understanding*) Master WILSON, Kags, (*an older Gentleman, with a strong one*) Mr. BROWN,
Barney, — (*a Lad, of "The Three Cripples;"*) — Master YOUNG,
Mrs. Maylie, (*a Widow in affluent circumstances*) Miss WILLIAMS, Rose Maylie, (*her Protegé*) Miss COLLETT,
Miss Nancy, — Miss MARTIN, Mrs. Corney, afterwards Mrs. Bumble, — Mrs. W. DALY,
Mrs. Mann, — (*a Matron*) — Miss YATES, Mrs. Bedwin, — (*Housekeeper to Mr. Brownlow*) — Mrs. LEWIS,
Mrs. Sowerberry, — (*a Lady, of an acidulated disposition*) — Miss YOUNG, Charlotte, — (*her Maid Servant*) — Miss SHARPE,
Susan, — Miss CHARTLEY, Peggy, — Miss BARTLET.

***Synopsis**, with **Extracts** and **Sketches** of the **Local Scenery**, and **Incidents** of the celebrated Novel of **Oliver Twist**.*

The SCENERY either from Designs made upon the spot by Mr. BRUNNING, or from the Etchings which so richly illustrate the Work, by the talented GEORGE CRUICKSHANK.

PARLOUR IN THE MANSION OF Mrs. CORNEY.

THE TEA TABLE.

"It was bleak, dark, and piercing cold—it was a night for the well-housed and fed to draw round the bright fire, and thank God they were at home; and for the homeless starving wretch, to lay him down and die. Many hunger-worn outcasts close their eyes in our bare streets at such times, who, let their crimes have been what they may, can hardly open them in a more bitter world."

"Mr. Bumble's conduct, on being left to himself, was rather inexplicable He opened the closet, counted the tea spoons, weighed the sugar-tongs, closely inspected a silver milk-pot, to ascertain that it was of the genuine metal; and having satisfied his curiosity upon these points, put on his cocked hat corner ways, and danced with much gravity four distinct times round the table."

THE EXTERIOR of Mr. SOWERBERRY'S, the UNDERTAKER.

THE CHARITY BOY—and—THE NEW APPRENTICE.

"For a second or two Oliver glanced up the street, and down the street, and over the way, impressed with the belief that the unknown, who had addressed him through the key-hole, had walked a few paces off to warm himself, for nobody did he see but a big charity boy, sitting on a post in front of the house, eating a slice of bread and butter, which he cut into wedges, the size of his mouth, with a clasp knife, and then consumed with great dexterity."

THE UNDERTAKER'S SHOP.

THE PAROCHIAL COFFIN.

"It's only about young Twist—a very good looking boy that, my dear.' 'He need be,' says she, 'for he eats enough.' 'There's an ex-expression of melancholy in his face, my dear, which is very interesting—he would make a delightful mute—not a regular mute to attend grown up people, but only for children's practice—it would be very new to have a mute in proportion, my dear.'"

"Mr. Bumble entered the shop, drew forth his pocket book, from which he selected a scrap of paper, which he handed over to Sowerberry—'Aha!' said the undertaker, with a lively countenance, 'an order for a coffin, eh?' 'For a coffin first, and a parochial funeral afterwards,' replied Mr. Bumble, fastening the strap of the leathern pocket book, which like himself, was very corpulent."

A WRETCHED GARRET IN AN OBSCURE STREET.

THE STARVING FAMILY.

"'Ah,' said the man, bursting into tears, 'I say she was starved to death. I never knew how bad she was till the fever came upon her, and then her bones were starting through the skin. There was neither fire nor candle; she died in the dark—she could not even see her children's faces, though we heard her gasping out their names. I begged for her in the streets, and they sent me to prison; when I came back, she was dying—and all the blood in my heart has dried up, for they starved her to death.'"

THE UNDERTAKER'S HOUSE.

THE PAYMENT—and—THE RECEIPT.

"'Meat, ma'am,' said Mr. Bumble, 'if you give him meat you'll over feed him—you'll raise an artificial spirit in him, unbecoming a person of his condition.'"

"'Well, Oliver,' said Mr. Sowerberry, 'how do you like this business?' 'Pretty well, I thank you. Not much, Sir,' said Oliver."

Mr. SOWERBERRY'S KITCHEN.

THE BRAWL—and—THE BLOW.

"'Work'us,' said Noah, "how's yer mother?' 'She's dead,' replied Oliver, 'don't you say anything about her to me.' 'But yer must know,' continued Noah, 'work'us, yer mother was a regular right down bad un.' 'What did you say?' inquired Oliver, looking up quickly. 'A regular right down bad un,' replied Noah, coolly. Crimson with fury, Oliver started up, overthrew chair and table, seized Noah by the throat, shook him in the violence of his rage till his teeth chattered in his head, and collecting his whole force in one heavy blow, felled him to the ground."

EXTERIOR of the PAROCHIAL ORPHAN ASYLUM.

THE RUN-AWAY.

"He had come a long distance, and had lost a great deal of time in doing so—his heart beat quickly when he bethought himself of this, and he half resolved to turn back, but he still walked on."

"A child was weeding one of the little garden beds, and, as Oliver stopped, he raised his pale face, and disclosed the features of one of his former companions. 'Kiss me,' said the child, flinging his little arms round Oliver's neck. 'Good bye, dear, and God bless you.'"

THE HIGHGATE GATE-HOUSE.

THE ARTFUL-DODGER—and—THE EARLY BREAKFAST.

"'Hollo, my covey, what's the row?' Oliver thought that the young gentleman who thus addressed him was one of the queerest looking boys that he had ever seen; he was short of his age, with rather bow legs, and little sharp ugly eyes. He wore a man's coat, which reached nearly to his heels. He had turned the cuffs back half way up his arm to get his hands out of the sleeves, apparently with the ultimate view of thrusting them into the pockets of his corduroy trowsers, for there he kept them. He was altogether as roystering and swaggering a young gentleman as ever stood four feet six, or something less, in his bluchers."

FAGIN's DEN, in the Neighbourhood of FIELD LANE.

THE INTRODUCTION.

"When they reached the bottom of the hill, his conductor catching him by the arm, pushed open the door of a house near Field Lane, and drawing him into the passage, closed it behind them. 'Now then,' cried a voice from below, in reply to a whistle. 'Plummy and slamm,' answered the Dodger—this seemed to be some watchword, or signal that all was right. 'There's two on yer,' said the man, 'who's the t'other one?' 'A new pal,' replied Jack Dawkins, pulling Oliver forward. 'Is Fagin up stairs?' said he. 'Yes,' said the other, and sorting the wipes,—up with ye.'

"In a frying pan, which was on the fire, and which was secured to the mantel shelf by a string, some sausages were cooking, and standing over them, with a toasting fork in his hand, was a very old shrivelled Jew. Oliver ate his share of the supper, and the Jew then mixed a glass of hot gin and water, telling him he must drink it off directly; Oliver did as he was desired, and then sunk into a deep sleep."

Figure 2.3. *Oliver Twist! Or, the Parish Boy's Progress* (Source: © Victoria and Albert Museum. 2011FB0362-01).

'The SCENERY [was developed] either from Designs made upon the spot by Mr. BRUNNING, or from the Etchings which so richly illustrate the Work, by the talented GEORGE CRUIKSHANK.'[69] On the one hand, both the script and playbill suggest that the set design is location-specific. Scenes are set in '*Mutton-hill, in the neighbourhood of Hatton-garden*' and on '*London Bridge*'.[70] This indicates that certain scenes will realise specific places in the contemporary city and give playgoers vicarious access to hidden criminal locations – even if, in reality, this was achieved only by audiences' associations between the place names and their memories of these sites or their representation in the novel. On the other hand, this supposed topographic realisation is combined with deliberately pictorial effects. The technique of realising illustrations was ubiquitous in nineteenth-century dramatisations of Dickens's novels, and continued well into the mid-nineteenth century:[71] 'the effect depended on the apparent literalness and faithfulness of the translation'.[72] However, juxtaposing *tableaux* and set designs drawn from recognisable images with supposedly realistic portrayals of London meant that *Oliver Twist* and the city were reimagined through a combination of real and imagined referents. In this, the theatre sought to satisfy contradictory desires for armchair slum tourism and pictorial effects. The result was that the setting became a complex of competing remediations of fiction, image and the city, and that the Surrey's representation of space was dynamically responsive to competing agendas.

One example of how the Surrey realised, but also departed from, Cruikshank's illustrations is in their representation of the Jacob's Island scene. A comparison between Cruikshank's illustration 'The Last Chance' and an engraving of the Jacob's Island scene published in printed editions of the script reveals a direct line of influence from the print to the *mise en scène* (Figure 2.4). If we suppose that the engraving 'by Pierce Egan the Younger, from a drawing taken during the representation' is a reasonably faithful record, then the set design is recognisable from the print.[73] One can trace consistent details between the scenery and Cruikshank's engraving. The rooftop is nearly identical and its distinctive features are preserved, such as the T-shaped guttering that runs beneath the tiles. Conversely, while the set was evidently inspired by Cruikshank's image, 'The Last Chance' is not realised as a *tableau vivant*. The scenery alters the print by giving a cut-out view inside the house. The cut-out set enables the action to continue on two separate levels simultaneously, as Egan's engraving depicts: Sikes mounts

Figure 2.4 Frontispiece to *Oliver Twist. A Serio-Comic Burletta* (Source: © The British Library Board. 2304.b.9).

the set to attempt his escape, while the other characters struggle below. The set contributes to heightening the dramatic tension, as it ensures that the scene can be played as fast-paced and action-packed. Tributes to Cruikshank's images thus intersect with dramatic conventions and the demands of the plot.

Further differences between Cruikshank's image and Egan's engraving suggest that realisation of the illustrations was combined with visual tourism to this notorious slum in the production. The play script states that the scene should depict the '*interior of an old house situated on Jacob's Island with view of the Thames by moonlight*'.[74] Likewise, instead of the closely packed houses in the background of Cruikshank's print, the backdrop displays the river. In Egan's engraving, rooftops and a church spire along the opposite bank evoke the larger cityscape rather than the confined slum space. The real Jacob's Island was surrounded by tidal waterways and so the alterations to Cruikshank's image in the set design allude to its distinctive topography, even if it did not aim for topographic verisimilitude. The scenery thus mingled actual and symbolic spaces by evoking the illustration, Jacob's Island and London more widely.[75]

The playbill and engraving suggest that the drama will realise Jacob's Island in accordance with the audience's prior expectations of this nefarious locale. However, part of the scene's appeal is in the fact that it offers audiences the opportunity to see a notorious place that they would otherwise be unlikely to frequent. Jacob's Island is described as 'hidden' location in the novel, 'wholly unknown, even by name' to many London residents (*OT*, p. 416). The synopsis of the scene given on the playbill quotes from Dickens's description of the site as well as detailing Sikes's death, and so implies that the topography contributes to the titillating attraction of the scene and the dramatic excitement. Painting the backcloth to represent a view of the Thames and the wider city likely heightened this effect, because it emphasises the fact that Jacob's Island is locatable in London. Playgoers are invited to imagine that dangerous criminals and spaces coexist in the same city as themselves, so adding to the thrilling effect of the criminal scenes. The real and the imagined are thus realised dialogically to construct a multi-layered representation of space that evokes fiction, image, and the actual built environment at once, even while each of these composite elements are also conceived through the dialectical interaction of symbolic and material referents.

Oliver Twist at Sadler's Wells Theatre, December 1838

Sadler's Wells is mentioned in Dickens's description of Oliver's first arrival in London, which details how he and Dodger cross 'from the Angel into St John's road, and struck down the small street which terminates at Sadler's Wells theatre' (*OT*, p. 63). Oliver's journey ends at Fagin's den, located 'near' to Field Lane, less than a mile from Sadler's Wells (Plate 5) (*OT*, p. 63). Nearby locations are regularly mentioned in this theatre's adaptation to emphasise their proximity to the criminal settings. Even if patrons were not personally familiar with these specific locations, then, they were nevertheless invited to imagine themselves as physically adjacent to nefarious criminal hide-outs. A contemporary reviewer indicates that this technique was a significant attraction for audiences:

> the principal incidents in the novel are supposed to have taken place in the immediate vicinity of this theatre, its performance was as much a matter of policy as it has since proved of interest. Although coming late in the field, and in some measure forestalled by adaptations from the novel at other minor theatres, this does not seem to prove less effective on that account; its *locale* imbuing it with an interest which no previous theatre had possessed, and thus in some measure compensating for the want of novelty in the treatment of its incidents.[76]

The reviewer suggests that the proximity of Sadler's Wells to the places represented on stage becomes part of the audience's experience. In her or his account, the theatre's neighbourhood distinguishes this adaptation from alternative productions, and even makes it more authoritative than other versions, despite its similarity in other respects. The dialogue that Sadler's Wells constructs between their dramatisation and the contemporary cityscape allows the theatre to create a distinctive representation of London, which made their play stand out from the crowd of other Dickensian adaptations.

Foregrounding the dramatic appeal of both London and urban crime, Sadler's Wells imaginatively maps melodramatic associations on to the neighbouring built environment by adapting *Oliver Twist* as a local drama. Local dramas are plays based close to the theatre and are a common feature in Sadler's programmes in the 1830s. These include Thomas Wilks's *The Red Crow* (1834) and George Almar's *The Clerk of Clerkenwell* (1834).[77] The theatre's proximity to sites made notorious by crime satisfied contradictory popular tastes for realism and melodrama, or, as Holder puts it, '[t]he enduring desire for intensely localised plays suggests that the audience's enjoyment was not only in seeing the recreations of urban spaces, but more precisely in the embedding of melodrama in such a fully realised world, a visual realm that authenticates the action on stage'.[78] This is best illustrated by the staging of gruesome real-life murders – like *The Ruby Ring; or, The Murder at Sadler's Wells* (1840) – in which excessiveness in reality accords with the demands of melodrama.[79] Portraying London as both a known locale and the stage for surprising or criminal activities, this adaptation offers a different kind of metatheatrical engagement with contemporary London than the Surrey's production. Where the Surrey's representation purports to introduce its audience to the drama's slum settings for the first time, Sadler's Wells emphasises the recognisability of these specific urban locations.

Despite the supposed verisimilitude of the urban scenes, akin to the Surrey's staging techniques, the production at Sadler's Wells realised Cruikshank's illustrations alongside allegedly realistic representations of the contemporary cityscape. For instance, the script details that the scene of Oliver's first introduction to Fagin's gang opens with 'Fagin [being] discovered frying sausages, and the whole picture as much like the print as possible'.[80] However, rather than overlaying and combining pictorial and topographic realisation in a single scene, Sadler's Wells dramaturgy alternates quickly and indiscriminately between *tableaux vivants* and *tableaux architecturaux*. Detailed stage directions given in the play script indicate that potentially familiar local scenes were reconstructed on stage. Oliver and Dodger's arrival in Saffron Hill is a very short scene, and the slum vista is quickly replaced by the interior of Fagin's den. Nevertheless, the on-stage action is minutely described:

> Saffron Hill.[81] House P.S.2.E / Dark / Slow Music – Enter from house cautiously, a figure enveloped in a cloak. He looks round to see if he is observed and Exits L.H.I.E.
>
> Enter Dodger leading in Oliver alarmed Dodger intimates all is right – sees a light in the upstairs window – intimates that is the place – goes to door and whistles – the light is removed and a voice within says
>
> 'Now then?'[82]

This scene is almost exclusively pictorial, and it does not significantly contribute to the development of the plot. This, added to the fact that Saffron Hill is located near to Sadler's Wells, suggests that this scene is included to reinforce the drama's local setting for, just as the 'effect of a realisation depended on recognition', the appeal of representing adjacent areas on stage probably also derived, in part, from the familiarity of the scenes.[83]

In addition to the stagecraft, both the script and the advertising emphasise the proximity of the criminal scenes. Those set in nearby locations – 'Field Lane', 'Clerkenwell', 'Saffron Hill', 'Hatton Garden', 'Field Lane' – are named one after the other on the playbill (Figure 2.5).[84] The repetition of Field Lane signals that nearby sites were supposed to occasion audience interest, particularly as the locales were typeset in larger print than the (presumably exciting) dramatic content of these scenes, such as 'the chase'.[85] Meanwhile, the characters' dialogue emphasises the immediacy of the action. For example, in the novel, Fagin counsels Oliver that Dodger will 'be a great man himself, and make you one too, if you take pattern by him' (*OT*, p. 72). The play script extends this advice to indicate its specifically local applicability: 'And do you mind my dear only make Mr Dawkins your model, and you'll be a great man *in these parts* before you've done depend on it.'[86] Performed in front of a set that portrayed the neighbouring area, the exchange is likely to have been staged as a metatheatrical nod to local members of the audience.

Verisimilitude may not have been an achievable or a desired effect, however. The playbill and the stage directions imply specificity but it is possible that these sets may have been reused from other productions, rather than produced specially for *Oliver Twist*. There are multiple references to stage flats in the script, particularly for generic interior scenes. Flats were regularly recycled between productions, and audience members may have even recognised scenery from other plays. Indeed, Jerome's memoir recounts how multiple reuses of a cottage interior in the same play provoked the audience to '[greet] its second appearance with cries of kindly recognition'.[87] Nevertheless, local scenes were brought into focus *both* because they were potentially knowable places *and* because they were the setting for exciting events. Even if the set design was evocative rather than realistic, the review of the Sadler's production shows that Saffron Hill's closeness to the theatre was perceived to accentuate audience interest in these scenes. Therefore, even if a patron did not have the first-hand knowledge to recognise the topography, or the set was not sufficiently detailed, the thrill of proximity meant that this was not necessarily a barrier to the dramatic effect. The staging of London in local dramas oscillated dialectically between physical, perceived and represented spaces.

Audiences also consumed *Oliver Twist* as part of an intertheatrical experience (Figure 2.5). The playbill that survives for this

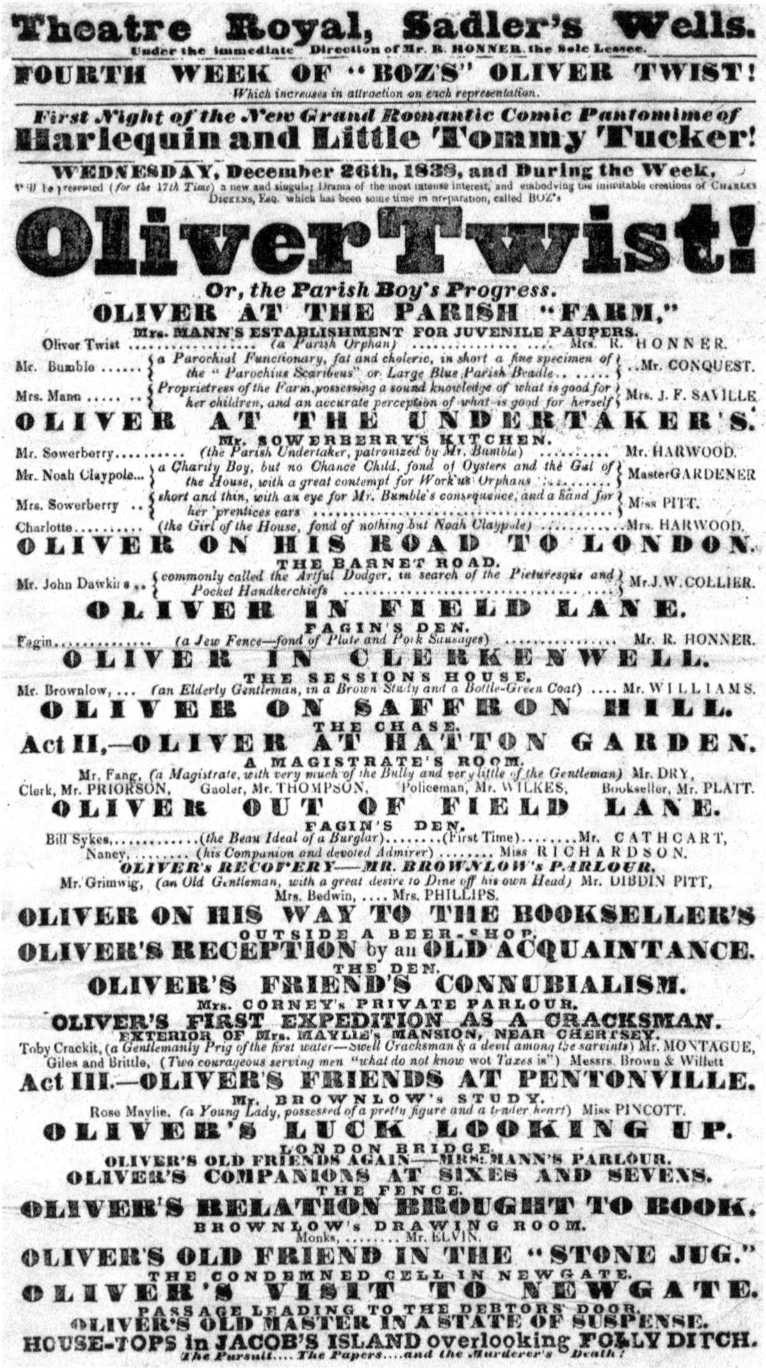

Theatre Royal, Sadler's Wells.

Under the immediate Direction of Mr. R. HONNER, the Sole Lessee.

FOURTH WEEK OF "BOZ'S" OLIVER TWIST!

Which increases in attraction on each representation.

First Night of the New Grand Romantic Comic Pantomime of

Harlequin and Little Tommy Tucker!

WEDNESDAY, December 26th, 1838, and During the Week,

Will be presented (*for the 17th Time*) a new and singular Drama of the most intense interest, and embodying the inimitable creations of CHARLES DICKENS, Esq. which has been some time in preparation, called BOZ's

Oliver Twist!

Or, the Parish Boy's Progress.

OLIVER AT THE PARISH "FARM,"

MRS. MANN'S ESTABLISHMENT FOR JUVENILE PAUPERS.

Oliver Twist .... (*a Parish Orphan*) .... Mrs. R. HONNER.
Mr. Bumble ...... { *a Parochial Functionary, fat and choleric, in short a fine specimen of the "Parochius Scarибeus" or Large Blue Parish Beadle* ...... } ..Mr. CONQUEST.
Mrs. Mann ...... { *Proprietress of the Farm, possessing a sound knowledge of what is good for her children, and an accurate perception of what is good for herself* } Mrs. J. F. SAVILLE

OLIVER AT THE UNDERTAKER'S.

MR. SOWERBERRY'S KITCHEN.

Mr. Sowerberry.......... (*the Parish Undertaker, patronized by Mr. Bumble*) .... Mr. HARWOOD.
Mr. Noah Claypole... { *a Charity Boy, but no Chance Child, fond of Oysters and the Gal of the House, with a great contempt for Work'us Orphans* ...... } MasterGARDENER
Mrs. Sowerberry .. { *short and thin, with an eye for Mr. Bumble's consequence, and a hand for her 'prentices ears* .... } Miss PITT.
Charlotte.......... (*the Girl of the House, fond of nothing but Noah Claypole*) ....Mrs. HARWOOD.

OLIVER ON HIS ROAD TO LONDON.

THE BARNET ROAD.

Mr. John Dawkins .. { *commonly called the Artful Dodger, in search of the Picturesque and Pocket Handkerchiefs* .... } Mr.J.W.COLLIER.

OLIVER IN FIELD LANE.

FAGIN'S DEN.

Fagin.............. (*a Jew Fence—fond of Plate and Pork Sausages*) .... Mr. R. HONNER.

OLIVER IN CLERKENWELL.

THE SESSIONS HOUSE.

Mr. Brownlow, ... (*an Elderly Gentleman, in a Brown Study and a Bottle-Green Coat*) .... Mr. WILLIAMS.

OLIVER ON SAFFRON HILL.

THE CHASE.

Act II,—OLIVER AT HATTON GARDEN.

A MAGISTRATE'S ROOM.

Mr. Fang, (*a Magistrate, with very much of the Bully and very little of the Gentleman*) Mr. DRY,
Clerk, Mr. PRIORSON, Gaoler, Mr. THOMPSON, Policeman, Mr. WILKES, Bookseller, Mr. PLATT.

OLIVER OUT OF FIELD LANE.

FAGIN'S DEN.

Bill Sykes,............(*the Beau Ideal of a Burglar*)........(First Time)........Mr. CATHCART,
Nancy,........ (*his Companion and devoted Admirer*) .... Miss RICHARDSON.

OLIVER's RECOVERY—MR. BROWNLOW's PARLOUR.

Mr. Grimwig, (*an Old Gentleman, with a great desire to Dine off his own Head*) Mr. DIBDIN PITT,
Mrs. Bedwin, ... Mrs. PHILLIPS.

OLIVER ON HIS WAY TO THE BOOKSELLER'S

OUTSIDE A BEER-SHOP.

OLIVER'S RECEPTION by an OLD ACQUAINTANCE.

THE DEN.

OLIVER'S FRIEND'S CONNUBIALISM.

MRS. CORNEY's PRIVATE PARLOUR.

OLIVER'S FIRST EXPEDITION AS A CRACKSMAN.

EXTERIOR OF MRS. MAYLIE's MANSION, NEAR CHERTSEY.

Toby Crackit, (*a Gentlemanly Prig of the first water—Swell Cracksman & a devil among the sarvints*) Mr. MONTAGUE,
Giles and Brittle, (*Two courageous serving men "what do not know wot Taxes is"*) Messrs. Brown & Willett

Act III.—OLIVER'S FRIENDS AT PENTONVILLE.

MR. BROWNLOW's STUDY.

Rose Maylie, (*a Young Lady, possessed of a pretty figure and a tender heart*) Miss PINCOTT.

OLIVER'S LUCK LOOKING UP.

LONDON BRIDGE.

OLIVER'S OLD FRIENDS AGAIN—MRS. MANN'S PARLOUR.

OLIVER'S COMPANIONS AT SIXES AND SEVENS.

THE FENCE.

OLIVER'S RELATION BROUGHT TO BOOK.

BROWNLOW's DRAWING ROOM.

Monks, ... Mr. ELVIN.

OLIVER'S OLD FRIEND IN THE "STONE JUG."

THE CONDEMNED CELL IN NEWGATE.

OLIVER'S VISIT TO NEWGATE.

PASSAGE LEADING TO THE DEBTORS' DOOR.

OLIVER'S OLD MASTER IN A STATE OF SUSPENSE.

HOUSE-TOPS in JACOB'S ISLAND overlooking FOLLY DITCH.

The Pursuit.... The Papers....and the Murderer's Death!

HARLEQUIN
AND LITTLE
TOMMY TUCKER!
OR, THE
Christmas Feast & Giant's Supper.

"Little Tommy Tucker sung for his supper, What shall he have? White bread and butter.
How shall he cut it without ere a knife? How shall he marry without ere a wife?"

The Machinery and Changeable Scenes, by Mr. B. SLOMAN. The Decorations, Properties and Physiognomy, by Mr. DEARLOVE.
The Dresses, by Mr. SMITHYES, Miss BAYLEY, and Assistants.

The Overture and Pantomimic Music, composed expressly for the occasion by Mr. HERBERT.
The Pantomime Composed and Arranged, by Mr. H. YOUNGE and Produced under the immediate Direction of Mr. R. HONNER
The Scenery, by Messrs TELBIN, MEADOWS, W. MARSHALL, FENWICK, and Assistants.

Abode of Old Winter in the Regions of Eternal Frost!
Old Winter, — — Mr. BROADFOOT,
Attendant Snowballs, — Masters Freeze, Frost, Bluenose, Pinchemup, Chilblain, and Verycold,

PUDDING PALACE, THE DWELLING OF CHRISTMAS!
Christmas, — Mr. DRY, Jack Pudding, — *(his Attendant Sprite)* — Mr. STILT,
Attendants on Christmas, Mesdames HARWOOD, ROSE, PRIORSON, THOMPSON, PHILLIPS, LOUISE, &c.

Left Wing of Turkey Terrace, *leading to the* ***Mansion of Lady Bountiful***
Grumbo Gobble Kid, *(a Juvenile Giant, with a ravenous appetite both for Love and Meat)* Mr. C. MONTGOMERY,
Little Tommy Tucker, *(a Juvenile Vender of Ballads)* Mr J. W. COLLIER,
Tabitha Turnspit — *(Cook Extraordinary to the Lady Bountiful)* — Mr. GRAMMANI,
Rufus & Grufus, *(his Particular Friends and Associates, Partners in his Toils and Pleasures)* Messrs. Thicknob & Strongarm

BOUNTIFUL BOUDOIR—Hon. Lady Bountiful *(much given to Charity & the Brandy Bottle)* Mad. HARWOUDIEN
Rosalie, *(her Daughter, full of Beauty and Benevolence)* Madlle. WIBER.
Messrs. Pryall & Gotobed, *(Footmen to the Hon. Lady before-mentioned)* Messrs. Neverwork & Nothingdo.

Giant's Wicket, leading to the Castle of Master Grumbo's Papa!
Gigantic Guards, Messrs. Tenfoot, Stretchem, Tallboy, Growlast, Longbody, and the Illegitimate Sons of Gog and Magog.

THE GIANT'S SUPPER!
Displaying his Table after his Christmas Eve's Feast!
Goliah Gobblekid, (the respected Parent of Master Grumbo) by [illegible].
But his name's a secret—the extraordinary size of this Gentleman is so great, that it has been found practicable only to introduce his HEAD and SHOULDERS for public inspection; therefore imagination must picture the rest.

PALACE OF CHRISTMAS.
Harlequin, (his First Appearance in that Character) **Mr. J. W. COLLIER,**
Columbine, - Mademoiselle WIBER,
Pantaloon, Mr. GRAMMANI, Jack Pudding, Mr. STILT,
Clown, (his 1st Appearance in that Character at this Theatre) **Mr. C. MONTGOMERY**

View of Windsor Castle from the Park!
Nurseryman, Mr. Mundungus Marygold, Milkmaid, Miss Skyblue.

The "Old Joe's Head" and "Grimaldi" Tavern!
Landlord, Mr. J. Grim, Ostler, Mr. Geeup, Haymakers, Messrs. Longgrass, Newmown-Rye, & Early Dew,
Waiters, Messrs. Nevercome, Callagain, Twopencetake, & Collarall, Lady, Mrs. J Grim, Old Maid, Miss Starch.

THE RISING SUN AND SHIPPING POST OFFICE.
Postmaster, Mr. Letterall, Passengers, Messrs Goalong, Neverstop, Runaway, &c.

Court Card Manufactory and Surgeon's Shop.
Surgeon, Mr. Loplimb, Card Maker, Mr. Oldnick, Cobbler, Mr. Welt, Officer, Mr. Noservice.

GRAND NUKTERIDOPALIAN EFFECT; INTRODUCING
TWO SPLENDID DIORAMIC PAINTINGS,
Executed by **Mr. W. MARSHALL & Mr. MEADOWS,** of the T. R. Covent Garden—illustrating
The Coronation of Her Majesty, Queen Victoria!
DISPLAYING THE
Exterior & Interior of Westminster Abbey!
On THURSDAY, the 28th of June, 1838, from Drawings taken on the spot.

MARINE PAINTER'S AND EXHIBITION ROOM!
Hindoo Apartment in the Exhibition Room, with the
BAYADERES' DAGGER DANCE!
A Well-known Eating-House and Country Cage!
Fat Beadle, Mr. Union, Starved Paupers, Messrs. Nothingeat & Sorryfare.
The CAVERN of COLD and DAMPS of FOG!
REALMS OF JOY.

Boxes 2s. Pit 1s. Gal. 6d. Half price to the Boxes only, at the end of the First Piece
The Box-Office under the direction of Mr. FREEMAN, open from Eleven o'clock till Three.
Manager, Mr. H. YOUNGE, of the Theatre Royal, Covent Garden
ORGAN to whom all Communications relative to that Department, must be addressed at the Stage Door, of the Theatre.
Doors open at a Quarter before Six—commence at Half-past
S. G. Fairbrother · Garrick Printing Office, 31, Bow Street, Covent Garden

Figure 2.5 *Oliver Twist! Or, the Parish Boy's Progress* (Source: © Islington Local History Centre. GB1032 S/SWT1/3/4/3).

production details that its seventeenth performance was staged alongside the Christmas pantomime *Harlequin and Little Tommy Tucker! Or the Christmas Feast & Giant's Supper*. On the same night that contemporary slums were represented in *Oliver Twist*, Sadler's Wells also staged fantastical places like the 'Palace of Christmas', and displayed 'Two Splendid Dioramic Paintings', which included a 'View of Windsor Castle from the Park' and the 'Exterior & Interior of Westminster Abbey!'[88] Markedly different views of London are presented in these adjacent productions. Audiences would have been able to reflect on the contrast between slums and monumental architecture, and map these differences in wealth and grandeur specifically and locally. In addition to encoding criminal associations into the modern built environment, the localised representation at Sadler's Wells reinforced the disparity of wealth in London. Therefore, similarly to the Surrey's representation of Jacob's Island, the Sadler's Wells adaptation of *Oliver Twist* as a local drama combined competing views of London that were mediated through contemporary knowledge and association, as well as through fiction and the visual arts.

Portability

Adaptations of *Oliver Twist* juxtapose scenes of the capital with others based outside of London. This faithfully replicates the settings of Dickens's novel but also provides a cache of contrasting images. One of the ways that dramatisations create and reinforce an urban imaginary was through its visual dissimilarity to rural scenes. However, staging the city meant something different again when productions toured out of London to the provinces or overseas. When the Surrey's adaptation was taken to Bristol, for instance, a reviewer described 'Mr. Stephens, as *Fagin*, [as] one of the low Jews who abound in some of the metropolitan districts'.[89] Unlike ephemera relating to the London shows, this review does not situate Fagin in a specific slum location, even while it conceives the capital through topographically localised social stereotypes. This review is misleading because it implies that London is evoked as a symbolic space when productions were transported out of the capital, and shows were unable to realise localised representations of place. It suggests that the metropolitan was conceived in relation to the action in these scenes and the broad cultural connotations evoked by certain kinds of urban space, as popularised by the contemporary press. Conversely, London was still conceived in contradictory terms in touring productions. While slum tourism was certainly one appeal, a review of a dramatisation of *Oliver Twist* performed in Edinburgh in 1840 gives special mention to the monumental architecture that audiences saw represented. 'The view of the Thames and part of London by moonlight, seen through the arch of London Bridge, is one of the most beautiful and picturesque scenes that could well be imagined.'[90] Provincial and overseas audiences could thus enjoy different kinds of visual tourism. London was evoked flexibly, depending on what aspects of the plot the dramatisation chose to emphasise, or which material properties were available at the theatre.

Impact

Both place and text were diversely represented in these early adaptations. There was more than one *Oliver Twist*, and more than one version of London on stage at the same time. Actual spaces and their symbolic connotations were multiply reimaged alongside Dickens's text and Cruikshank's images, and this compound evocation of perceived, conceived and lived spaces was differently constructed, depending on the theatre's location and audience. *Oliver Twist* was thus adapted in dialogue with the contemporary city, but London was also reimagined in parallel with differing adaptations of Dickens's plot and characters. However, some people thought that this did more than simply embed imaginative associations in certain places. *Oliver Twist* was seen by some to have a real impact on life in London.

Oliver Twist was caught up in wider reactions against Newgate fiction when it was first serialised in the 1830s. Evolving from the records of real-life criminals in the *Newgate Calendar*, by the mid-1830s the Newgate novel was an established, if disreputable, genre. At first these stories were generally rollicking adventures, but the genre developed into a conduit for social and political critique. By the time that *Oliver Twist* was published, Newgate fiction frequently addressed experiences of dislocation, poverty and alienation among poorer social groups.[91] Particularly after the New Poor Law was passed in 1834, and the deliberately cruel workhouse test made the victimisation of the poor a matter of public policy, tales of individual resistance to imposed hierarchies and the established order were understandably attractive. Conversely, reactionary opposition to the genre argued that exciting depictions of the criminal underworld could degrade public morality. Newgate fiction was broadly accused of glamorising criminality. Some people worried that it could incite imitative behaviour and so make London more dangerous. Similar arguments resurface periodically. One might compare these fears to the outcry against Sensation fiction in the 1860s, or more recently to concerns that violent computer games will heighten aggressive impulses in users.[92] In the 1830s, as in the modern day, such worries were not ubiquitous. Nevertheless, concerns voiced by certain high-profile individuals (including the Prime Minister, Lord Melbourne) prove that this was not the view of an obscure minority.[93]

In his preface to the 1841 edition of *Oliver Twist*, Dickens explains that he had tried to intervene in debates about Newgate fiction by representing criminals 'as they really are' rather than as 'amiable', 'seductive fellows', in the hope of 'warning' people against any misguided attraction.[94] While some reviewers still criticised Dickens's subject matter, others praised the novel's representation of criminals 'in all their wretchedness'.[95] Reviewing *Oliver Twist* after it was published as a complete volume in November 1838, the *Examiner* states that '[f]ew writers have achieved a nobler moral than that which is embodied here – not simply the scorn of vice but the "pity of it" too'.[96] However, dramatisations of *Oliver Twist* were perceived by some as an even greater threat than the novel. William Makepeace Thackeray famously complained that when

> these heroes stepped from the novel on to the stage [. . .] the whole London public, from peers to chimney-sweeps, were interested about a set of ruffians whose occupations are thievery, murder, and prostitution. A most agreeable set of rascals, indeed, who have their virtues, too, but not good company for any man.[97]

Thackeray's complaint is focused less on the content of the play than on the fact that it was watched by a mass audience. The supposed risks are intensified by the indiscriminate, and potentially indiscriminating, makeup of theatre audiences.

The urban crowd is threatening because it is not a knowable community. Thackeray's concerns therefore posit a view of popular culture that is opposite to Benedict Anderson's concept of imagined communities, which explores how unknown numbers of people can be imaginatively connected by a shared cultural experience. In contrast, Thackeray's 'whole London public' is an anonymous mass, and he reinforces his fears that dramatisations could put *Oliver Twist* into the wrong hands in his plea: 'in the name of common sense let us not expend our sympathies on cut-throats and other such prodigies of evil!'[98] Thackeray's use of the word 'sympathy' is a telling indicator about why he felt that theatre audiences' identification with criminal characters was dangerous. In *The Romantic Crowd*, Mary Fairclough explores how sympathy was conceived as a mode of political communication in the late eighteenth and early nineteenth centuries. It did not relate only to emotion. Sympathetic engagement with criminal characters could facilitate the spread of subversive ideas and social behaviours, and so, Thackeray implies, audience members had to have developed skills of critical thinking to be able to resist the pull of sympathetic identification. As urban populations grew at an alarming rate, the number of people who might be negatively affected by exciting representations of criminality was increased. Moreover, the physical space of the theatre exacerbated its dangers. Individuals were crowded into a theatre's auditorium, and so could be influenced both by the drama and by the diverse public with whom they shared the space.

In contrast to fears that dramatisations of *Oliver Twist* would incite criminal behaviour, other prominent individuals made contradictory claims that these dramas would make London a safer place. In 1838, the Surrey's manager, G. B. Davidge, published a lengthy treatise that claimed that the play would 'forcibly inculcate the great moral lesson, that vice, however prosperous for a time, will sooner or later meet with punishment and disgrace, while virtue, whatever be its trials and temptations, will ultimately secure a lasting and just reward.'[99] This moral lesson is universal, Davidge implies, yet the public that he addresses is not an undifferentiated crowd. Indeed, Davidge's claims that *Oliver Twist* will provide a social and moral education to its audiences are based on the presumption that it will have different effects on different patrons.

> The Stage is never devoted to a more noble or better purpose than when it lends its powerful aid to improve the morals, and correct the vices of the age. It is this conviction which has led to the adaptation of the impressive Work upon which this Drama is founded, opening one of the darkest volumes of life, and revealing facts that must startle the more strongly, from the previous total ignorance of their existence, even by those persons residing in the very heart of the scenes in which they are daily and nightly passing.[100]

Although the vividness of the criminal scenes in Dickens's novels, particularly in contrast to his more clichéd representation of the Maylie household, indicates the author's fascination with London's underworld, the novel is 'recognisably on the side of the law'.[101] Aligning the Surrey's production with Dickens's moral stance, Davidge suggests that the Surrey's dramatisation will benefit less reputable playgoers by performing, and so reinforcing, middle-class values. Moreover, excusing the fact that the theatre is capitalising on the exciting depiction of urban crime, Davidge implies that these scenes will serve to enlighten his upright audience members about the seedy facts of London life. The bill even goes so far as to suggest that watching *Oliver Twist* will help people to take precautionary measures to ensure their safety in the city, so while, like Thackeray, Davidge declares that dramatising *Oliver Twist* will have an impact on public morality, his claims about its positive effects are established because of his oppositional view of the public as interconnected and discriminating.

Davidge claims that his bombastic assertions are authoritative by contextualising his statements in line with contemporary concerns about the inability of the new metropolitan police force to control the capital adequately. Quoting from an article on the subject published in *The Times*, he states:

> Nothing can be more useful and salutary than the knowledge of such facts to the Public at large [than] 'giving to the respectable inhabitants of every parish a general acquaintance with what goes on in the little alleys near them, and thus enabling them to exercise with the more advantage that local vigilance, which is the best, and, indeed, almost the only check upon these haunts of vice. Evidence of complete offences committed by the tenants against any specific law is not easily obtained, but constant observation, and active declared suspicion, will do a good deal in the way of prevention. Disorderly people grow cautious how they behave when they know that their practices are understood and watched. Few pockets are picked under a gas lamp.'[102]

The article quoted by the bill reports on an investigation into the state of the metropolitan police commissioned by the government in 1837.[103] This 'Report from the Select Committee on Metropolis Police Offices' concludes that 'Metropolitan police have not been useful in preventing crime [and] Police never attempt to meddle with receivers of stolen goods, though perfectly well known to them.'[104] The report gives further details of how the police had allowed Ikey Solomon (a notorious East End fence on whom, it was long presumed, the character of Fagin was based) to escape justice on multiple occasions.[105] The Surrey's dramatisation reinforces these contemporary fears about the city's lawlessness, and so appears to confirm Davidge's paratextual representation. London scenes constantly threaten to dissolve into disorder and, unlike in the St James's adaptation, the police are directly critiqued:

> *But.* Oh, here cums a policeman.
> *Mr. B.* Who generally is the last person who does come on such occasions. (*mutteringly*)[106]

The police have no power to control the criminal characters and are represented as either ineffective or abusive: '*Mr. B.* Don't hurt him, officer. D-mn it, sir, I say, don't hurt the boy, or, by the Lord! I'll thrash the dust out of your blue jacket.'[107] Still, seeking to appeal to a broad public, Almar's dramatisation offers both topical critique and reassurance. Davidge's bill suggests that providing an education about London's underworld will encourage and facilitate the surveillance of the poor by the wealthy, and so implies that *Oliver Twist* will help the middle class to take control of the city.

Despite Davidge's assertions, the belief that dramatisations of *Oliver Twist* could have a negative impact on London intensified in the 1840s. In 1848, the Lord Chamberlain banned theatres from performing adaptations of the novel, and attempted to suppress productions over the next two decades by extending licences selectively and infrequently: once to the Pavilion Theatre in 1855, then to John Oxenford's version at the Queen's Theatre in 1868.[108] Although the Lord Chamberlain's ban did not ultimately prevent unlicensed productions of *Oliver Twist* from appearing in London and elsewhere, this sustained interest in preventing further dramatisations shows that Dickens's works were perceived to have a perceptible impact on life in London during his lifetime.

The different representations of London in these early adaptations reveal that Dickensian afterlives were mobilised to construct multiple images of the city, and linked social issues, even before Dickens had completed the novel. Adaptation of the novel was one vehicle through which contemporaries could use Dickens as a platform to popularise and disseminate their own interpretations and agendas. Early adaptations thus model practices of mobilising Dickensian afterlives in improvement debates, which became more widespread over the following decades. Multiple remediations between the physical and the symbolic in early dramatisations of *Oliver Twist* realise Dickens as an affective bridge between imaginative representation and material reality, for, while place had an impact on the style of each drama, adaptations also affected how the perceived cultural identities of actual places and symbolic spaces were communicated to a wider public.

Notes

1. Bolton, p. 104. Three plays by Dickens premiered at the St James's Theatre in the 1836–7 season: *The Strange Gentleman*, *The Village Coquettes* and *Is She His Wife? or, Something Singular!*
2. Ibid., p. 109.
3. Ibid., p. 109. The number of performances expected in a theatre run increased in the mid-nineteenth century, but in the 1850s there were still 'only thirteen productions in the West End [that] ran for 100 consecutive nights or more' (Booth, *Theatre in the Victorian Age*, p. 13). In his memoir of the short time he spent as an actor, Jerome K. Jerome comments that 'an unusually long run' in minor theatres in the latter decades of the nineteenth century would last 'a month or six weeks' (p. 46). Jerome's account is no doubt exaggerated for comic effect, but it nevertheless indicates that long runs were not typical in minor theatres during the nineteenth century.
4. This is evidenced by theatre listings in newspapers in December 1838. For example: Anon. (1838), 'Public Places of Amusement', *Figaro in London,* 363, 3 Dec., p. 106.
5. A surviving handwritten script of the Sadler's Wells adaptation gives J. L. Greenwood's name as the adapter, but a review attributes the adaptation to the theatre's manager at this time, Robert Honner. Both the script and review are located in the Islington Local History Centre, London.
6. Bolton, pp. 112–13.
7. As on the playbill for the Sadler's Wells version of *Oliver Twist* (London, Islington Local History Centre, GB1032 S/SWT1/3/4/3. *Oliver Twist! Or, the Parish Boy's Progress*, at Sadler's Wells Theatre (3 December 1838), playbill). Marc D. Cohen has, however, examined how Dickens tried to counteract unauthorised adaptations by attempting to impose a hierarchical value system, in which he authorised some adaptations and not others 'like a royal patent [. . .] in exchange for productions arranged and produced more in keeping with his wishes' ('How Dickens Co-opted the British Theatrical Adaptation Industry in 1844: Part I', p. 133).
8. An evening at the theatre in nineteenth-century London required stamina. Offering multiple entertainments every evening, the full programme often lasted for at least four hours (Moody, p. 165).
9. *Bumble's Courtship* extracts the scene in which Bumble proposes to Mrs Corney as a short interlude piece, without making significant changes to the dialogue or progress of events. The only marked alteration is in Bumble's final speech, which, in line with nineteenth-century stage conventions, addresses the audience directly: 'If there happens to be any bashful gentleman present this evening, who is thinking of making an offer of matrimony to some fair lady, and doesn't quite know

the way to set about it, I hope the manner in which my future partner here, (*looking lovingly at* MRS. CORNEY) Mrs. Corney, and myself have settled our affairs will have given him a practical lesson' (p. 11).

10. London, Islington Local History Centre, GB1032 S/SWT/1/2/1/15. [J. L. Greenwood], *Boz's Oliver Twist. Or, the Parish Boy's Progress*, handwritten play script, III, vii, f. 60.
11. Jacky Bratton, Marc Brodie, Elaine Hadley and Michael Ragussis (among others) have examined how theatrical performances played a role in both establishing and questioning social and political identities outside of the playhouse (J. S. Bratton, 'Theatre of War: The Crimea on the London Stage 1854–5', in David Bradby et al. (eds), pp. 119–137; Brodie, 'Free Trade and Cheap Theatre'; Elaine Hadley, 'Storming the "Bastile" [*sic*]: *Oliver Twist* and Melodramatic Resistance to the New Poor Law of 1834', in *Melodramatic Tactics*, pp. 77–132; Michael Ragussis, '"Family Quarrels"', in *Theatrical Nation*, pp. 1–42).
12. Approximately two miles away on the south bank of the River Thames.
13. As set out in contemporary acting handbooks, such as Siddons, *Practical Illustrations of Rhetorical Gesture and Action*.
14. Bratton, p. 38.
15. Almar, I, i, p. 5. Italics in original.
16. Barnett, I, ii, p. 7.
17. The licensing copies of scripts submitted to the Lord Chamberlain, for example, usually offer sparse evidence about the setting. This allowed copyists to complete the scripts as quickly as possible to meet licensing deadlines.
18. Eltis, p. 7.
19. Toy theatre publishers produced juvenile versions of popular dramas to coincide with their representation on the London stage. As such, toy theatre sheets have often been seen as a unique visual record of nineteenth-century theatrical scenery and costumes. However, I explore how these juvenile adaptations in fact present very different interpretations of source dramas, even when they are based on the same performance event, in an article in the *Journal of Victorian Culture*, '"Kaleidoscopes of Changing Pictures": Representing Nations in Toy Theatre'.
20. Minor theatres were diminutive only in name; by 1866, many of them had capacities comparative to Covent Garden and Drury Lane (each at 2,500). In *Curiosities of London*, John Timbs states that the Pavilion in Whitechapel could hold 2,300 people, and the Britannia in Hoxton 2,400. These estimates vary throughout the nineteenth century, as fires resulted in the destruction and subsequent rebuilding of a number of theatres. Nevertheless, minor theatres commanded both a wide appeal and the ability to house a multitude of patrons per night (*Curiosities of London*, p. 789).
21. Anne Humphreys, 'Victorian Stage Adaptations and Novel Appropriations', in Sally Ledger and Holly Furneaux (eds), pp. 27–34, p. 27.

22. Moody, p. 6.
23. Moody explains that 'rhyming couplets and dramatic recitative, accompanied by music, provided two important kinds of illegitimate speech at the minor theatres. Then, from the 1790s onwards, playhouses began to circumvent the ban on spoken dialogue by the use of linen scrolls, also known as flags or banners. The scrolls were inscribed with small portions of dramatic speech (idiosyncratic spellings often provided a source of amusement for some educated spectators) and held aloft on stage by the performers for the audience to read' (pp. 28–9).
24. Sos Eltis explains in *Acts of Desire* that, under the terms of the 1737 Licensing Act '[a]ny theatre found guilty of performing an unlicensed play could have its performance licence revoked and be closed down. These laws remained essentially unchanged until the Theatres Act of 1968 [. . .] The risks of prosecution and loss of livelihood for theatre managers were clear, while playwrights faced the frustration and expense of writing a play only to have it refused a licence. The power of the censorship system to ban the performance of any play deemed offensive to public decency and morality thus provided an inbuilt incentive for writers and managers to conform to orthodox standards' (p. 4).
25. Bolton, pp. 109–15.
26. As Jim Davis and Victor Emeljanow emphasise in *Reflecting the Audience*, theatres self-consciously engaged in dialogues with contemporary contexts, and productions addressed their target audiences directly. Nevertheless, as Davis and Emeljanow stress, theatre audiences remained reasonably unpredictable, partly because many London theatres were within easy walking distance of each other (p. 16). Theatres also encouraged a variety of custom by selling tickets at different prices, and by allowing people the opportunity to buy discounted tickets if they attended only a part of the evening's entertainment (Moody, p. 165). Still, each theatre had a distinct identity, which, in the 1830s, was at least partly determined by the socio-economic spectrum represented in its target audience.
27. Anon. (1839), 'Theatricals', *Figaro in London*, 372, 21 Jan., pp. 20–1, p. 21.
28. Anon. (1837), 'Amusements', *Court Magazine and Monthly Critic*, 2, 1 Aug., p. 95.
29. Davis and Emeljanow, p. 19.
30. Jerome, pp. 59–60.
31. Spectacle was a celebrated feature of productions at Sadler's Wells throughout its history and the watercolour depicts one of its famed 'aquatic dramas', in which water from the New River and the mineral well on its site were directed into a tank under the stage (Timbs, *Curiosities of London*, p. 787).

32. Heidi J. Holder, 'Nation and Neighbourhood, Jews and Englishmen: Location and Theatrical Ideology in Victorian London', in Davis and Holland (eds), pp. 105–20, p. 105.
33. Michael R. Booth, 'The Metropolis on Stage', in Dyos and Wolff (eds), pp. 211–24, p. 212.
34. Holder, p. 49.
35. As in Wilkie Collins's *The New Magdalen: A Dramatic Story, In a Prologue and Three Acts* (London: published by the author, 1873), which picks up on discussions about prostitutes' reintegration into mainstream society.
36. Meisel has noted that, as the century progressed, 'the appetite for truth and fact shared the stage with the appetite for wonder' (p. 33).
37. Booth, *Victorian Spectacular Theatre*, pp. 3–4.
38. Panoramas were a popular mode of entertainment from the 1790s until well into the 1850s. The first panorama exhibition in London, by Robert Barker and his son Henry Aston Barker, included a view of *London from the Roof of Albion Mills* (1794). (For a discussion of the first panoramas see, for instance, Denise Blake Oleksijczuk (2011), 'Introduction: Robert and Henry Aston Barker's Panorama', in *The First Panoramas*, pp. 1–22.) Subsequent exhibitions displayed a variety of landscapes. Topical subjects, such as scenes of battle and exotic landscapes, were popular, but the exotic was depicted alongside the recognisable. Views of London and other British landscapes and cityscapes were regularly represented through the first half of the nineteenth century (Hyde, pp. 61 and 37). Panoramas were adopted by scene painters and mechanists in some productions – one of many exchanges between the stage and other visual arts in the period. Martin Meisel's authoritative *Realizations* long since explored manifold interactions between visual and theatrical cultures, while Richard Altick's *Shows of London* exposes pathways of influence between distinct and distinctive entertainments.
39. Buckley, p. 434.
40. Booth, *Theatre in the Victorian Age*, p. 74.
41. Booth, *Victorian Spectacular Theatre*, p. 17.
42. Jerome notes in his memoir: 'Fresh scenery is a very great rarity at the minor theaters. When anything very special is produced, and an unusually long run is expected, say, of a month or six weeks, one or two scenes may, perhaps, be specially painted, but, as a rule, reliance is placed upon the scenery, the gradual growth of years, already in stock, which, with a little alteration, and a good deal of make-shift, generally does duty for the "entirely new and elaborate scenery" so minutely described in the posters' (p. 46).
43. Tunbridge, p. 212.
44. Anon. (1835), 'The Political Man Fred', *Figaro in London*, 167, 14 Feb., p. 31.

45. See 'A Map of London Theatres and Similar Places of Amusement from 1800 to 1870', in Ernest Bradlee Watson (1926), *Sheridan to Robertson*, available on *arthurlloyd.co.uk* (last accessed 28 Apr. 2017).
46. London, British Library, Lord Chamberlain's Collection, Add MS 42945, ff. 683–707b. Anon., *Oliver Twist. A Burletta in Two Acts* (St James's Theatre; Licensed 26 Mar. 1837), play script, f. 689.
47. Bumble It's a long time Maam, since I've passed such a very pleasant evening as I've done to night [*sic*]
Mrs B = I'm glad of it Sir – I'm sure you've made yourself very agreeable
Bum You see Maam – I can do these things out of the parish that I couldn't do in it –

(BL, LCC, Add MS 42945, *Oliver Twist*, f. 704.)

48. Ibid., f. 707.
49. Ibid., f. 707.
50. Vernon, p. 66.
51. Moody, p. 38.
52. John Timbs described the Pavilion as 'one of the largest theatres in the metropolis, cover[ing] nearly an acre of ground: it is nearly 60 feet high, yet has but two tiers of boxes and one gallery; depth and width, nearly 50 feet each; decorations, dead-white, gold, and crimson'. In a survey detailing which theatres were licensed by the Lord Chamberlain in 1866, the Pavilion has a seating capacity of 2,300, only 100 less than the Britannia. The old patent theatres, Drury Lane and Covent Garden, are the largest, with capacities of 2,500 (*Curiosities of London*, pp. 786 and 789).
53. Davis and Emeljanow, p. 55.
54. Barnett, I, ii, p. 7.
55. See Hadley, 'Storming the "Bastile"', pp. 77–132.
56. Ibid., pp. 80–5.
57. Barnett, III, v, p. 37. In this adaptation, Monks also murdered Oliver's father.
58. Forster, p. 105.
59. Anon. (1838), 'Drama', *Literary Gazette*, 1140, 24 Nov., pp. 747–8, p. 748.
60. Bolton, p. 109.
61. Davis and Emeljanow, p. 5.
62. Anon. (1837), 'Amusements', *Court Magazine and Monthly Critic*, 2, 1 Aug., p. 95.
63. Almar, I, ii, p. 10.
64. Ibid., II, ii, p. 29.
65. Ibid., II, vi, p. 39.
66. Anon. (1838), 'Drama', *Literary Gazette*, 1140, 24 Nov., pp. 747–8, p. 748.
67. Almar, I, ii, p. 10, and I, v, p. 15.
68. Anon. (1838), 'Theatrical Examiner', *Examiner*, 1608, 25 Nov., p. 742.

69. London, Victoria and Albert Museum, 2011FB0362-01. *Oliver Twist! Or, the Parish Boy's Progress*, at the Surrey Theatre (19 Nov. 1838), playbill.
70. Almar, I, xi, p. 27, and III, viii, p. 67.
71. Bolton, p. 108.
72. Meisel, p. 30.
73. Almar, p. 1.
74. Ibid., III, xii, p. 57.
75. This technique can be compared to later composition photography. Daniel Novak explains that composition photography 'set out to restore aesthetic unity, and in the process it produced realism itself as a photographic fiction [. . .] blur[ring] the boundary between realism and fiction [. . .] by using photography to represent scenes and encounters that never occurred' (p. 4).
76. London, Islington Local History Centre, GB1032 S/SWT/1/2/1/15. Anon., 'Review' (hand-dated 22 Dec. 1838), newspaper cutting.
77. Moody, p. 171.
78. Holder, p. 106.
79. Moody, p. 171.
80. ILHC, [Greenwood], *Boz's Oliver Twist*, I, v, f. 21.
81. The playbill and the script are not consistent, locating the action variously in Field Lane and Saffron Hill. However, the two places were adjacent in London. Dickens's description is deliberately obscure, stating that Fagin's den is in 'a house *near* Field-lane' (*OT*, p. 63. Italics my own). This permits various interpretations of its exact location. The discrepancy between the Sadler's documents may result simply from the adapter and the scene painter having interpreted the text differently, or from various opinions about which view could be more successfully 'realised'.
82. ILHC, [Greenwood], *Boz's Oliver Twist*, I, iv, f. 20.
83. Meisel, p. 251.
84. ILHC, *Oliver Twist!* Playbill.
85. Ibid.
86. ILHC, [Greenwood], *Boz's Oliver Twist*, I, v, f. 23b. Italics my own.
87. Jerome, p. 59.
88. ILHC, *Oliver Twist!* Playbill.
89. Anon. (1839), 'The Theatre', *Bristol Mercury*, 2553, 2 Feb., p. 3.
90. Anon. (1840), 'The Theatre', *Caledonian Mercury*, 18755, 26 Mar., p. 3.
91. Buckley, pp. 430–1.
92. Paul J. C. Adachi and Teena Willoughby's 2011 study in *Psychology of Violence* suggests that it is the element of competition in video games that elevates aggressive behaviour, rather than violent content.
93. Juliet John, 'Contextual Overview', in Juliet John (ed.), *Charles Dickens's Oliver Twist*, pp. 7–18, pp. 15–16.

94. Dickens, 'The Author's Introduction to the Third Edition (1841)', pp. 457–8.
95. Ibid., p. 457.
96. Anon. (1838), 'The Literary Examiner', *Examiner*, 1607, 18 Nov., pp. 723–5, p. 723.
97. William Makepeace Thackeray, qtd in Hotton et al., *Charles Dickens*, p. 28.
98. Ibid., p. 28.
99. Los Angeles, Huntington Library, Rare Books 217462. [G. B. Davidge], 'Copy of the Surrey Bill', in *Oliver Twist; or, The Parish Boy's Progress. A Drama, in Three Acts. Adapted from the Celebrated Novel, by Mr. Charles Dickens* (London and New York: Samuel French, [187-?]), pp. 2–8, p. 3.
100. Ibid., p. 2.
101. Buckley, p. 431.
102. [Davidge], 'Copy of the Surrey Bill', p. 2.
103. The report was written by Edward Gibbon Wakefield, who had a personal insight into London's penal system, having been imprisoned for abducting an heiress named Ellen Turner. Wakefield subsequently campaigned against capital punishment, and in favour of colonisation as a means of combating crime (David J. Moss, 'Wakefield, Edward Gibbon (1796–1862)', *Oxford Dictionary of National Biography*, available at <http://www.oxforddnb.com/> (last accessed 16 Feb. 2014)).
104. Benjamin Hawes, 'Report from the Select Committee on Metropolis Police Offices; with the minutes of evidence, appendix and index', *House of Commons Parliamentary Papers*, available at <http://parlipapers.chadwyck.co.uk/> (last accessed 4 Mar. 2014), p. 225 (p. 27 of appendix).
105. John, 'Contextual Overview', p. 15.
106. Almar, I, xi, p. 23.
107. Ibid., I, xi, p. 23.
108. Anon. (1848), 'The Lord Chamberlain', *Trewman's Exeter Flying Post*, 4294, 30 Mar., p. 4; London, Victoria and Albert Theatre Archive, outsize 8. *Oliver Twist; or, the Life and Adventures of a Parish Boy*, at the Pavilion Theatre (17 Sept. 1855), playbill; Hotton et al., p. 28.

Chapter 3

Dickensian Afterlives and the Demolition of Field Lane

Field Lane was hidden in plain sight. Centrally located in the heart of London but still obscure, it was a confined and dilapidated byway 'too narrow for vehicles to use', which led north off the busy thoroughfare of Holborn Hill to meet Saffron Hill.[1] Field Lane was a gateway to a network of labyrinthine slum streets and overcrowded courts. However, the space also prevented outsiders from accessing these areas easily, as the trade carried out in the street obstructed direct paths of communication. Field Lane was closely associated with the traffic in stolen goods and second-hand clothes. A pedestrian's progress would have been hindered by stalls selling these wares, and clear lines of sight veiled by shop awnings bearing rows of fluttering handkerchiefs.[2] This made monitoring or policing Field Lane's supposed criminal population difficult, particularly given the sparse resources of metropolitan police forces in the early nineteenth century. Until its partial demolition opened the remaining side of the street up for the observation of passers-by, shops with seedy reputations and brothels thrived among its closely packed tenements.[3] Fearful of assaults upon their persons and property, some wealthier people were afraid to enter Field Lane.[4]

Dickens responded to Field Lane's already iniquitous reputation when he decided to locate Fagin's den in this area in *Oliver Twist* (1837–9). The street was so notorious it could be used as a byword for urban danger prior to its widely popularised association with Fagin and Bill Sikes. For instance, detailing the disruptive conduct of several young boys at a crowded fair in 1820, the *Morning Post* comments sardonically, '[t]hey call themselves the "youths of the metropolis", we believe; but from their appearance, we should suspect them to be the youths of St Giles's, Field-lane, and Saffron-hill'.[5] Listing Field Lane alongside other infamous slums, the article signals that these areas were perceived by many to be the worst in London, and were imaginatively connected with rough, potentially violent, behaviour. Field Lane's association with threatening individuals was reinforced repeatedly in the press. Among many damning newspaper reports in the 1820s and early 1830s, Field Lane is named as the location of an '*Audacious Street Robbery*'; the residence of a desperate woman driven to attempt the double murder of her child and herself; and as the place where 'the London Burkers – Bishop and Williams' (so named because they repeated Burke and Hare's techniques) acquired provisions for their crimes.[6] Judging by the widespread dissemination of similar associations across a large number of newspapers and periodicals, based in and out of London, it appears that Field Lane's reputation as a dangerous locality was widespread. Indeed, during a trial for pickpocketing at the Old Bailey in 1838, George Bird's retreat down Field Lane was presented by one witness as indicative of his guilt.[7] Bird was convicted and, aged thirteen, was transported for ten years. Popular representations thereby resulted in clusters of extreme connotations, which, as Julian Wolfreys argues in *Dickens's London*, allowed Dickens's fictional mapping to carry socio-historical intertexts for nineteenth-century readers.[8]

Field Lane was envisioned as a nexus of crime, overcrowding, foreignness, social unrest and insanitary conditions in representations of the district in multiple media and contexts in the mid-nineteenth century.[9] In London more widely, these anxieties helped to shape how improvements were conceived, and which places were targeted for demolition. Given Field Lane's reputation, it is not surprising that arguments in favour of its destruction appeared repeatedly in newsprint from at least the 1820s; however, this was not commissioned until the late 1840s, and the site was cleared in a piecemeal fashion from 1848 into the 1870s. The space occupied by Field Lane was a meeting point for numerous publicly and privately funded developments, and the delays attending its demolition were due, in part, to competition between different interests. The lane was demolished to make way for several infrastructural road and rail projects, including: the extension of Farringdon Street northwards from the City from the 1840s and through the next two decades; the building of new railway lines above and below ground, to run into a new terminus at Farringdon Street over the same period; and the construction of the Holborn Viaduct, which opened in 1869. Nevertheless, linking these diverse initiatives was the promise that the destruction of Field Lane would have a socially ameliorative impact. Even when projects were driven by commercial gain, then, developers and commentators portrayed these improvements as ideologically valid because they claimed that development would 'produce an extraordinary effect' on the supposedly criminal population of the area, as well as the cityscape itself.[10]

This chapter presents evidence that the social improvements promised by advocates of Field Lane's redevelopment were repeatedly articulated and conceptualised through references to *Oliver Twist*. It traces a proliferation of Dickensian afterlives in commentaries on Field Lane's improvement before, during and after its demolition. Dickens's account of the site was multiply appropriated in campaigns for its material redevelopment by writers and politicians, and repurposed as a legible representation of Field Lane to elucidate why its demolition was a necessary intervention. One appropriative mode was the republication of descriptive passages, which were evoked as representative yardsticks against which users compared its real conditions or measured the impact of physical changes in the district. Another strategy was to mobilise characters or themes from the novel to comment on linked social problems, which – advocates imagined – would be ameliorated if Field Lane were improved. Of course, as is the case with all the Dickensian afterlives analysed in this book, the novel was variously appropriated, even when users commented on the same site or descriptive passage. However, it is in this instability that we can see how Dickensian afterlives were put to work in arguments for Field Lane's demolition. Far from suggesting that people believed Dickens's descriptions and characters were documentary accounts of contemporary urban conditions – although they were often re-presented in this way – the portability and mutability of Dickensian afterlives reveal the many ways in which his fiction was manipulated to serve numerous interests.

Appropriations of *Oliver Twist* in debates about London's improvement entered dynamic relations with the contexts of their re-presentation. The physical or textual spaces into which the appropriation was redeployed, the genre it was reworked for, the audience it was addressed to, and the personality of the appropriator all had an impact on how the afterlife was received and interpreted. Two of the major fora analysed in this chapter are press commentaries and parliamentary debate. Appropriations of Dickens by politicians are significant to Field Lane's demolition because each improvement had to be authorised by the passing of a new parliamentary act in the mid-nineteenth century. Rhetorical uses of Dickens's fiction in government were thereby addressed to the people who had the power to sanction large-scale material change in London. The press, on the other hand, both represented and stirred certain currents in popular opinion. Tony Bennett rightly cautions us in 'Media, "Reality", Signification' that '[t]o show that the media propose certain definitions of reality is one thing; but it cannot be inferred from this that such definitions are necessarily accepted in the sense that they are effectively taken for real and acted upon'.[11] That is certainly true, and we should approach Dickensian afterlives in both the press and parliament with this caution in mind. I do not make a case that a direct, causal chain connects Dickens with Field Lane's demolition: first, because these appropriative discourses were ephemeral, and second, because they were not systematic or used to promote a single cause. Conversely, the frequency of appropriations across various debates, spaces and media indicates that *Oliver Twist* provided a rhetorically effective vocabulary with which contemporaries with public voices articulated connected social issues, and spurred and supported Field Lane's demolition.

Bennett's caution is appropriate to analyses of the public impact of the press; still, it is occasionally possible to discern the instrumentality of press campaigns in material legacies or the movement of capital. The influence that journalists could exert over contemporary causes or issues is signalled by the significant amount of money subscribed in response to *The Times*'s campaign for 'The Homeless Poor' in London in 1858, for example. The cause was taken up by various other London and provincial newspapers after *The Times*'s initial feature, and subsequent articles in numerous publications record a huge influx of charitable donations over the following weeks as a direct response.

> The recent articles in the *Times* [*sic*] on the sufferings of the homeless poor of London, have resulted in the munificent sum of £7917 14s 3d having been subscribed up to Wednesday for the various refuges and reformatories established for the relief of destitute outcasts, the greater proportion £5500, being for the Field Lane refuge.[12]

The newspaper campaign had material and social effects because it raised money to improve conditions in the Field Lane Refuge. Lord Shaftsbury, who was the charity's president, gave a speech in which he acknowledged the contribution made by the press in drawing the public's attention to the refuge: 'He felt exceedingly grateful to all the papers, and especially to that great paper, *The Times*, for the judgement and the perspicuity with which they had advocated this cause.'[13] The money subscribed after the campaign substantiates Shaftsbury's statements. Nevertheless, journalists also reinforced the impression that they were a uniquely influential group by reprinting his speech in the very media he praised. By quoting affirmations from high-profile individuals, publishing eye-catching headlines that boast about 'The Power of the Pen', and creating dialogues between publications and issues by cross-referencing newspaper campaigns, nineteenth-century journalists present reportage as reliable and effective.[14] In fact, 'news could be premature, provisional, chronologically out of sequence, and disconcerting rather than unifying. As a heterogeneous mix of special correspondence and official dispatch, eyewitness account and hearsay, reportage was often contradictory and sometimes just plain wrong.'[15] Dubious self-congratulation aside, however, the circulation of the story and the money subscribed reveal that channels of influence and exchange flowed between the press, political power and the public.

The 'messy networks of print culture' are given textual form in practices of reprinting quotations from other publications, transcribing parliamentary speeches and publishing public letters.[16] Instead of categorising the news as *either* a passive reflection of dominant opinions *or* as an active agent in directing popular trends, therefore, encounters between the press, parliament and the public expose dialogues between these potentialities, as well as between publications and their target readership. Of course, some journalism was overtly didactic yet, as James Mussell argues, a two-way exchange between journalists and their readers is embedded in newspaper form. Continuities between issues, such as dividing content into digestible sections that are similarly formatted in each edition, meant that the press presented fresh topical content in a mode that appeared consistent with readers' existing worldview or expectations. The form of newsprint or periodicals thus 'allowed the new to be accommodated within existing bodies of knowledge', and so could equally buttress established opinions or shape readers' responses to new content.[17]

Dickensian afterlives were similarly used both to consolidate and reinforce existing opinions, and to pose new interpretations of contemporary affairs. Politicians and journalists each deployed Dickensian afterlives rhetorically, and so caused popular fiction to intersect dynamically with political and topical contexts, and different visual and textual genres published adjacent in newsprint. Responding to a public letter that the MP Sir Edward Bulwer Lytton published in the Corfu *Government Gazette* in 1858, for example, a journalist writing for *The Times* mocked Bulwer's high-flown diction through a comparison with *Oliver Twist*:

> If the late Mr. Fagin, of Field Lane, when in trouble for receiving the proceeds of the Dodger's adroitness, had been reminded by the Clerkenwell judge of the genius of Isaiah and the heroism of the Maccabees, he could not have been more dead to the touching appeal than are the Ionian patriots to Sir E. Lytton's classical allocution.[18]

Allusions to Fagin's and Field Lane's infamous reputations are mobilised in this article to mediate encounters between current government affairs, the media and the newspaper's readership. The appropriation was then circulated further afield. This article was subsequently reprinted by provincial newspapers, including the *Glasgow Herald* and two issues of the *Liverpool Mercury*.[19] Therefore, this example reveals that Dickensian afterlives were repurposed to comment on press commentaries and parliamentary addresses, and that specific afterlives could be widely disseminated. Such intersections between the press, parliament and fiction are significant to the study of metropolitan improvements because they reveal diverse encounters and discourses between public interests and different textual genres.

Of course, the effectiveness of Dickensian afterlives to confirm or shape public opinion in improvement debates depended on who witnessed or deployed his fiction as a rhetorical tool. Users were able to repurpose Dickensian afterlives to argue for material alterations in Field Lane because they chiefly addressed a wealthy audience. As the evidence presented in this chapter will suggest, references to *Oliver Twist* were often used to convince people that Field Lane's infamous reputation was an accurate reflection of its community. Consequently, Dickensian afterlives could appear to confirm existing worldviews and social prejudices against its poor population. By contrast, readers can infer from George Godwin's investigations of the Field Lane region in the 1850s that the population were aware that they were being linked with social problems and did not consider this a fair portrait:

> The smells which come from this district are sickening. If, however, you venture in the course of inquiry to mention to any manufacturer the complaints heard from the neighbours, you will probably be laughed at, and told, 'This is a *nuisance neighbourhood*. What business have you to interfere? Leave us alone – we neither hurt ourselves nor anybody else.'[20]

Despite Godwin's inclusion of this terse statement, his mission was to advocate sanitary reform in the district and his account emphasises its unwholesome characteristics. Therefore, even apparently sympathetic accounts do not really allow Field Lane residents to have any input into discussions about the street's demolition. Appropriations of Dickens's works similarly eschewed the voices of Field Lane's actual inhabitants, as its population were identified with fictional characters and frequently demonised by association. The literary was mobilised to confirm or direct the opinions of people who could campaign for or otherwise influence topographic alterations, rather than the Londoners who were directly affected by them. Even though the Dickensian afterlives that proliferated in discussions about Field Lane's improvement were not systematic, then, the evidence presented in this chapter, taken collectively, indicates that Dickens's fiction provided a common terminology through which individuals linked the site to social problems addressed by its improvement.

Field Lane in *Oliver Twist*

Dickens layers different descriptive modes to create an unstable effect in his first description of Field Lane. On one level, he provides explicit topographic details. A curious reader could have walked the route that Dodger and Oliver take to Fagin's den by following street signs:

> They crossed from the Angel into St John's road, struck down the small street which terminates at Sadler's Wells theatre, through Exmouth-street and Coppice-row, down the little court by the side of the workhouse, across the classic ground which once bore the name of Hockley-in-the-hole, thence into Little Saffron-hill, and so into Saffron-hill the Great [. . .] (*OT*, p. 63)

Mapping the narrative on to London's real built environment imaginatively identifies Dickens's criminal community with specific, and locatable, places. However, Dickens juxtaposes this exactness with Oliver's impressionistic perspective, gathered from 'a few hasty glances on either side of the way as he passed along' (*OT*, p. 63). Field Lane is thus evoked through a combination of apparently objective geographic details and the subjective response of a frightened child.

> The street was very narrow and muddy, and the air was impregnated with filthy odours. There were a good many small shops; but the only stock in trade appeared to be heaps of children, who, even at that time of night, were crawling in and out at the doors, or screaming from the inside. The sole places that seemed to prosper amid the general blight

> of the place were the public-houses, and in them, the lowest orders of Irish (who are generally the lowest orders of anything) were wrangling with might and main. Covered ways and yards, which here and there diverged from the main street, disclosed little knots of houses where drunken men and women were positively wallowing in the filth; and from several of the doorways, great ill-looking fellows were cautiously emerging, bound, to all appearance, upon no very well-disposed or harmless errands. (*OT*, p. 63)

Oliver's sense that the area is dangerously unpredictable is reinforced by the restless motion of the scene. Active verbs litter the passage: people are 'crawling', 'screaming', 'wrangling', 'wallowing' or 'emerging' (*OT*, p. 63). Dickens thus evokes an overwhelming and overcrowded space. A series of close-up vignettes given in rapid succession further emphasise Oliver's feelings of horror, as his focus shifts between 'heaps of children', 'drunken men and women' and 'great ill-looking fellows'. This technique creates a nauseating effect, as the different sights 'disclosed' to Oliver as he progresses down the lane appear to surge in and out of focus. Although his journey to Field Lane is precisely mapped, therefore, the disorder of Field Lane itself presents the conditions of the city as disorientating and threatening to pedestrians. Moreover, unlike Dodger and Oliver's route to Field Lane, Fagin's den – the focal point of these urban dangers in the text – cannot be mapped. We only know that it is 'near' Field Lane (*OT*, p. 63). Even after Oliver enters the room, his impressions are dream-like and unspecific. There are '[s]everal rough beds' and 'four or five boys': a numerical slipperiness that indicates the area's capacity to render these people hidden and anonymous, as though in defiance of contemporary impulses to measure populations and social problems through statistical analysis (*OT*, p. 64). Still another layer to this description is in the interjections of the narrator. The comment about the Irish, for example, is given in parentheses, which mark this observation as exterior to Oliver's viewpoint. Consequently, an additional perspective is added to Dickens's representation, further emphasising that cities defy singular interpretations. Dickens's representation of Field Lane thus picks up on multiple contemporary genres of text, including reportage, government reports, cartographic maps and Newgate fiction, and explores the disarray of the urban scene by not resolving the conflicts that this generates.

Field Lane's unruliness in Dickens's first description reinforces negative social stereotypes already associated with the area, and with slum living generally. In 1838, the year of *Oliver Twist*'s full publication, Field Lane was described in the House of Commons as 'one of the very worst streets of that part of the metropolis'.[21] In the novel, Field Lane is presented as a complex of myriad dangers – a style of representation that responded to beliefs that the social problems associated with slums were interdependent and exacerbated each other.[22] Overcrowded with violent and disreputable individuals, *Oliver Twist* buttresses contemporary fears that drunkenness and immorality were inevitable consequences of poor living conditions and indiscriminate mixing between criminal and impoverished social groups. The space is unclean and confined, 'filthy odours' indicating the spread of disease by miasma. Meanwhile, foreign Others and criminals heighten the threatening tenor of Dickens's portrayal because these people reinforce his depiction of Field Lane as simultaneously alien to Victorian London's growing prosperity and troublingly located at the heart of the city. Field Lane is a chaotic space, containing a lawless population who pose dangers to the wider city in their uncleanliness, criminality and violent mob behaviour.

Oliver Twist could be easily appropriated in arguments for Field Lane's improvement because the novel enforces the idea that criminal activities are enabled by the area's labyrinthine topography in the novel. Field Lane prevents easy interference by authoritative bodies or the free movement of the uninitiated. Fagin's den is a space that helps to keep outsiders out:

> Oliver, groping his way with one hand, and with the other firmly grasped by his companion, ascended with much difficulty the dark and broken stairs which his conductor mounted with an ease and expedition that showed he was well acquainted with them. (*OT*, p. 64)

Then, after Oliver is captured on suspicion of stealing Brownlow's handkerchief, Charley and Dodger employ their superior knowledge of London's streets to their advantage and easily avoid capture, 'their course indeed being rather to lengthen the distance by various circumlocutions and discursive staggerings' (*OT*, p. 95). The corollaries Dickens draws between criminality and the built environment reinforce widely held contemporary beliefs in the environmental determination of social problems. Dickens's representation of Fagin's den as an alternative domestic space also contributes to his portrayal of the area as a place where crime is both facilitated and produced. The route to Fagin's den is dirty and foreboding but Oliver's first view of its interior is more welcoming than anything he has previously experienced. Particularly given the contrast between the brutal workhouse scenes and the enticing humour and food provided by Fagin and the boys, Dickens indicates that a criminal career could be a favourable option for children like Oliver. In juxtaposing institutionalised cruelties with urban dangers, Dickens emphasises his critique of the workhouse. Nevertheless, the momentary appeal of Fagin's den is one indication of why *Oliver Twist* was variously interpreted as a warning against criminality and as a means of inciting and encouraging it.[23]

The second description of Field Lane in *Oliver Twist* presents a remarkably different view to Dickens's anarchic first portrait:

> a narrow and dismal alley leading to Saffron Hill. In its filthy shops are exposed for sale huge bunches of second-hand silk handkerchiefs of all sizes and patterns – for here reside the traders who purchase them from pickpockets. [. . .] Confined as the limits of Field Lane are, it has its barber, its coffee-shop, its beer-shop, and its fried-fish warehouse. It is a commercial colony of itself, the emporium of petty larceny, visited at early morning and setting-in of dusk by silent merchants, who traffic in dark back-parlours, and go as strangely as they came. (*OT*, p. 204)

The lane is still dark, unwholesome and criminal but, unlike Oliver's montage-like impressions, this second representation portrays an ordered – if alternative – commercial centre. While the first description depicts Field Lane as a chaotic and overcrowded space, the second account reveals that it is the residence of an organised and close-knit community that coexists with conventional society. Fagin runs his racket of pickpockets like a business. There is a formal hierarchy among the boys, with Dodger at the top. It is a criminal meritocracy, which can facilitate social advancement within this group. Fagin informs Oliver that Dodger is on course to be 'a great man himself, and [will] make you one too, if you take pattern by him' (*OT*, p. 72). Dickens often presents the poor as victims. The presence of a workhouse in the list of landmarks that Dodger and Oliver pass on their way to Field Lane implies that these institutions served only to propel people towards further impoverishment or criminality. Conversely, the economic and power relations between the criminal characters resist sentimental treatment.

The organisation of Field Lane's community indicates other urban dangers to those foregrounded in the first description. While these people are far from constituting an unruly mob, contemporary fears about working-class unrest (which were occasionally drawn into focus by European revolutions or Chartist agitation) were spurred equally by the prospect of the poor being efficiently mobilised and by the threat of riot. Cohesion could equal anarchy because it implied that subversive, foreign revolutionary ideals could be effectively circulated and gather support in London. Partly because slums were associated with communities of foreign migrants, and partly because living conditions in these areas were 'almost unimaginable to those of any substantial means', slums were commonly perceived as foreign spaces within London.[24] Particularly as political unrest in other European countries sparked fears of rebellion in Britain, these alien zones were often perceived as conduits for the transmission of continental revolutionary sentiments to Britain. Thomas Beames expresses these concerns in *The Rookeries of London* (1852):

> when rebellion recruits her forces she is fed by the denizens of these retreats. It is on record that during the combats in Paris in 1848, and on the famous 10th of April here, multitudes of strange figures issued from these lurking places, distinguished by their appearance from the rest even of the poor population. [. . .] St. Antoine, riddled by bullets as when we last saw it, still remains; shall we neglect our duty, because St. Giles and Saffron Hill, unscathed by war, crumble peacefully beneath the hand of Time?[25]

Beames identifies Saffron Hill, a street connected to Field Lane, as a major cause for concern in Britain. Field Lane's improvement is portrayed as an issue of national importance because it is envisioned as a preventative measure against revolt. Therefore, the multiple portraits of Field Lane that Dickens draws in *Oliver Twist* – as both organised *and* lawless – probably contributed in different ways to readers' interpretations of it as a subversive locale.

Dickens's layered and shifting representation meant that users could produce afterlives linking Field Lane to a variety of perceived social problems without appearing to stray far from the text. In public commentaries on Field Lane's demolition, two of the major issues that *Oliver Twist* was used to conceptualise were crime and the presence of communities of foreign Others in the area. Dickensian afterlives provided an attention-grabbing and accessible vocabulary through which contemporaries could examine these supposed concerns and link them to this specific place. For example, one of the ways that other writers repurposed *Oliver Twist* to represent Field Lane as dangerous was to suggest that Dickens had brought Field Lane to the public's notice, and so enabled the site and its criminal inhabitants to be scrutinised. Beames suggests that *Oliver Twist* is equivalent to reportage. He argues that Field Lane is obscure, despite its central location, and the public's knowledge of the place

> is indebted to Mr. Dickens, whose researches have dragged it into light: some of the scenes of his Oliver Twist are laid there; there, if we remember, the poor friendless boy is enticed into a den of thieves. The place is connected in the minds of many with the disappearance of pocket handkerchiefs [. . .][26]

Beames indicates that Dickens's work had an instrumental effect on the work of other social explorers and campaigners, and so influenced later encounters with the site. He provides a model of the practice he describes. Beames supports his own investigations by cross-referencing *Oliver Twist* as a documentary account that tallies with and validates his own observations. His report thus exemplifies how *Oliver Twist* was mobilised to facilitate commentary in other texts and contexts, by linking fiction to current social anxieties and specific metropolitan places.

Improving Field Lane

Walking around the Field Lane area in modern London reveals no clues of the street's previous existence. The spot is now occupied by a section of Charterhouse Street, and by a part of some large, modern offices with cafes and restaurants underneath. If we want to know where to look, we must compare different maps. In *Cruchley's New Plan of London 1838*, published concurrently with *Oliver Twist*, Field Lane is shown extending north off Holborn Hill until it connects with Saffron Hill (see Plate 5). It is at the centre of a district that is not bisected by any major roads for just over a mile. Developments are evident in *Cross's London Guide* (1844), which depicts the large cut made by Farringdon Street being driven through this area. At this point, Farringdon Street runs parallel with Field Lane, and the street does not appear to have been touched. Maps produced in 1857 and 1861 still label Field Lane as a separate street, indicating that it remains a distinctive locality, despite alterations. However, the name is effaced from *Stanford's Library Map of London and Its Suburbs* (1872). By the time that the George W. Bacon atlas is published in 1886, the map shows only a blank space where Field Lane used to be.[27] Today there are steps leading down to a small cobbled area at the southern end of Saffron Hill, but the surrounding buildings and the cobbles are of recent construction and no traces of Field Lane remain. It has literally been wiped from the map.

As early as 1824, a 'Constant Reader' of the *Morning Chronicle* wrote a letter to the editor to complain that 'the removal of Fleet Market [. . .] did not extend further', and opined that a 'great public improvement would thus be effected' by the demolition of Field Lane.[28] Advocates of its destruction imagined this action would produce multiple positive effects, including sanitary reform, better communication between metropolitan areas, and the *embourgeoisement* of Field Lane's populace. None the less, Field Lane was not entirely neglected by developers or local government in the early decades of the nineteenth century. Plans of the Field Lane sewer held in the London Metropolitan Archives (dated between 1814 and 1847) reveal that there were limited efforts made to improve sanitation in the area.[29] Still, conditions were dreadful. The lane backed on to the Fleet River, or Fleet Ditch, which was used as an open sewer in some places well into the mid-nineteenth century.[30] Maps that detail the district prior to its redevelopment also indicate closely confined living conditions. The sewerage plans portray Field Lane as narrower than adjoining byways, and the houses just over half of the size of those in nearby streets like Ely Place and Hatton Garden, or even those in courts like Bleeding Heart Yard or Union Court.

The wider area around Field Lane started to undergo considerable change in the 1830s, when large parts of the Farringdon Street district were demolished to make way for the new road.[31] Despite previous arguments for the beneficial impact of further slum clearance, however, the plan for the continuation of Farringdon Street produced for the House of Commons in 1839 did not have an impact on Field Lane.[32] The street is also untouched in early proposals for the Holborn Viaduct. John Turner and James Moon's 1832 and 1839 plans for a new carriage road running along the southern side of Holborn Hill and Skinner Street barely affected the street.[33] Moreover, Francis Whishaw's *Proposed Plan and Elevation for Holborn Viaduct* (1839) proposes that the viaduct should cut across Farringdon Street and Shoe Lane horizontally, before curving round to meet Holborn Hill at Fetter Lane. This plan locates the development to the south of Field Lane, and does not intersect with that byway.[34] Although a bill was approved by the House of Commons 'for the continuation of the New Farringdon Street' in February 1838, no immediate action was taken.[35] In the 1830s, therefore, its destruction was not a foregone conclusion.

By the 1840s, commentators used the press as a platform to argue that demolishing Field Lane and redeveloping the area was a matter of urgency. A correspondent to *The Times* complained in 1842 that the Farringdon Street development:

> has been contemplated for the last 20 years, and four years have elapsed since an act was obtained for the purpose, [yet] we are now apparently as far off as ever, to the great detriment of trade and the depreciation in value of property in the immediate neighbourhood, independently of the importance, in a public point of view, of so direct a communication from the city to the northern parts of London.[36]

Echoing the *Morning Chronicle*'s earlier correspondent, this 'Old Inhabitant of the Locality' states his 'eager[ness] to effect a radical improvement in the neighbourhood in question', which is currently allowed to '[flourish] in all its luxuriant rankness with as much security as if it were to go on fattening till doomsday'.[37] Paradoxically, the desirability of Field Lane's demolition was one reason why large works were delayed. In 1846, *The Times* reported a debate in the Court of Common Council in which it was noted that 'Field-lane was one of the greatest abominations in the whole metropolis; and it was absurd to think of proceeding with the buildings in Farringdon-street until such a nuisance was removed.'[38] In fact, a local act was passed in 1842 authorising Field Lane's demolition to enable the expansion of Farringdon Street.[39] However, competition between different interests appears to have impeded progress and it remained unclear when this improvement would happen or what new infrastructure would take its place.

In addition to plans to widen and extend Farringdon Street, there were also proposals for a 'project for connecting the great lines of railway from all parts of England, to one general terminus in Farringdon-street', and the construction of the first underground railway running into this station.[40] Therefore, while some reports state that the demolition of Field Lane was intended 'to widen and improve the thoroughfare [Farringdon Street]', there is a parallel narrative that names the 'erection of temporary depots for merchandise and goods coming by railway from the manufacturing districts' as the chief driver of the area's redevelopment.[41] With Farringdon Street advancing from the south and railway lines reaching into the area from the north, Field Lane was a meeting point of two of the most significant forces altering London's cityscape in the nineteenth century. Meanwhile, diverse commentators repeatedly portray the lane as 'extremely wretched' and 'filled with all sorts of filthy abominations', and agree that improving the area was a necessary intervention, regardless of which project ultimately drove its clearance.[42] In 1845, for instance, the *Standard* argued that 'greatly beneficial' though the various developments in the area 'doubtless would be, [they were] insignificant in comparison to the vast improvement which it would lead to in the vicinity by the removal of the horrible nuisances round about, and the demolition of the acclivities of Holborn-hill and Snow-hill'.[43] There was no investment in building or maintenance while developers waited for the site to be cleared, and the condition of its built environment continued to decline.[44]

The slow pace and complications attending Field Lane's demolition were exacerbated by the fact that it was unclear to whose jurisdiction the area belonged. Although located in the parish of St Andrew, Holborn, the street was bisected by the border of the City of London: 'The southern end only [was] in Farringdon Ward Without, the greater portion lying outside the City boundary.'[45] The City was administered separately to the rest of London, and the improvements planned by different local government bodies and by Her Majesty's Office of Works were not effectively linked to the works pursued by the Corporation.[46] As a result, the efforts made by the City to remove slum districts during the building of Farringdon Street extended only so far, and this explains why Farringdon Street halted for so long at the City's border. In the end, the City paid £25,000 towards continuing the demolitions in Field Lane in 1848, and any '[d]efficiencies [were] paid out of the Chamber of London'.[47] Nevertheless, further proposals for the Holborn Viaduct in the 1840s and 1850s show that the site's redevelopment remained in flux for many years after demolitions began. Plans were put forward by J. Belcher (c. 1842), Peter Jefferys (1847) and John Phillips (1851).[48] These, in addition to several more undated designs for the viaduct, show that its route was unsettled into the 1850s, despite the fact that architects had discussed the development for two decades already. The plans detail various incarnations of the viaduct; some include Field Lane in proposed demolitions and some do not. As late as 1854, its route was still so undecided that Robert Hesketh published a pamphlet entitled *Shall the New Street Which is to Form the Grand Communication between the Eastern and Western Parts of the Metropolis be Straight or Crooked?*[49] Both the real space of Field Lane and plans for its improvement were disordered throughout its redevelopment.

The impact that improvements had on Field Lane's inhabitants is not usually noted by commentaries published in the press. Looking back on a previous 'great demolition' in 1861, Lord Derby remarked in parliament that '1,000 houses were displaced, which had sheltered 4,000 families, comprising 12,000 individuals; and very nearly the whole of those were driven into the adjoining tenements'.[50] Conversely, earlier reports focus on the ameliorative effects that its demolition would have for the economy, society and the built environment.[51] A broadside advocating 'Street Improvements in Connexion with the Central City Terminus' in 1853 cited a list of twenty-five reasons 'in Favour of the Bill', which needed to be passed to authorise the project. These include removing a 'noisome neighbourhood' and benefits to local trade, which it conceives as socially as well as economically beneficial.[52] Even Dickens, who wrote about Field Lane's redevelopment in 'A Sleep to Startle Us' (1852), envisions its demolition as a positive change. He imagines that a 'thriving street [. . .] will arise upon this spot' to replace 'obscene Field Lane and Saffron Hill' with their 'mounds of earth, old bricks, and oyster-shells – the arched foundations of unbuilt houses – the backs of miserable tenements with patched windows – the odds and ends of fever-stricken courts and alleys – which are the present features of the place'.[53] Field Lane's redevelopment was piecemeal and slow but – continuous with his negative representation of the place in *Oliver Twist* and contemporary arguments for its reform – Dickens's article indicates that its demolition was widely conceived as being in the public's best interest (Plate 6).[54]

Appropriating *Oliver Twist*

The 1840s: before demolition

Commentators did not immediately appropriate Dickensian afterlives to argue for Field Lane's demolition. The frequency with which *Oliver Twist* was employed in these debates gathered pace in line with the perceived urgency of the street's improvement, which heightened in the late 1840s. Nevertheless, both the novel and its multiple remediations reinforced Field Lane's already infamous reputation by identifying it with criminal characters. For instance, theatrical playbills proclaim that **'FIELD LANE'** is the location of **'FAGIN's DEN'** in bold typeface.[55] More widely, Dickensian tropes were used to stir public worries about larger problems and dangers that the lane's demolition was later supposed to ameliorate. In 1840, W. C. Taylor wrote in *Bentley's Miscellany*:

> The fact cannot be too strongly stated, that the Fagins of the Metropolis seek invariably the children of honest parents, because they believe that such will be most faithful to their infamous employers. An Oliver Twist is a much more valuable acquisition than a Noah Claypole.[56]

Taylor picks up on the business-like practices of Fagin's gang. He posits that this organisation threatens the social order because it permits criminals to manipulate middle-class values for their own gain. Fears for readers' safety and property are crystallised and concentrated by the characters, who are transformed into symbolic carriers of specific anxieties by the pluralisation of their names. He introduces the characters as representative figures to persuade readers that his ominous vision is justified. Pointedly relocating the characters from fiction to the contemporary city, Taylor uses *Oliver Twist* to describe what interactions middle-class and poorer social groups could have in the streets of the capital. Such appropriations helped to popularise the practice of using Dickensian afterlives to discuss contemporary London, and by the mid-1840s there were direct links made between *Oliver Twist* and cases for Field Lane's improvement.

Another reason why Dickensian afterlives were used more regularly as a representative currency to describe Field Lane from the 1840s on was that, by this time, Dickens was not alone in having used its already notorious reputation to titillate readers. W. H. Ainsworth presents the area as a site of mob activity in *Jack Sheppard* (1839–40), and G. W. M. Reynolds makes it the location of murder and child abuse in the first series of *The Mysteries of London* (1844–6). As Chapter 2 explored, not only was Newgate fiction seen as a genre that represented metropolitan crime, but also some commentators believed that it would inspire imitative behaviour. These fears intensified in the 1840s when, on 5 May 1840, a valet named Courvoisier murdered his 72-year-old master, Lord William Russell, apparently claiming 'that the idea of the crime had come to him upon reading *Jack Sheppard*'.[57] Public anxieties about Newgate fiction overlapped with, and were reinforced by, the volatile political climate of the 1840s. In the context of Chartist demonstrations, European revolutions, famine in Ireland, and a trade depression that left many people starving, it is easy to see why fears of urban disorder were heightened, particularly as mass inward migration made the streets even busier and fears of the potentially riotous urban mob coalesced with reactionary rejections of foreign Others. Apparently concerned that working-class audience members would be tempted to imitate the criminal or revolutionary behaviours they witnessed, in 1848 the Lord Chamberlain forbade theatrical adaptations of both *Oliver Twist* and *Jack Sheppard* under the same interdiction as 'pieces founded on subjects illustrating recent events in France, designed for representation in the minor theatres in London'.[58] In drawing a specific link between urban danger and Field Lane, then, Dickens's, Ainsworth's and Reynolds's wildly popular narratives both reinforced existing fears and allowed them to be precisely mapped.

The demolition of a building invested with sensational connotations in 1844 also helped to focus popular attention on fictional and melodramatic representations that linked the Field Lane district with crime. Slum tourists flocked to see the Red Lion Tavern in adjacent West Street prior to its demolition. The *Illustrated London News* reports that '[t]his extraordinary place has been inspected by his Royal Highness the Duke of Cambridge, Lord Lonsdale, parties of magistrates, and a crowd of visitors, for some days past'.[59] The building concealed trapdoors and secret passages to facilitate criminals' escape, or to capture those who threatened their interests. According to the *Illustrated London News*, '[t]he eagerness [. . .] with which crowds have flocked to this den of infamy, proves that the morbid taste for Jack Sheppardism is not yet extinct'.[60] In other words, cheap, popular fiction, and dramatisations of it in minor theatres, melodramatically reimagined real places in ways that could appear to glamorise crime. Reports of the Red Lion's demolition reveal that press accounts of improvements in the area combined fictional references with coverage of current events. Particularly when two skeletons were discovered beneath a trapdoor, newspapers evoke fictional representations of the area to speculate about its perceived lawlessness.[61]

The *Illustrated London News* maps a broad range of fictional associations on to the real cityscape in their account of the Red Lion's demolition. The writer plots the proximate locations of the Red Lion Tavern, the 'house (No. 3) [which was] the abode of the notorious Jonathan Wild',[62] and Fagin's den, even though the Red Lion is not named in *Oliver Twist*.[63] The area's connection to fictional criminals allows the city to be melodramatically reimagined in a way that is attuned to the literary and slum tourism that this writer affects to dislike, for, while the *Illustrated London News* uses the titillating appeal of the site's sensational associations to intrigue readers, she or he also mobilises *Oliver Twist* to make a moral argument that links urban decay in the area to crime.

> It is impossible to look upon the place, seated upon the bank of a foul ditch, without reflecting upon the two-fold pestiferous influence of this moral and physical nuisance in the very heart of our metropolis; and it is only in this view, and as a fragment of old London, that the place is entitled to illustration in our columns. [. . .] West-street, by the way, debouches into Field-lane, that notorious region of Bandana, admirably described by Mr. Dickens in his master-piece, 'Oliver Twist'.[64]

The writer entwines fiction with how she or he conceives and portrays metropolitan 'nuisances': *Oliver Twist* is evoked as a symbolic vocabulary for the representation of crime. This technique is repeated in other newspaper articles that comment on Field Lane's disreputable and dangerous reputation prior to its demolition. Indeed, *Oliver Twist*'s multiple appearances in the press allow journalists to implant an apparent objectivity into their fictional references, as such pieces frequently cross-reference both *Oliver Twist* and each other, and so validate the novel's suitability in reportage. Moreover, the *Illustrated London News* often refers readers to previous issues of the newspaper to create a sense of a unified purpose between editions, despite the paper's miscellaneous form. In the account of the Red Lion's demolition, for example, the writer invites readers to compare the improvements documented in the article with an illustration 'engraved in No. 95 of our Miscellany'.[65] The form of news reportage thereby allows Dickensian afterlives to be embedded in ongoing arguments for targeted material change.

One year prior to the first demolitions in Field Lane in 1848, the *Illustrated London News* published another feature that conflated the real and the imagined. The significance of the piece is signalled by the fact that the paper devoted most of a page and two large illustrations to argue for the necessity of improving sanitary and living conditions in Field Lane, and referred readers back to previous issues to suggest that the piece was part of a rolling campaign.

> Of the vile old places which formerly occupied the site cleared in our Illustration, we gave two effective views in a former No. of our Journal. The narrow avenue, known as Field-lane, with its tempting premiums for thievery, the pocket-handkerchief display, still exists: but will, we hope, shortly be cleared away by force of the wholesome doctrine, which enjoins cleanliness as next to godliness.[66]

In this anonymous piece dealing with topical content, the journalist affects a posture of self-abstraction common in nineteenth-century media at this time, which obscures her or his personal motivations and interests. As Richard Salmon observes, this pose is persuasive because it allows 'the journalist [to write] both within and to "the public"'.[67] However, despite the objectivity suggested by the removal of the journalist's identity, and the article's juxtaposition with supposedly realistic visual representations of the site, the writing is littered with emotive adjectives and direct statements about the bad moral condition of the place. '[T]he notorious Field-lane' is called 'a specimen of the wretched house-accommodation for the working classes, and of the frightful moral results to which this foul neglect unquestionably conduces'.[68] As Chapter 1 explained, overcrowding was a major concern for nineteenth-century improvers. It had a negative impact on residents' health but was also frequently seen to produce licentious or immoral behaviour, as a lack of private space meant that people mixed indiscriminately. Overcrowding appeared to create an environment in which respectable working-class people would inevitably come into frequent contact with dangerous criminals. The journalist makes similar assumptions when she or he presents the demolition of Field Lane as a material expression of society's moral and social duty to the poor. So, she or he combines apparently objective observations with didactic campaigning.

The journalist co-opts *Oliver Twist* both to reinforce the moralistic tenor of the article and to authenticate her or his representation of the site. The novel is presented as a recognisable point of reference that further elucidates Field Lane's perceived identity for readers, as well as exposing why its demolition is necessary: 'Every reader of Mr. Dickens's novel of excellent purpose, "Oliver Twist", will remember how vividly he has sketched this locality; but the picture is so good a lesson of morality that we shall quote it [. . .]'[69] Reportage is thus interrupted by the quotation of an extended fictional description and so, added to the illustrations, the page combines at least three generic forms and muddles various representative modes to make a memorable case. The journalist presents the extract from the book as evidence that supports her or his position – both because it is presented as realistic representation and because she or he believes that it conveys a similar didactic argument. The journalist thus substantiates her or his position by claiming an affiliation with the popular author well known for his concern with urban conditions. As such, the inclusion of fiction is not presented as a barrier to the potential potency of the journalist's argument. She or he does not dwell on the fact that Dickens's description is fictionalised, but establishes her or his position in the debate by comingling various generic and representative forms. Field Lane's improvement is thereby conceptualised in relation to *Oliver Twist*, even though these Dickensian afterlives built on long-established concerns about the area's sanitary and moral conditions, an understanding that demolition could be used as a defence against insurgency or immorality, and popular receptions of Dickens's novels.

The 1850s and 1860s: Field Lane in transition

In 1848, the demolition of Field Lane's east side opened the remains of the street up for observation. An engraving made of the site in the 1850s even depicts three figures lounging against a railing to gaze into the lane.[70] Martin Daunton long since argued that desires to subject the working class to surveillance helped to drive demolitions in slum districts: 'The aim was to "open up" the city in order to make it visible for inspection.'[71] Certainly, the fact that users mobilised Dickensian afterlives to map urban dangers on to specific slums indicates that contemporaries were nervous about what activities were going on in London unseen. By contrast, familiar characters and descriptions create the impression that Field Lane is a known space. Nevertheless, any spatial policing effected by cutting paths through tangled and dilapidated streets was not straightforward. Once commentators were able to scrutinise these areas, they were horrified by what they saw:

> Just enough had been done to lay bare the sore places of the great City. Field Lane was exposed to the passer-by, – the worst dens and courts of Saffron Hill, the Fleet Ditch, and the purlieus of Cow Cross were brought into prominent public view, – low and crowded dwellings, windows without glass, roofs from which the tiles have fallen long ago, children with pale and ghastly faces, forms hideous with disease and ugly with crime, were revealed.[72]

The shameful failure of Victorian society to support the poor adequately was suddenly made more obvious than ever, and its visibility forced people to imagine what further hidden spaces still existed beside respectable areas. Moreover, the slow pace of nineteenth-century improvements meant these 'sore places' were subject to lengthy periods of display and suggested an anarchic counter-narrative to the city's progress and economic growth. Even though demolitions were envisioned partly as a means of erasing problem areas from the cityscape, they frequently intensified the fears associated with these sites. The criminal populations many contemporaries assumed these districts contained were scattered by demolitions, so disseminating their corrupting influence and making them more difficult to monitor than before: 'Field-lane and the Rookery are gone, but their former inmates remain. They have been dispersed into quarters once tenanted by the more decent among the poor.'[73] The street thus remained a site of considerable anxiety even after its demolition began. This commentator argues that demolitions neither halted the growth of a criminal population nor improved the surrounding area. Field Lane's perceived Otherness was thereby reinforced by its partial demolition.

Other public commentators praised Field Lane's partial demolition in subsequent representations but it was still perceived to be a dangerous locale and many continued to agitate for further reforms. During this transitional phase, users mobilised Dickensian afterlives to conceptualise desired improvements to the built environment. In 1854, for instance, a deeply anti-Semitic article written for the *Daily News*, signed 'Argus', celebrates the idea of its total destruction because it would supposedly reform a place that

> has long been one of the main haunts of London criminals – the pet locality of Israelite receivers of stolen goods, and of their particular friends, the housebreakers. Here Dickens places the residence of the amiable *Jew Fagin*; and here, in very fact, many Bill Sikeses of real flesh and blood have lived and are still living, holding out obstinately till the last [bricks and] mortar shall be swept away, and looking with jealousy upon the invasion of their domain.[74]

Like W. C. Taylor in 1840, and Lord Monteagle who, declaiming on juvenile criminality in parliament in 1851, warned that 'juvenile offenders might fall into the clutches of the Fagins',[75] this writer evokes Dickens's characters as symbols of real criminal practices and types. Field Lane's redevelopment was slow, and 'Argus' repurposes Dickensian afterlives to argue that Field Lane's demolition needs to continue. Similarly, in 1865, an article in *Once a Week* states that:

> When it was thought proper for the public good to connect Clerkenwell and Blackfriars Bridge, what a pulling down of old, dilapidated, worm-eaten, ramshackle hovels took place. Field Lane – where Oliver Twist served his apprenticeship under the accomplished Mr. Fagin, archpriest of pocket-picking – was half-demolished, and Saffron Hill, sacred to organ-grinders and gilders, exposed to the naked eye. Would that the whole of Field Lane had been pulled down. The western side still remains, dirty, slovenly, inodorous, swarming with miserable croons and idle children reeking with filth, and hideous with every physical deformity.[76]

Throughout the course of the site's piecemeal transition, therefore, Dickensian afterlives were mobilised to map criminal associations on to the site and argue that its continued redevelopment would help to combat these problems. Therefore, even though the opportunity to gaze into Field Lane after 1848 made its dilapidated conditions more obvious, Dickensian afterlives were still a means of making these disturbing sights legible.

At the same time as these commentators mobilised *Oliver Twist* to express their frustration with the slow pace of reform, others referred to the novel to invest Field Lane's protracted redevelopment with a sense of purpose. Dickens's first description of the site was repeatedly republished as an isolated extract and used as a representative yardstick against which the scale of the city's physical change could be measured. In these instances, users appropriated the novel's first description as a faithful account of the area's prior condition. In so doing, users cast *Oliver Twist* as a justification of later improvements that had displaced so many people. In an article discussing the need for new working-class homes in 1865, a writer for the *Era* comments that '[i]n the Farringdon-road, where costermongers congregate, there is a Model Lodging-house, and in the vicinity of Field-lane and Saffron-hill, the locality of FAGIN, the Jew, in "Oliver Twist", may now be seen great improvements'.[77] The article's central argument is philanthropic. It seeks to encourage 'the higher classes [to] extend a helping hand to raise their fellow creatures from filth and misery'.[78] However, apparently anticipating some resistance to this mission, it encourages readers' charitable feelings for Field Lane's residents by melodramatically reimagining the area's past through its fictional associations, and so suggesting that the horrific conditions made visible by demolitions are redeemable because they are less frightening than its previous criminal identity. *Oliver Twist* is thereby presented as a realistic representation, at the same time as the article uses it to sensationalise Field Lane's past. This dichotomy is repeated in *Leisure Hour* in 1869:

> The vicinity of Fleet Ditch and the Holborn Valley was notorious as a rookery of the most infamous classes of the population. The description which Dickens, in 'Oliver Twist', in 1837, gave of Field Lane, may serve as a picture of the whole region of the Holborn Valley.[79]

Juxtaposing fiction with specific details about the engineer responsible for the works, *Leisure Hour*'s intertextuality allows the writer to conceptualise the improvements as evidence of social as well as topographic progress: 'No region of the metropolis more demanded improvement in a sanitary and moral aspect.'[80] *Oliver Twist* is presented as both sensational and realistic, and so permits the commentators in *Leisure Hour* and the *Era* to evoke imaginative and specific topographies simultaneously. Both before its demolition and during its transition, therefore, Dickensian afterlives were used to conceptualise Field Lane's improvement as a didactic intervention.

Some contemporaries recognised the impact that representations of specific areas in popular culture and newsprint had on improvement agendas. In 1861, for instance, John Hollingshead commented on the role played by imaginative works in shaping received perceptions of place, and its material consequences in the built environment.

> We have been too much accustomed of late years to look upon certain notorious localities as representing the only plague-spots in London. They have been visited by day, inspected by night; have formed the text-books of preachers, the back-bones of sanitary reports, and the building materials of popular authors. They have attained an exaggerated importance in the public mind, and have been erroneously regarded as the tumours of our social degradation. The sweepings of society have seldom been carefully traced to their hiding-places, and fancy neighbourhoods have been created upon paper, and peopled with the phantoms of imagination.[81]

Hollingshead suggests that multiple representations of particular places in different genres of print media reinforce each other, as apparently continuous concerns across various modes authenticate their shared negative imagery in the public imagination. Consequently, print culture popularised partial, or inaccurate, impressions of London areas. Hollingshead argues that this has a material impact. In shining a spotlight on to certain areas, others are cast into shadow and so obscured from view:

> The close, crowded borders of the city of London have been touched upon too frequently in some parts, too little in others. We have heard enough of Saffron Hill, and have been lectured about a certain refuge in Field Lane until we have almost forgotten that there are any more refuges in the world.[82]

Thus, while Hollingshead acknowledges that written commentaries are a driving force for urban improvement, he argues that this practice facilitates only partial progress. It leads to targeted demolitions but, he implies, these are ultimately ineffectual because they fail to tackle broader issues. Other slums remain concealed behind new streets, and social problems are preserved and accentuated in left-over neglected spaces. Conversely, Hollingshead's commentary still suggests that fiction is an indirect contributor to urban change. The reoccurrence of Dickensian afterlives in commentaries on Field Lane's improvement certainly indicates that later users recognised the effectiveness of literary rhetoric.

Users continued to mobilise Dickensian afterlives as a tool for contemporary comment, even when the prospect of further demolitions caused contemporaries to recategorise Field Lane's remains from a current problem site to vestiges of London's past. Although parts of the street still existed and were used by Londoners throughout its transitional stage, its redevelopment permitted contemporaries to revise their perception of the site from a pressing concern to a relic of a bygone time. As early as 1855, John Timbs republished Dickens's first description of Field Lane in *Curiosities of London* to illustrate the degree to which the built environment and its perceived social identity had altered in the intervening years: 'An infamous rookery of "the dangerous classes," extended from the foot of Holborn-hill, northward, parallel with the Fleet Ditch, but has been mostly taken down since it was thus vividly painted in 1837.'[83] The improvements being made in Field Lane were still in progress when Timbs published this remark, but his use of the past tense decidedly situates *Oliver Twist* as a representational yardstick of its former conditions, against which the scale of its topographic change can be conceived. He fictionalises the past and so constructs a representation of place that overlays symbolic and real spaces, as well as multiple temporalities.

Building on this comingling of the real and imagined in another antiquarian retrospective of the capital published ten years later, Timbs evokes *Oliver Twist* again as a mediator between Field Lane's past and present:

> The romance of thievery has in a great measure departed, though much of the reality is left in another shape. The clumsy practice of criminal robbery has dwindled, and has chiefly fallen into the hands of boys, trained to their nefarious course by the fence, who takes the lion's share of the spoil. This character has been portrayed to the life by the author of *Oliver Twist*, in the admirable impersonation of Fagin, whose den is localised in Field Lane, which extended from the foot of Holborn Hill, northward, parallel with the Fleet Ditch: it was thus vividly painted in 1837 [. . .][84]

In this presentation as both a record of the past and a pertinent portrayal of ongoing criminal practices, Timbs constructs a palimpsestuous representation of the city. He juxtaposes an extract from *Oliver Twist* with other intertextual references 'in the *Spectator*; likewise by Pope, Gay, Fielding, and other authors of the last century'; historical contexts that link the site with 'bear and bull baitings, and gladiatorial exhibitions, from the time of Charles II'; and his own commentary on contemporary urban improvements. In so doing, Timbs comingles the real and the imagined, the past and the present, in his representation of Field Lane. More than any of Timbs's other literary or historical intertexts, *Oliver Twist* is invoked as a means of understanding and articulating both the city's past and present. In particular, he suggests that the novel enables contemporaries to measure how criminal practices have evolved over time: 'It is curious to find the initiatory processes of picking pockets, as taught by Fagin to Oliver Twist, practised in the metropolis nearly three centuries ago.'[85] Timbs's simultaneous evocation of multiple periods in Field Lane's history is thus achieved by his fictionalisation of the place and its cultural identity. Timbs's studies are examples of how Dickensian afterlives were used to reimagine the site as a historical artefact, instead of being appropriated as a tool to persuade audiences why Field Lane should be demolished. Yet, just as Timbs layers past and present, fiction and observation, so his historicised remediation of *Oliver Twist* was produced simultaneously with its appropriation as still relevant social commentary.

It was a long time before the demolitions begun in the 1840s were complete. During this time, Dickensian afterlives were regularly mobilised to construct legible representations of the disordered built environment and its crowded streets. References to *Oliver Twist* continued to be used to reinforce the perceived criminal identity of Field Lane and its population. In the *Methodist* in 1866, for example, an article describing a public execution asks readers,

> Do you remember the thrilling chapter of 'The Jew's last night alive' in *Oliver Twist?* Well, this was the scene! [meanwhile] Field-lane, where he kept his 'fence', lies a very little way off [. . .] I saw Charley Bates, and the Dodger, and Nancy, and Toby Crackit, and the rest, shying men's hats in the air, and looking out for the 'wipes' and the 'tickers'.[86]

The writer's excitement at apparently seeing literary characters realised in the flesh also records a shift towards another mode of afterlife, which became more prominent after Dickens's death in 1870 – that is, literary tourism. While earlier users appropriated tropes from *Oliver Twist* to identify Field Lane as a problem site in the contemporary city, when the built environment changed and improvement was less urgent, afterlives that connected the place to the novel tended to present visits to the area as pleasurable excursions. Like Timbs, who evokes the novel to articulate a historical shift, literary tourism 'is often not seen as representing a link to the Victorian past' but, in Juliet John's words, symbolises 'the difference or conflict between past and present'.[87] In 'Up and Down the London Streets' (1866), Mark Lemon mixes Dickensian afterlives indiscriminately with socio-historical intertexts and his observations of the contemporary city: 'On our right are the remains of Field Lane, where Mr. Fagan [*sic*] tutored the Artful Dodger and Charley Bates (as Wolton did years ago) in the art of picking pockets.'[88] Although, similarly to prior Dickensian afterlives, Lemon's references to *Oliver Twist* identify Field Lane as a criminal hub, his commentary marks the contrast between these scenes and the experience of his current journey through London. Dickens's account is, however, paradoxically reinforced by Field Lane's material dissimilarity to the scenes described in *Oliver Twist*. In this, literary tourism constructs symbolic spaces in the gap between the world of the novels and the material environment.

The 1870s and beyond: Conclusion

Real and symbolic spaces, the past and the present, are overlaid in commentaries on Field Lane's development through Dickensian afterlives. These out-of-sequence commentaries multiply revise how the place is perceived and presented in popular culture, and so give textual form to later urban theorists' interpretations of space as a product of human practices, never finished but constantly engaged in multiple processes of formation. Moreover, they confirm recent literary scholars' and historians' insistence on the coexistence of multiple modernities in nineteenth-century London, and how often these were conceived through, and in relation to, the past. The tracing of Dickensian afterlives reveals that this past is often evoked through literary representation, and fiction was likewise embedded in social processes of spatial production. Material alterations to the built environment were accompanied by numerous redefinitions of Field Lane's social and cultural identity, which influenced how its redevelopment was perceived and conceived. As the improvements that affected the area were completed, advocates continued to conceptualise its dangerous reputation by repurposing Dickensian afterlives. In 1870, for instance, an article campaigning for present-day social and urban reform in Field Lane identified the site as 'the very rookery of crime, where Fagin taught his boys to steal, and little Oliver was employed in picking out the marks in pocket-handkerchiefs'.[89] However, concurrently produced literary tourism, which reconceived *Oliver Twist* as historical rather than topical, became the more dominant mode for describing Field Lane after Dickens's death in 1870.

Retrospectives of Dickens's London are included in memorials for the author, as though his death marks a moment of fracture between Old and New London. In an obituary written for *Harper's Magazine*, Thomas Bucklin Wells comprehends Dickens's death through a comparison between his representation of the city in his novels and the modern, improved cityscape:

> most of all the genius of Dickens is associated with Field Lane, where Fagin had his den. [. . .] The alterations made by the Holborn Viaduct have almost completed the work begun by the Underground Railway, and Field Lane is now one dismal row of houses, from whose front the opposite row has been swept clean away, leaving all its wretchedness and filth exposed to view, and calling loudly to be swept into the biggest dust-hole that can be discovered. Eight years ago the wretched place was still what it had been when Dickens fixed it as the spot for Fagin's den. [. . .] In a year's time, probably, the Board of Public Works will have succeeded where the Board of City Missions failed, and every house that originally went to make up the terrors of Field Lane will have disappeared.[90]

Wells does not nostalgically reimagine Dickens's London. Instead, his account picks up on earlier intersections between Field Lane's perceived identity, specific social concerns, and their articulation in a Dickensian vocabulary. Restating the area's criminal associations, he recounts an anecdote about a missing handkerchief, which makes it 'plain that the Artful Dodger still lived thereabout'.[91] Wells thus employs similar rhetorical strategies to earlier commentators. He uses Dickensian afterlives to reinforce his observations of Field Lane's 'wretchedness and filth' by appropriating tropes and characters as shorthand for the ongoing issues he discusses. Intertextual references to Fagin's den, for instance, invite the reader to apply a web of criminal associations to his supposedly first-hand account, and prepare the reader to receive information linking Field Lane to crime. Yet Wells goes one step further than simply evoking Dickensian tropes as representational or rhetorical tools: he suggests that there are dialogues between Dickens's fictional descriptions, the author's social campaigning, and material changes to London's built environment. Wells reports that *Oliver Twist* made Field Lane 'much talked about' and sparked literary tourism to the area. He hints that imaginative curiosity led to targeted scrutiny and then changes to the real site. For example, the repetition of 'expose' in his account implies a connection between the way that the novel drew public attention to Field Lane as a criminal locale and subsequent demolitions that physically opened it to further surveillance.[92] Nor was Wells alone in naming Dickens's fiction as a driver of material reform. Charles Hindley's book *A History of the Cries of London, Ancient and Modern* (1881) also remarked that 'when Charles Dickens and Oliver Twist came in, Field-lane and Fagin went out'.[93] In the late nineteenth century, therefore, other writers measured Dickens's profound cultural impact in the simultaneous passing of both the author and his version of London. Wells asserts that Dickens's legacy is perceptible in the built environment and so recasts metropolitan alterations as a means of memorialising Dickens.

Not all literary tourists were as pleased by London's improvements. Walter Thornbury, a regular contributor to *Household Words*, explains in his book *Old and New London* (1872) that:

> Field Lane, extending from the foot of Holborn Hill northward, and in this way lying parallel with Fleet Ditch, used to be an infamous haunt of the 'dangerous classes'. Now, its site, entered off Charterhouse Street, may be visited by the inquiring stranger with somewhat of a feeling of disappointment that respectability is not half so picturesque as its opposite. In 1837, Field Lane was vividly sketched by Charles Dickens, in his 'Oliver Twist'.[94]

Thornbury's account still reinforces imaginative links between Dickens's criminal characters and Field Lane but he suggests that metropolitan improvements prevent enthusiasts from achieving a desired immersion in the world of the novel. Just as earlier appropriators had seen *Oliver Twist* as a tool to elucidate the material and social, for literary tourists the physical space offered further insights into the fictional. At the same time, Thornbury emphasises the supposed verisimilitude of Dickens's representation, which underpinned this kind of tourism by stressing the dissimilarity between *Oliver Twist* and the modern city.

Thornbury's book is not dedicated to literary representations of London. Nevertheless, intersections between imaginative portrayals and how the built environment is perceived are revealed and strengthened by an engraving that embeds Dickens's fiction in a purportedly faithful representation of the area's past (Figure 3.1). The elongated title of *Old and New London* states that it is *Illustrated*

Figure 3.1 *Field Lane About 1840* (Source: © Camden Local Studies and Archives Centre. 80).

with Numerous Engravings from the Most Authentic Sources, and the engraving also implies a specific, historically informed representation in its title, *Field Lane About 1840*. These tags suggest that the sketch is realistic; however, Fagin's name is depicted in large letters across the doorway in the middle of the image. The presence, let alone the centrality, of Dickens's narrative in the scene highlights the extent to which the street had become associated with *Oliver Twist*. However, the artist also used Dickensian afterlives to convey ideas about the area's social history. A placard above another doorway relocates Ebenezer Scrooge from *A Christmas Carol* (1843) to Field Lane. The combination of these avaricious characters within the engraving is likely to be an anti-Semitic reference to the mixed ethnic identity of the district, which Dickens's characterisation of Fagin as 'a very old shrivelled Jew' also emphasises (*OT*, p. 64).[95] The engraving thus illustrates that Dickensian afterlives were mobilised to identify the material and the social across multiple media and contexts.

Literary tourism elucidates numerous and ongoing interactions between Dickens's work and how people engage with London's material and social environments, even after the author's death and the street's demolition. For example, the impact that *Oliver Twist* has had on how Field Lane's history has been popularly perceived since its material redevelopment is indicated by the fact that numerous afterlives portray the novel as historical fiction. In 1888, John Ashton claimed that 'Fagin [. . .] was a real character' in his history of *The Fleet: Its River, Prison and Marriages*, and repeated this assertion in the *English Illustrated Magazine* in 1902.[96] In 1897, an article in the American newspaper the *Oregonian* even went so far as to construct a specific historical genealogy: 'Fagin was a real character, by name Isaac Touch, who, on being raided by the police, was found to possess a pack measure of watches.'[97] Moreover, the article maps specific fictional sites in relation to local improvements:

> at the bottom of Great Saffron hill, in what was once one of the most hideous and dangerous slums of London, still exists the relic of Fagin's kitchen. It is a part of a dirty and ruinous old tenement exactly coinciding with the famous den to which the Artful Dodger led Oliver Twist [. . .] From the outhouses any of the light-fingered gentry could easily have dropped into the street, while the adjacent house, recently condemned by the London county council, was easily accessible. The last-named tenement, formerly a haunt of vagrants, with all the conveniences of a thieves' kitchen, had associations of the worst kind, and has not a bit too soon come under the ban of the London parliament.[98]

The *Oregonian* registers the perceived social and moral imperatives for Field Lane's improvement by directly comparing their impact on the built environment with Dickens's supposedly accurate representation of real people and places in *Oliver Twist*.[99] Appropriations that present Dickens's description as realistic were present in British as well as American publications. In 1896, a writer for *Chambers's Journal of Popular Literature, Science and Arts* similarly maps fiction on to specific sites and improvements:

> 'Fagin's Kitchen', so graphically described by Dickens in *Oliver Twist*, with its filthy and insanitary conditions, has come under the ban of the London County Council, and is now closed. It was a registered lodging-house at Viaduct Chambers, Great Saffron Hill, Holborn. The premises consist of the main building and five cottages. The place had fifty-three beds in the main building.[100]

It is unclear from this account whether a real lodging house had adopted the sobriquet 'Fagin's Kitchen' as a joke because of its location and the novel's popularity, or whether this writer is building on the precise topographic details given in *Oliver Twist* to facilitate their interpretation of the built environment. Nevertheless, the uneasy interrelation between the fictional and the actual in the *Chambers's* article signals a more widespread trend of imaginative exchange. Particularly towards the end of the nineteenth century, when the area had been altered beyond recognition and readers could no longer compare Dickens's description with personal observations, Field Lane was regularly identified as 'the spot where Dickens located Fagin's den, in "Oliver Twist"'.[101]

The mutability of Dickensian afterlives, in addition to Dickens's multi-layered representation of Field Lane in *Oliver Twist*, meant that appropriating his fiction never offered representational stability. Instead, the multiplicity of Dickensian afterlives reveals practices of manipulation, which changed the novel and its characters into portable modes of signification. Dickens's description of Field Lane did not directly trigger the improvement of Field Lane, nor promote a single reading of the site. Even though later users often re-presented Dickens's works as a tool to aid the legibility of the city, therefore, the multiplicity and flexibility of Dickensian afterlives reveal that practices of appropriation in fact added to London's overwhelming illegibility. Still, the practice of appropriating *Oliver Twist* ensured that Dickens's fiction was mobilised regularly in connected debates, making the author a common feature of arguments for its demolition. Through this, we can see how processes that impelled material destruction and construction in London were both enabled and complicated by the literary for, while Dickens's fiction was used to argue for Field Lane's demolition, his enduring popularity also means that it has not been forgotten.

Notes

1. Tristan, p. 175.
2. See: Anon. (1847), 'Health of Towns', *Daily News*, 458, 16 Nov., p. 3.
3. Field Lane was known as a location of brothels and 'Molly Houses' from at least the eighteenth century. In 1726, there was a raid on a brothel kept by 'Mother Clap', after which one witness supposedly stated that he 'found between forty and fifty men making love to one another' (Anon. (1825), 'London: Saturday, August 27, 1825', *Morning Chronicle*, 17559, 27 Aug., pp. 2–3, p. 3. See also: Anon. (1833), 'Guildhall', *The Times*, 15123, 27 Mar., p. 7).
4. A transcript of the trial of Mary Ann King details how King 'asked' and then 'attempted to pull' her victim, George Alexander Brimmer, down Field Lane in order to rob him. Brimmer refused to enter Field Lane, however, as the area's reputation made him suspicious of King's intention (*Old Bailey Proceedings Online* (www.oldbaileyonline.org, version 7.2, 18 Oct. 2015), Oct. 1840, trial of MARY ANN KING (t18401019-2416)).
5. Anon. (1820), 'London. Tuesday, October 31', *Morning Post*, 15483, 31 Oct., p. 3.
6. Anon. (1821), 'London, Feb. 20', *Jackson's Oxford Journal*, 3540, 24 Feb., p. 4; Anon., 'Guildhall. – Catherine Carpenter', *Morning Chronicle*, 16056, 12 Oct., p. 3; Anon. (1831), 'The Burkers', *Belfast News-Letter*, 9859, 9 Dec., p. 1.
7. *Old Bailey Proceedings Online* (www.oldbaileyonline.org, version 7.2, 18 Oct. 2015), December 1838, trial of GEORGE BIRD (t18381217-330).
8. Wolfreys, *Dickens's London*, p. 133.
9. For some, Field Lane was comparable to 'the commercial resorts of Constantinople or Grand Cairo [. . .] rivalling them in its mingled aspect of brilliancy and squalor, its shady sunlessness, even in the dog-days, and its odours so genuinely Asiatic' (Anon. (1858), 'A Reminiscence of Field Lane', *Chambers's Journal of Popular Literature, Science and Arts*, 223, 10 Apr., pp. 231–4, p. 231).
10. Anon. (1845), 'Multiple News Items', *Standard*, 6626, 24 Oct., p. 7.
11. Bennett, pp. 297–8.

12. Anon. (1859), 'Domestic Intelligence', *Aberdeen Journal*, 5793, 19 Jan., p. 3.
13. Anon. (1860), 'Field Lane Refuge for the Destitute', *The Friend of India*, 1310, 9 Feb., pp. 131–3, p. 132.
14. Anon. (1859), 'The Power of the Pen', *John Bull*, 1998, 15 Jan., p. 41.
15. Broughton (para 4 of 28).
16. Turner, 'Companions, Supplements, and the Proliferation of Print in the 1830s', p. 131.
17. Mussell, 'Cohering Knowledge in the Nineteenth Century', p. 101.
18. Reprinted from *The Times* in: (1858) 'The Cabinet Drama', *Glasgow Herald*, 6006, 3 Dec., p. 3.
19. Anon. (1858), 'The Cabinet Drama', *Glasgow Herald*, 6006, 3 Dec., p. 3; Anon. (1858), 'Summary', *Liverpool Mercury*, 3368, 2 Dec., p. 4; Anon. (1858), 'Semi-Weekly Summary', *Liverpool Mercury*, 3369, 3 Dec., p. 9.
20. Godwin, *Town Swamps and Social Bridges*, p. 11.
21. W. Williams (1838), qtd in 'House of Commons. Friday, June 15', *The Times*, 16757, 16 Jun., p. 3.
22. Nead explains that '[d]isease and political sedition were not regarded as discrete problems; both were seen as the inevitable outcome of dirty and unhygienic living and working conditions. The moral condition of the poor was believed to correspond directly to their physical condition' (Nead, *Myths of Sexuality*, p. 118).
23. Please refer to Chapter 2 for further discussion of this topic.
24. Chase and Levenson, p. 149.
25. Beames, pp. 67–8.
26. Ibid., p. 52.
27. *Cary's New Plan of London and Its Vicinity* (1837), *Cross's London Guide* (1844), *Kelly's Post Office Directory Map of London* (1857), *Cross's New Plan of London* (1861) and *Stanford's Library Map of London and Its Suburbs* (1872), all available on *Map and Plan Collection Online*. See also Margary, *The A to Z of Victorian London*, p. 43, which is based on the George W. Bacon Atlas (1886).
28. Anon. (1824), 'Public Improvements', *Morning Chronicle*, 17334, 6 Nov., p. 3.
29. London, London Metropolitan Archives, HFCS/P. *Plans and Sections of the Main Line of the Field Lane and Hatton Garden Sewer Shewing its Dimensions and Depth from the Surface of the Ground and its Course and Fall from the Commencement at Christopher Street to its Junction with the River Fleet Sewer* [1814–47], sewerage plans.
30. White, pp. 50–1.
31. Stedman Jones, *Outcast London*, p. 167.
32. London, London Metropolitan Archives, SC/GL/PR/BM/F1/k1265901. J. Arrowsmith, *Plan for Improvements to Finsbury in the Form of Proposed Streets in Continuation of Farringdon Street to St John*

Street and Islington, and Communicating with Charterhouse (27 Mar. 1839), plan.

33. London, London Metropolitan Archives, COL/TSD/PL/04/05. John Turner and James Moon, *Design for the Improvement of Holborn Hill* (designed 1832, revised 1839), plan.
34. London, London Metropolitan Archives, SC/GL/PR/304/HOL/Q6011849. Francis Whishaw, *Proposed Plan and Elevation for Holborn Viaduct from North End of Fetter Lane to Old Bailey, also showing Plan for Improvement of Farringdon Market* (1839), plan.
35. London, London Metropolitan Archives, COL/CC/IMP/04/04/4. *Committee Papers*, Court of Common Council Improvements Committee, 'Committees: Improvement Farringdon New Street' (1838), minute book.
36. Anon. (1842), 'Metropolis Improvements', *The Times*, 18157, 3 Dec., p. 3. This time frame is confirmed by the papers of the Committee for the Improvement of Farringdon New Street, which show that as early as February 1838 a bill was issued to the House of Commons requesting its permission 'for the continuation of the New Farringdon Street'.
37. Ibid., p. 3.
38. Anon. (1846), 'Court Of Common Council', *The Times*, 19381, 30 Oct., p. 2.
39. London, Guildhall Library Archives, Acts Box. *An Act (5 & 6 Vict. cap. ci) for Further Extending the Approaches to London Bridge and the Avenues Adjoining to the Royal Exchange and for Amending the Acts Relating Thereto and for Raising a Sum of Money Towards Opening a Street to Clerkenwell Green in Continuation of the New Street from Farringdon-Street, in the City of London* (London: The Corporation, 1842), p. 28.
40. Anon. (1846), 'Railway News', *Daily News*, 96, 12 May, p. 7.
41. Anon. (1848), 'Opening of the National Assembly', *Hampshire Telegraph and Sussex Chronicle etc.*, 2535, 6 May, p. 8; Anon. (1845), 'Multiple News Items', *Standard*, 6626, 21 Oct., p. 7. This is also indicated in William Moseley's *Plan for Improvements. Holborn Hill & Skinner Street*, which offers a plan for a terminus at Farringdon and labels the area encompassing Field Lane as 'Property proposed to be taken for Warehouses' (London, London Metropolitan Archives, COL/PL/01/027/H/015. William Moseley, *Moseley's Plan For Improvements. Holborn Hill & Skinner Street* (undated), plan).
42. Anon. (1847), 'Health of Towns', *Daily News*, 458, 16 Nov., p. 3.
43. Anon. (1845), 'Multiple News Items', *Standard*, 6626, 21 Oct., p. 7.
44. There is no mention of Field Lane in any of the surveyor's returns for the parish of St Andrew, Holborn, from 1845 to 1852 (London, London Metropolitan Archives, MBO/DS/023. Office of Metropolitan Buildings, *District-Surveyors Returns, St Andrew, Holborn, &c.* (1845–52), record books).
45. Harben, p. 228.

46. Summerson, 'London, the Artifact', p. 314.
47. GLA, Acts Box. *An Act (5 & 6 Vict. cap. ci)*, p. 28.
48. London, London Metropolitan Archives, COL/TSD/PL. J. Belcher, *Mr Belcher's Plan for Improvements of Holborn Hill, by a Proposed Viaduct from Holborn to Skinner St* [? c.1842]; Peter Jeffreys, *Plan of an Improvement of Holborn Hill, by Reducing the Slope and by Forming a New Street from Victoria Street to King Street, West Smithfield* (1847), plans; and London, London Metropolitan Archives, COL/PL/01/027/H/013. John Phillips, *Plan and Section Shewing Proposed Street and Viaduct for Crossing the Valley of the Fleet, Between Holborn and Newgate Street* (2 Aug. 1851), plan.
49. London, Guildhall Library Archives, Pam 2468. Robert Hesketh, *Shall the New Street Which is to Form the Grand Communication between the Eastern and Western Parts of the Metropolis be Straight or Crooked? An Inquiry, with Suggestions, by an Architect* (London: John Weale and Letts, Son and Steer, 1854), pamphlet, p. 1.
50. Lord Derby (1861), qtd in 'Imperial Parliament', *Morning Post*, 27208, 1 Mar., p. 2.
51. The demolition of Field Lane and the consequent improvement of the district were promoted as an important facilitator of economic growth. The petition for the development of a terminus at Farringdon Street 'was signed by between 600 and 700 of the most eminent merchants, bankers, and wholesale and retail dealers in the City of London, who were aware of the importance of such a change as it recommended'. The continued existence of Field Lane not only stood in the way of the railway's physical development, but also made the district less attractive to potential investors (Anon. (1845), 'Multiple News Items', *Standard*, 6626, 24 Oct., p. 7).
52. London, Guildhall Library Archives, Bside 30.52. City Railway Terminus Company, *Street Improvements in Connexion with the Central City Terminus: Reasons for Signing a Petition in Favour of the Fleet Valley Railway and Farringdon Street Terminus, the Raising of Holborn Valley and other Street Improvements* (London: R. Clay, 1853), broadside, p. 3.
53. Dickens, 'A Sleep to Startle Us', p. 577.
54. Another article in *Household Words*, written by W. H. Wills, also remarked on improvements in the Farringdon area. Swiping at the mismanagement of London improvements in contrast to the systematic Hausmannisation of Paris, Wills gave the forestalled improvements around Field Lane as a typical example of the effectiveness of London developments: 'In our youth, a nest of rookeries was demolished on the Clerkenwell side of Holborn Bridge, under pretence of continuing Farringdon Street to be an open route for the Northern and Western Railways: we are now more than middle-aged, our second son has attained his majority, and Farringdon Street still stands where it did' (W. H. Wills, 'Paris Improved', *Household Words*, 12: 295, 17 Nov., pp. 361–5, p. 361).

55. V&A, *Oliver Twist!* Surrey playbill.
56. W. C. Taylor (1840), 'The Moral Economy of Large Towns', *Bentley's Miscellany*, 7, Jan., pp. 470–8, p. 473.
57. Qtd in Philip Horne, 'Introduction', in Dickens, *Oliver Twist*, pp. xiii–xliv, p. xxxii.
58. Anon. (1848), 'The Lord Chamberlain', *Trewman's Exeter Flying Post*, 4294, 30 Mar., p. 4.
59. Anon. (1844), 'Old House in Clerkenwell', *Illustrated London News*, 120, 17 Aug., p. 101.
60. Ibid., p. 101.
61. Anon. (1844), 'Occurrences', *Examiner*, 1907, 17 Aug., p. 13.
62. Wild was a historical figure as well as a now well-known character in Ainsworth's novel. The *Illustrated London News* was not alone in addressing a readership whose expectations were shaped by both historical and fictional accounts. The *Examiner* also noted that '[w]e can find no account of [the Red Lion] being the residence of Jonathan Wild, his houses being in the Old Bailey and Wych street. There is not the slightest doubt, however, that it was one of his principal hoards' (ibid., p. 13).
63. Anon., 'Old House in Clerkenwell', p. 101. Kathryn Chittick has shown in *Dickens and the 1830s* that there was a strong connection between these novels in the public imagination, and the *Illustrated London News* article certainly fits this wider trend.
64. Anon. (1847), 'Old House in Clerkenwell', p. 101.
65. Ibid., p. 101.
66. Anon. (1847), 'Health of Towns. – Improvement of London', *Illustrated London News*, 247, 23 Jan., p. 61.
67. Richard Salmon (2000), '"A Simulacrum of Power": Intimacy and Abstraction in the Rhetoric of the New Journalism', in Brake et al. (eds), *Nineteenth-Century Media and the Construction of Identities*, pp. 27–39, p. 32.
68. Anon., 'Health of Towns. – Improvement of London', p. 61.
69. Ibid., p. 61.
70. Godwin, *Town Swamps and Social Bridges*, p. 10.
71. Daunton, p. 204.
72. Anon. (1852), 'Our Weekly Gossip', *Athenaeum*, 1291, 24 Jul., pp. 800–1, p. 801.
73. Anon. (1858), 'London, Thursday, Dec. 2', *Daily News*, 3916, 2 Dec., p. 4.
74. Anon. (1854), 'Field-Lane and Saffron-Hill. Progress of the New Line', *Daily News*, 2604, 23 Sep., p. 3. Italics in original.
75. *Hansard*, 3rd ser., vol. 116 (9 May 1851), c. 765.
76. Harold King (1865), 'Our Unhoused Poor', *Once a Week*, 13: 321, Aug., pp. 246–9, p. 247.
77. Anon. (1865), 'A "New Site" for the Working Classes', *Era*, 1384, 2 Apr., p. 9.

78. Ibid., p. 9.
79. Anon. (1869), 'Holborn Valley Improvements', *Leisure Hour*, 890, 16 Jan., pp. 40–3, p. 42.
80. Ibid., p. 42.
81. Hollingshead, p. 13.
82. Ibid., p. 14.
83. Timbs, *Curiosities of London*, p. 336.
84. Timbs, *The Romance of London*, p. 265.
85. Ibid., p. 266.
86. Anon. (1866), 'An Execution in London', *Methodist*, 22, 2 Jun., p. 169.
87. John, *Dickens and Mass Culture*, p. 253.
88. Mark Lemon (1866), 'Up and Down the London Streets. Chapter VI', *London Society*, London: pp. 558–69, vol. 9, p. 559.
89. Anon. (1870), 'Refuge', *Englishwoman's Domestic Magazine*, 64, 1 Apr., pp. 221–3, p. 221.
90. Bucklin Wells, 'Footprints of Charles Dickens', pp. 611–12.
91. Ibid., pp. 611–12
92. Wells goes on to make a more decisive claim for a direct line of influence from Dickens's fiction to material change, stating that Dickens's *American Notes* 'probably [were] the first thing that led to the improvements of a region which had become almost impassable – which have ended in the railway': 'that old Acquia road' in northern Virginia (ibid., p. 612).
93. Hindley, p. 9.
94. Thornbury, p. 542.
95. Multiple migrant communities lived in Field Lane, as well as people who were born in Britain. The 1841 census reveals that there was an equal division between residents who had been born in England and those who had not. It records 50 residents in Field Lane: 25 state that they were born in Britain and 25 state that they were 'Born in Scotland, Ireland, or Foreign Parts'. This exactly even spread is rather suspect and possibly denotes an incomplete or invented record; however, it still reveals that the district probably had a mixed demographic, accordant with its popular identity ('Field Lane' (1841), in *England's Census, Ancestry* <www.ancestry.co.uk> (last accessed 12 Apr. 2012)).
96. Ashton, p. 158. John Ashton (1902), 'The Fleet River and its Associations', *English Illustrated Magazine*, 231, Dec., pp. 283–9, p. 285.
97. Anon. (1897), 'Fagin's Kitchen', *Morning Oregonian*, 7, 14 Feb., p. 16.
98. Ibid., p. 16.
99. The journalist also appropriated the fiction to convey new meanings and different contexts. Isaac Touch, the article reported, 'had the name of being a confederate in even worse crimes than training young thieves and buying stolen property'. Fagin's criminality was thus recontextualised for an American readership, adding further nuances to character to make a political comment (ibid., p. 16).

100. Anon. (1896), 'Better Homes for Working People', *Chambers's Journal of Popular Literature, Science and Arts*, 13: 664, 19 Sep., pp. 601–3, p. 603.
101. James Strang (1899), 'The Italian Colony in London', *Good Words*, 40, Dec., pp. 119–25, p. 124.

Chapter 4

Paperwork and Philanthropy: Dickens's Involvement in Metropolitan Improvement

The last chapter examined appropriations of Dickens's fiction by politicians and the press. Whether to support their own arguments or merely to enliven a dry speech, these users mobilised Dickensian afterlives to facilitate modes of communication that implicitly spoke for a larger group, journalists and politicians each being, in their way, supposedly answerable to the public. Moreover, as slum clearance was aligned with the amelioration of social and environmental problems, these Dickensian afterlives were used to argue that improvements would benefit the general populace, as well as specific communities or target districts. Dissenting voices always challenged these claims. Still, Dickens's works were valuable rhetorical tools through which such users spoke for, evoked or directly addressed a wider public. This chapter steps back from public arenas. Instead, it examines the roles that individuals could play in driving alterations to the built environment. Although practical building or reform projects were necessarily collaborative endeavours – requiring the participation of various tradesmen and financial backers, for instance – philanthropic initiatives prove that individuals could and did effect change.

I begin with Dickens himself. By investigating Dickens's personal involvement with a charitable scheme to improve London's provision of housing stock for the East End poor, this chapter suggests that he was directly involved with making changes to the built environment in his lifetime. Dickens's philanthropic works and interest in social and environmental reform have long been a subject of critical enquiry. For example, Patrick Brantlinger, Lauren Goodlad and Jenny Hartley have each examined intersections between Dickens's fiction and his advocacy of contemporary causes or practical reform projects, such as Urania Cottage.[1] Meanwhile Sajni Mukherji, Louise Penner and Bruce Robbins, among others, have analysed Dickens's imaginative representations of charity and charitable individuals.

This chapter adds to the research presented in these fine studies by framing his interests and activities in the context of his social network, which included important philanthropists and government reformers. It then considers how his administration of material projects instigated by these people affected how he conceived the utility of writing, and what kinds of texts could have an impact on society and the built environment.

Examination of Dickens's involvement with practical charitable projects provides another window on to how the circulation of texts overlapped with metropolitan improvements. The textual processes of paperwork were instrumental to the implementation of charitable schemes, as different kinds of documentation were required in the processes of planning a new development: communicating with specialist advisors, fundraisers or artisans, or seeking government authorisation for a project. Dickens's letters reveal that he regularly acted as administrator for practical improvements conceived by members of his social network. In particular, he worked closely with the wealthy philanthropist Angela Burdett Coutts for over two decades, and his bureaucratic work was instrumental to the success of a number of her ventures during this period.[2] Ironically, Dickens's letters also expose points at which communications broke down and the mismanagement of paperwork caused frustration and delay. Taking the Columbia Square development in Bethnal Green – a block of model dwellings in London's East End – as an example, this chapter traces Dickens's involvement in the project from its conception through to completion. Its progress was not smooth. Dickens's experiences were typical of the slow pace and complexity of most metropolitan improvements in the mid-nineteenth century. Contemporaneously with his involvement in this project, he explored the tensions between the effectiveness and ineffectiveness of paperwork in *Bleak House* (1852–3). Thus, this chapter suggests that Dickens's practical and administrative involvement in charity work informed his imaginative representation of the utility and futility of paperwork, and how he conceptualised the effectiveness of different forms of writing.

Despite Dickens's first-hand experience of the formal textual processes that accompanied material reform, he continued to reinforce the potential of 'fancy' to drive social and environmental change. In the 'Preliminary Word' to *Household Words*, for instance, he laid out his mandate to 'tenderly cherish that light of Fancy [. . .] to bring the greater and the lesser in degree, together, upon that wide field, and mutually dispose them to a better acquaintance and a kinder understanding'.[3] His 'success as a social reformer has been disputed', yet, as Catherine Waters notes, the changes he envisions in his writing did help to stir a 'groundswell of pressure for government action on urgent issues'.[4] Dickens regularly campaigned for pet causes in his fiction and journalism. Nevertheless, the various ways in which Dickens's works were appropriated by other people, and recontextualised to promote or to criticise philanthropic projects, prove that his writing was not always useful in the sense that he imagined. Other people carried on repurposing Dickens's novels in unpredictable directions, regardless of his involvement in urban reform, or of how he represented the roles texts could play in driving material or social change.

One reason for this diversification was users' different societal positions and the spaces in which they worked. Dickensian afterlives carried altered cultural connotations when they were mobilised by contemporary philanthropists than when they were employed rhetorically by politicians and journalists. Male voices dominate improvement debates in the press and parliament. Women were not permitted to be politicians and, although female journalists were published throughout the nineteenth century, the common practice of anonymising contributors made their participation in reporting metropolitan developments less obvious. Philanthropy, on the other hand, was commonly gendered as feminine. Dickensian afterlives were deployed rhetorically by female philanthropists in a similar way to male commentators but, as Anthony Trollope's satire of Dickens as 'Mr Popular Sentiment' suggests, contrary to their male counterparts, such afterlives inspired derogatory criticism when they were produced by women: 'Namby-pamby in these days is not thrown away if it be introduced in the proper quarters.'[5] Dickensian afterlives could reinforce pejorative assumptions that women's charity work was amateur, emotionally rather than intellectually driven, and misguided. Conversely, as the final section of this chapter will argue, Trollope's satire is contradicted by female philanthropists' strategic uses of Dickensian afterlives.

The apparent male bias in improvement debates obscures the impact that women's philanthropic works had on the development of London's built environment. Indeed, the material legacies of these initiatives are still frequently neglected in critical studies. Histories of female contributions to changing urban conditions have generally been limited to experiential practices, such as visiting the poor in their homes or providing education or community support. Anne Anderson and Elizabeth Darling even interpret Octavia Hill's social housing schemes as exercises in 'space-making' rather than material developments because Hill focused on improving the existing urban fabric, rather than building new homes from scratch.[6] Nevertheless,

Anderson and Darling's study also redresses the neglect of women's participation in metropolitan improvements by its 'identification and reclamation of female counterparts to the canon of "dead white males"'.[7] While refocusing 'the canon' is useful, as Darling and Lesley Whitworth remark, studies that approach the field through this method are ultimately 'self-delimiting' because they inevitably concentrate on high-profile and wealthy individuals. Consequently, there needs to be further research into other channels and locations of female involvement: for example, 'patronage, criticism, and women's associative capacities'.[8] Although women-centred histories correctly address a gender imbalance, they also risk exceptionalising female involvement, and so maintaining the impression that women's contributions were always separate from other initiatives, did not involve a mixed network, or depended on certain financial or social advantages. My analysis of Dickens's philanthropic network goes some way towards establishing a more integrated view of women's participation. Although limitations placed on women in the nineteenth century certainly prevented them from occupying certain spaces or roles, Dickens's letters reveal a mix of women and men, amateurs and professionals, working together to implement practical projects.

Dickens's voice drove material change to London's built environment, both directly and indirectly. As we have seen in the case of Field Lane, his fiction was mobilised by other commentators to promote specific urban improvements. Dickens also urged contemporary alterations himself. In both his administrative and imaginative work, he used his writing as a platform from which to organise or encourage urban and social change. Exploration of the different ways in which contemporary philanthropists and Dickens brought his writing into dialogue with practical charitable projects in London reveals considerable intersection between official and unofficial channels for reform and collaborations between women and men. Dickens thereby focuses a wider investigation of the instrumentality of texts and the sometimes unlikely agents who used them to promote metropolitan improvements.

Philanthropy

Comparison of campaigns for urban improvement in parliamentary speeches and the press to personal endeavours to impel reform relates to a broader renegotiation of the individual's relationship and responsibility to the state over the course of the nineteenth century.

Certain individuals' rights were increased. The Reform Acts of 1832, 1867 and 1884 extended the franchise to create a larger, though obviously far from representative, voting public. Meanwhile, the 1834 Poor Law Amendment Act made the inhuman treatment of the poor national policy. The Act introduced the infamous 'workhouse test', as a supposedly standardised method of testing individuals' needs and providing state aid. The test was designed to minimise variations between the help offered to different people by government bodies. Previously, local boards had decided how best to distribute poor relief but the test reduced their powers to make personal judgements. While the act depersonalised those in need, then, it also reduced the degree to which public servants could intervene in individual cases. In practice, the New Poor Law did not have as totalising an effect as its Utilitarian aims imply.[9] Nevertheless, both the implementation of the Poor Law and the public outcry that followed are indicative of wider concerns with what level of paternalistic care, or state intervention, was appropriate in a 'self-consciously liberal society'.[10]

Charity was a way for individuals to intercede when the state failed to make adequate provision for those in need, but philanthropic work took many forms in the mid-nineteenth century. The 'Lady Bountiful' model recalled a paternalistic system of feudal responsibility, in which a wealthy landowner performed philanthropic activities as a duty of care to their tenants. Burdett Coutts exemplifies this mode. She built a model village on her estate at Holly Lodge in Highgate; designed and funded local projects in areas of London with which she was connected, such as building St Stephen's Church in her father's old constituency of Westminster; and organised poor relief during economic downturns.[11] Burdett Coutts also intervened by demolishing slums. The construction of her model dwellings at Columbia Square began only after Nova Scotia Gardens was cleared out of the way.[12] Despite the impact Burdett Coutts's projects had on contemporary London, however, the Lady Bountiful figure was itself outdated. The mobility of workers and the division and development of aristocratic estates in London made this personal method inappropriate to contemporary urban social and monetary relations. Burdett Coutts perceived the need for a flexible and broad approach, and so did not limit her generosity to local causes. Although her deep pockets meant that she was commonly referred to as 'Lady Bountiful' in the nineteenth-century press, her interests were wide-ranging.[13] She funded far-reaching projects in Britain and abroad, such as endowing churches in Adelaide and Cape Town in the 1840s, and setting up stores selling basic foodstuffs at a minimal price in Ireland in the 1860s.[14]

Wealthy sponsors enabled practical philanthropic projects by making huge financial contributions, but charitable societies also raised large sums of money by collecting subscriptions or organising fundraising events.[15] Records that detail which charities attracted the largest number of female subscribers indicate that women were discriminating about which causes they chose to support.[16] F. K. Prochaska reveals that '[w]omen preferred to contribute to those charities which dealt with pregnancies, children, servants, and the problems of aging and distressed females'.[17] The urban impact of such charitable bodies is traceable in new construction – such as setting up refuges, schools or hospitals – or the demolition of former slums. Therefore, even if women did not have the means or status to make large contributions, organised societies still allowed women to play instrumental roles in funding and fundraising for improvements. Exceptionally wealthy women like Burdett Coutts made large donations, but smaller subscriptions, casual charity and fundraising also meant that bourgeois and working-class women impelled material reforms.[18] Burdett Coutts pays tribute to the contributions women made through such action in *Woman's Mission*:

> To women the country owes many of its educational foundations. Hospitals and almshouses have been generously endowed by them. The records of old doles, orphan charities, and other pious benefactions carry their names, connecting the feeling of protection for the young and comfort for the old which is the spring of so much benevolent action in our time.[19]

The material legacies of individual philanthropists and charitable societies thus prove that women made a tangible impact on the development of London's built environment.

Women's charity work also draws attention to the effects that women had on the built environment as space-makers. Prominent female philanthropists published treatises that emphasise how important ordering and improving domestic and urban spaces were in ameliorating the poor's living conditions. Burdett Coutts stresses the value of domestic economy and cleanliness in *Common Things* (1865), for example, and Octavia Hill argues that attractive urban aesthetics have a significant benefit on people's wellbeing and behaviour in *Homes of the London Poor* (1875). These philosophies underlie Burdett Coutts's and Hill's practical building and redevelopment projects. However, space-making activities, such as offering aid or education, were often informal and unsystematic. As

Dorice Williams Elliott notes in *The Angel Out of the House*, by the mid-century 'thousands of women visited the poor regularly, in their homes as well as in workhouses, hospitals, and even prisons'.[20] Recent analyses of nineteenth-century philanthropy rightly state that practices such as home visiting, didactic instruction and ordering of space according to bourgeois social codes are extremely patronising. It cannot be known how the poor reacted to such interventions, but Dickens's portrait of Mrs Pardiggle in *Bleak House* suggests that modern disquiet about nineteenth-century philanthropic practices echoes contemporary unease. Nevertheless, the fact that many people chose to administer aid through personal contact with those in need rather than through financial support also emphasises the fact that philanthropic work was undertaken not only by the wealthy.

Charity was not always something that was 'done' to the poor, rather than with or through them. Prochaska notes that

> [p]ropping up family institutions and the local community were intimately associated with a woman's role, whatever her class. [. . .] Such activities were part of the day-to-day, unadministered lives of the poor; [but] for the historian they rarely leave a trace behind.[21]

Online archives, unavailable when Prochaska published his study, now provide glimpses of working-class philanthropy. Transcripts of trials on the *Old Bailey Online* are one such resource. While simultaneously revealing tensions within slum communities, the trial in 1831 of Mary Ann Lee – who had been arrested for stabbing her neighbour Ellen Foulkes – reveals that the communal style of court living, with partition walls 'so thin I can hear anything', could build strong communities.[22] Foulkes's testimony indicates her participation in a supportive social network, in spite of Lee's subsequent actions: 'I quarrelled with her through her being ungrateful, for I have been a good friend to her, by giving her a home and victuals when she could not support herself – I had done that that very week.'[23] The home visiting performed by members of the middle classes thereby mimicked and built on the support already offered within working-class communities, even though the power dynamics in these exchanges were inevitably different.[24]

Philanthropy was increasingly formalised throughout the course of the nineteenth century, yet despite the high-level organisation required to marshal large charitable societies and the budgets of practical reforms, many continued to view women's charity work as amateur. Women were only gradually accepted on the management committees of charities in the second half of the nineteenth century, even though they had served on sub-committees and in associative capacities for many decades.[25] Men were involved in philanthropic projects but their contributions were conceptualised differently. Helen Meller argues that differences in men's and women's approaches to urban development are the reason why their work was often valued differently in cases of metropolitan reform. She suggests that women's space-making activities were 'a crucial element in the civic experience of urban living. [But w]omen's emphasis on the experiential aspect of urban life was at odds with their male counterparts' primarily physical and interventionist approach to planning.'[26] This bifurcation certainly emphasises how contrarily men's and women's contributions were perceived in the nineteenth century. Unlike women's supposedly recreational involvement, men's interests were frequently seen as an extension of professional work or expertise. In *Bleak House*, for instance, Alan Woodcourt's kindness to Jo and other slum-dwellers is interwoven with his role as physician, though he performs his professional services gratis. In practice, however, this presumed gender divide was less straightforward. Indeed, men's and women's activities often fall into similar categories. Like 'Lady Bountiful', some men endowed large-scale material improvements: for instance, George Peabody's social housing scheme in London. Still, others emphasised space-making – offering education and opportunities to the poor. Lord Shaftsbury, for example, was President of the Ragged School Union. Therefore, both men's and women's philanthropic works sought to ameliorate the lives of the poor through environmental and social interventions.

A gendered view of philanthropy and urban development is further complicated by collaborations between individuals. Charitable initiatives to improve the built environment brought amateur philanthropists into contact with the emerging class of professional specialists. Calling up Dickens's unflattering portraits of Mrs Jellyby and Mrs Pardiggle, Williams Elliott interprets the frequent hostility conveyed in written and artistic representations of female philanthropists as evidence that some men 'were uneasy about the challenge that systematised female philanthropy posed not only to accepted gender roles and class relations but also to their own position as experts'.[27] No doubt this was true in some instances but it was not universal. First, as my analysis of Dickens's network in the next section of this chapter will prove, professional men sometimes worked with women to effect topographic reforms. Second, these individuals used similar methods when carrying out their work. Akin to the home visits made by amateurs, Dickens remarks in a letter to Burdett Coutts that '[t]he knowledge that the [government's General] Board of Health has acquired [is] founded upon their personal inspection of the abodes of the poor in all parts of the country'.[28] Dickens suggests that these specialists' professional knowledge of urban conditions qualifies them to recommend reformatory initiatives. However, their expertise was achieved by the same method of home visiting that female philanthropists undertook when interceding through space-making activities. Finally, both professionals and amateurs, women and men, struggled to push through systematic reforms. Goodlad has already explored the frustrations faced by Edwin Chadwick when he tried to drive through legislative changes to effect public health improvements.[29] Similarly, delays and frustrations beset Louisa Twining's attempts to implement a Workhouse Visiting Society, as her proposals were initially rejected by the local Poor Law Board.[30] By the late nineteenth century, the division between professional and amateur charity work was further obscured, as philanthropic ventures were increasingly rationalised and organised. Burdett Coutts records how differently women's charity work was conceived by the end of the century from what it was at the start. In *Woman's Mission*, published in 1893, she presents the female contributors to the volume as recognised specialists or ambassadors in their fields, terms that were previously applied only to men. Professionalising philanthropy was thus one way in which women's roles, and the value of their work, were revised.

Dickens and his Network

Dickens's personal participation in metropolitan improvements took place on that side of his life that was not always recorded. His activities as a public figure and social campaigner must be reconstructed from fragments. Traces from his letters, public speeches and reports nevertheless reveal his wide-ranging and longstanding involvement in reform. Most famously, perhaps, this included his hands-on and administrative connection with Urania Cottage for more than a decade.[31] Still further initiatives are evident in his committee work, his support of petitions to government, and his attempts to influence a network of people who worked toward making physical developments to London's cityscape. This section explores Dickens's administrative involvement in material reform and the contributions he made to these projects behind the scenes.

Dickens had access to individuals with powers to effect urban change. This is recorded in documents such as guest lists of public dinners. A regular speaker at public events, Dickens was propelled on these occasions into the company of other well-known philanthropists and reformers who were involved in implementing large-scale metropolitan alterations: for example, Lord Ashley, MP (Lord Shaftsbury from 1851), who was an advocate for numerous charitable projects, including schemes to improve working-class housing in London.[32] The list of the men who acted as stewards at a public banquet given in Dickens's honour in 1867 provides evidence of the relationships he built with powerful people over his career, as well as the opportunities that he had to address them – formally and informally – about his concerns. Amongst the famous writers, actors and artists that one might expect (such as Wilkie Collins, W. C. Macready and J. E. Millais), there were also several aristocrats (like the Duke of Argyll), politicians (including William Gladstone), government inspectors (Professor Owen), and important members of London's local government (the Lord Mayor) and the legal profession (the Lord Chief Justice of England).[33] The account of this dinner notes that

> [i]t was a List made up almost entirely of Representative Men. It comprised within it upwards of one hundred celebrities. There, among that gathering of great names, Science, Art, Statesmanship, Heroism, Commerce, the Law, the Church, Literature, and Philosophy, each had its most notable representatives.[34]

Proximity is not a measure of influence, of course, but this list emphasises that Dickens's access to a network of leading men was not just at a local committee level.

Dickens's contact with influential people responsible for material improvements is specifically traceable in his relationships with the members of various sanitary boards, which incorporated changes to the built environment in their policies of reform.[35] In addition to being a member of the Metropolitan Sanitary Association (MSA),[36] a voluntary committee, Dickens was variously a colleague, friend or relation of the individual members of central government's General Board of Health (GBH).[37] These connections allowed Dickens to become involved with the GBH's endeavours, by spearheading supportive written campaigns and advising on administrative decisions, such as staffing.

In addition to Chadwick, with whom Dickens was acquainted, other major figures on the GBH in the 1850s included Dickens's brother-in-law, Henry Austin, and Octavia Hill's grandfather, Dr Thomas Southwood Smith.[38] Dickens had read Southwood Smith's publications with interest from at least 1842 and approved of his approach. For instance, he wrote to congratulate the doctor after reading his report 'On Extramural Sepulture' (1850), stating that the reforms proposed were 'a monument of good sense, moderate reasoning to demonstration, and noble feeling'.[39] Their relationship was both personal and professional. In addition to a shared interest in sanitary reform, Dickens sought Southwood Smith's opinion on delicate family medical matters, including Catherine's (presumably postpartum) nervous condition.[40] Dickens was even more intimately connected to Austin, who was secretary to the GBH over a four-year period. Aside from their familial connection, the two were in close and frequent contact in the early 1850s and clearly respected and valued each other's opinions. Austin, for instance, advised Dickens on a prospective purchase of a house in Highgate in January 1851, and later Tavistock House.[41] This closeness spilled into their professional lives. Austin sought out Dickens's knowledge of London's intellectual milieu when it became necessary to replace Alexander Bain as the Assistant Secretary to the GBH, and wrote to Dickens for advice about a suitable replacement.[42] Dickens replied: 'My Dear Henry / I *ought* to know the kind of man. Give me another day to try to remember him in.'[43] This exchange was not an isolated occurrence. The first person whom Dickens suggested refused the post, and Austin consulted with him again.[44] Dickens's involvement is behind the scenes; however, his interactions with Austin indicate that his opinion had an impact on the administration of the GBH. My next chapter examines sanitary reform more closely, but these connections are worth noting here because the public health scares of the 1840s were instrumental in sparking philanthropic interventions in housing provision for the poor in London and elsewhere, with which this chapter is concerned.[45]

Dickens's personal and professional relationships with the members of the GBH had an effect on how he organised Burdett Coutts's practical housing initiatives. He used his network strategically to secure the participation of people who he felt would bring appropriate and useful professional expertise to the project. Nevertheless, it is likely that he was also conscious that the involvement of central government representatives would help the project to obtain necessary parliamentary authorisation. In the terminology of current network theory, Dickens was the 'node' that connected government representatives, wealthy philanthropists and professional specialists, and facilitated their collaboration.[46] Dickens thus used his network to promote material change in London's housing stock.

Dickens's involvement in model housing projects began because of his friendship with Burdett Coutts. Biographers are unsure whether the two met in 1837 or 1838,[47] but agree that he was quickly and 'firmly established as Miss Coutts's unofficial almoner'.[48] Before many years had passed, Dickens could confidently apply to Burdett Coutts for money to support causes in which he was interested. On 16 September 1843, for instance, he wrote:

> On Thursday night, I went to the [Field Lane] Ragged School; and an awful sight it is. I blush to quote Oliver Twist for an authority, but it stands on that ground, and is precisely such a place as the Jew lived in.[49]

Unlike other commentators who appropriated his novels to elicit sympathy or notice, Dickens was already assured of Burdett Coutts's attention and had no need to use his fiction tactically.[50] Dickens habitually enlivens his letters with references to his works. However, in this instance, Dickens's allusion to *Oliver Twist* (1837–9) perhaps reflects an awareness that his access to, and ability to influence, Burdett Coutts was predicated on her receptiveness to the social causes and sympathies propounded by his novels, and on the fact that many people interpreted his fiction as evidence of his first-hand, specialist knowledge of London's conditions.[51] In 1899, an interview with Burdett Coutts for *The Young Woman* claimed that she had declared 'the novelist [. . .] had much to do with inspiring her intense sympathy with the poor'.[52] Certainly, his letters commanded her attention. Burdett Coutts responded by beginning to make enquiries about purchasing ground to build other utilities for the poor in that area, including a wash house.[53] The letter is thus an early example of how Dickens's and Burdett Coutts's friendship resulted in multiple physical changes to London's built environment, and how these were impelled by the mobilisation of different forms of writing.

The Columbia Square development is an example of the material legacies left by women philanthropists in London's built environment, but also of the instrumentality of administrative agents to the successful completion of these projects. The scheme was Burdett Coutts's idea. In the 1850s, she wrote to consult with Dickens about the building of model lodgings in Nova Scotia Gardens in Bethnal Green, later known as Columbia Square, and in Westminster, close

Figure 4.1 'Model Lodging-Houses, Columbia-Square' (Source: © The British Library Board, London. ZD.9.d.149).

to St Stephen's Church. Ultimately, the Westminster project was not carried out but building work on the model dwellings in East London, though delayed, began in 1859 and was completed in 1862 (Figure 4.1).[54] Philanthropic organisations started to address the problem of inadequate working-class housing in London around a decade before Burdett Coutts first mooted her idea. The Metropolitan Association for Improving the Dwellings of the Industrious Classes was founded in 1841, and the Society for Improving the Conditions of the Labouring Classes in 1844. These associations had high-profile support from Lord Ashley and Prince Albert.[55] The mid-1840s saw experimental schemes trialled in London: for example, converting lodging houses into self-contained flats. Then, in 1849–50, a block of 'Model Houses for Families' was erected in Streatham Street, Bloomsbury.[56] Conversely, Burdett Coutts did not simply seek to replicate former endeavours, but analysed how her buildings could improve on them. Dickens's letters to her indicate that she maintained a central role in planning Columbia Square, even though she often acted through, and consulted with, agents.[57]

Burdett Coutts is certainly not representative of women's involvement with philanthropy and urban developments as a whole. She did not marry until late in life and so retained control over her extraordinary wealth. This enabled her to make monetary contributions beyond the means of almost any other individual in the country. Her money gave her a unique autonomy to fund and plan philanthropic schemes as she saw fit. In addition to the benefits of aristocratic status and education, her wealth allowed her to command a degree of creative control that was unusual for any individual, regardless of gender. Records held at the Westminster City Archives reveal how she satisfied her personal tastes in the building of St Stephen's Church. For example, the *Account for Making the Chancel Carpet and Other Church Furnishings for St Stephen's Submitted to Miss Burdett Coutts by Elizabeth Besserier, Embroideress, of 9 Judd Street, Brunswick Square* lists and costs the decorations being embroidered for the interior décor individually.[58] These include coats of arms relevant to Burdett Coutts and her immediate circle, and others representing her wide-ranging charitable concerns, such as the bishoprics she endowed in Cape Town and Adelaide. One entry details the price for 'Square of Fleur de lys, worked entirely, to replace one worked wrong'.[59] It seems unlikely that the embroideress would have billed for this square if it were her own mistake. Besserier presents herself as '**Embroideress,** To Her Majesty the Queen and Her Royal Highness the Duchess of Kent' and includes a royal insignia on her receipt.[60] One assumes, then, that her reputation would have been worth more to her than a single *fleur de lys*. The receipt indicates that Burdett Coutts requested a new square, redesigned to suit her vision for the church's décor more exactly. This suggests that she maintained control over her projects down to the finer details.

Burdett Coutts certainly played a significant role in planning Columbia Square, but her working practices were collaborative and Dickens was her chief ally. He communicated with her regularly about the project throughout the planning stages, and his letters reveal that he was involved in surveying the district prior to any demolitions, in recommending practical measures to be implemented in the construction of the dwellings, and in seeking the advice of professional specialists about the project. Diana Orton notes that although 'Dickens was not involved in the architectural planning, Columbia Square was built on the principles laid down by him in a letter to Angela of April 18, 1852.'[61] Dickens's advice follows what was coming to be the dominant contemporary opinion about what style of housing was suitable and healthy for the urban working classes.[62] Nevertheless, his letter goes into considerable detail justifying why: 'I have no doubt myself (after long consideration of the subject) that the large houses are best.'[63] His opinions are attuned to popular perceptions of the environmental determination of social problems. Citing benefits for sanitation, residents' easy access to employment, better construction and the economic advantages of large houses, Dickens suggests that these changes to the built environment will have a positive impact on inhabitants' lives and spatial practices.

Dickens's advisory role is one way in which his influence is traceable in the completed Columbia Square development. We can perceive what a significant victory this was for him because he was by no means the only person who could have influenced Burdett Coutts's project. Her former governess and close friend Hannah Meredith (later Mrs Brown) was instrumental in developing Burdett Coutts's religious convictions and the way in which she approached philanthropic work. Meredith's importance is recognised in later commemorations of Burdett Coutts's life and work. In 1947, for instance, a hilariously sycophantic centenary play celebrating the foundation of St Stephen's, titled 'A Goodly Heritage', gives Meredith a large part and does not feature Dickens at all, even though the play draws attention to Burdett Coutts's friendships with other eminent men, such as the Duke of Wellington.[64] Meredith's strong religious faith undoubtedly influenced how Burdett Coutts conceived the building of St Stephen's, and the two were later buried in a shared crypt in this church with Meredith's husband.[65] However, Dickens's influence commanded a more powerful sway in the Columbia Square project. Unlike Dickens, Meredith preferred small houses.[66] Although Burdett Coutts continued to discuss the relative benefits of small or large houses with her collaborators during the 1850s, she ultimately favoured Dickens's advice.

In spite of his close involvement with Columbia Square, Dickens could not presume his ability to influence Burdett Coutts, and he knew it. Regardless of the cultural bias that favoured male, supposedly expert opinions on urban improvement, Dickens recognised Meredith's high standing with Burdett Coutts, and referred to her (only semi-jocularly) as 'my perpetual contradicter, who I suppose is laying up a stock of illustration and argument that will utterly defeat me for the rest of my life'.[67] Correctly perceiving the need to work with Burdett Coutts's inner circle to maintain his position, Dickens proposes making 'an expedition to the spot' with Meredith's husband after making his initial survey of Nova Scotia Gardens, and *before* consulting with his own close network of professionals and government representatives.[68] Unlike the control Dickens maintained over his literary collaborations, he adopted a deferential attitude in his dealings with Burdett Coutts and was quick to emphasise his respectful adherence to her opinions.[69] Her vision, and purse, were in command. Nevertheless, Dickens's careful management of their relationship indicates his recognition that working with Burdett Coutts also gave him opportunities to drive tangible improvements that reflected his values and opinions.

The letter Dickens wrote to recommend the benefits of large houses enables modern scholars to perceive intersections between his views and the completed project. Dickens stresses the importance of space-making activities as well as bricks and mortar. Recalling model towns built by industrialists in the north of England, Dickens notes the 'humanizing' affect created by 'paying schools, savings banks, little libraries, &c' as well as 'by establishing decent houses'.[70] Reading rooms were later built on the top floor of the Columbia Square dwellings, with a 'library of five hundred standard volumes [. . .] provided'.[71] Dickens's recommendations speak to Burdett Coutts's own concerns as well as his belief in the importance of 'fancy' (he had earlier noted the 'humanizing influence of a few leaves and flowers in [St Stephen's Church]', which, he states, 'will suggest to the commonest mind that you wish to please the poor'[72]); still, his clear proposals for the East London site allow us to trace how Dickens's suggestions were taken up and realised. This tells us something about the degree to which his participation in material reforms was expected and accepted by the other people involved in the project. Amateurs as well as professionals could influence the redevelopment of physical spaces.

Columbia Square is one example of how philanthropists, public servants and specialists collaborated to push through practical reforms but Dickens's involvement was instrumental to making these alliances successful. The author was responsible for recruiting the various people involved, introducing them to each other and acting as a mediator frequently thereafter. His first task was to decide whom to enlist. Dickens believed in the project – '*certain* that a scheme like [this] is the only hopeful way of doing lasting good, and raising up the wretched' – and so considered whom to involve in the project carefully.[73] The following letter is worth quoting at length, because it reveals Dickens's central role in forging the network behind the Columbia Square development:

> I saw Inspector Field last night. I could only approach the subject afar off, in consequence of his horrible sharpness, but I am disposed to doubt the efficacy of his peculiar sort of knowledge and sagacity in this stage of the matter. A locality chosen, I have no doubt that, at a small expense, his assistance in the beginning would be of immense service; or, a locality suggested, that his observations upon it would also be very important – for, if there were a serious objection, he would be certain to know it. But the habits of his mind hardly lead him (I think I observe) to the present point before us.
>
> I have been thinking a good deal about it, and it seems to me that Dr. Southwood Smith is the man of all others, to consult first. His fever-practice has made him, for many years, well acquainted with all the poor parts of London; he is in possession of all the reports made to the Board of Health in the late Survey; and he knows what work there is in this or that place; and how the people live; and how their tenements are held; and all about them. I am well acquainted with him – have both advised him and advised with him in many delicate matters – and can implicitly trust him. Not that I should think it necessary to mention you, or to proceed beyond generalities, but I mean, I can trust his interest in such a subject and his giving an opinion on sound knowledge and careful consideration and well regulated humanity.[74]

Despite Dickens's respect for Inspector Field, he does not deem him an appropriate collaborator for the Columbia Square project. Field's 'horrible sharpness' suggests both his intelligence and a cold, analytical approach. Although he has specialist knowledge of London conditions, Field's 'habits of [. . .] mind' do not suit Dickens's object to recruit people whose sympathies and ideals are aligned with the project. Southwood Smith is also presented as an expert in London's conditions, whose insights would be useful to ensure that Columbia Square addressed working-class needs appropriately. Moreover, Dickens notes that he is usefully connected to the GBH and so has access to up-to-date research completed in 'the late Survey'. In contrast to Field, however, Southwood Smith's professional knowledge is balanced by his 'well regulated humanity'. This indicates that Dickens thought philanthropy required emotional investment, as well as money, time and expertise. The completed Columbia Square was to be a material representation of jointly held ideals. He wanted people who could make useful contributions to the scheme but proposed that empathy was also central to its successful execution.

Dickens's strategic networking demonstrates the power that individuals could wield in directing the course of larger, collaborative endeavours. Given his personal relationships with the members of the GBH, Dickens was the point of connection between Burdett Coutts and members of government bodies. He then facilitated their cooperation by circulating papers and reports, and writing letters to the different people involved. Dickens's letters show that both Austin and Southwood Smith were regularly consulted during the planning of Columbia Square, and their contributions are evident in the project's up-to-date sanitary provisions.[75] The combined efforts of Burdett Coutts and her team were realised in large-scale material change. They began by clearing Nova Scotia Gardens of its dilapidated property and removing a huge dust mound, of the kind described by Dickens in *Our Mutual Friend* (1864–5). New dwellings were then erected on the site and rented to members of the working class. After the success of Columbia Square, Burdett Coutts initiated further (though less fruitful) schemes in the area, including building the cathedral-like Columbia Market and new road and rail infrastructure. Dickens's role as unofficial administrator thus helped to impel the development of the built environment in East London.

Conversely, Dickens's letters also reveal points at which collaboration became difficult or opinions clashed. Burdett Coutts initially intended to employ Philip Hardwick as architect, and Dickens's correspondence makes multiple references to the fact that he has 'gone over the plan carefully, with Mr. Hardwick, on the ground'.[76] As in his letter about the size of the dwellings, these exchanges show that Dickens was personally involved with the detailed planning of the physical site. He did not trust Hardwick's capabilities and advised Burdett Coutts:

> Before you sanction any plan of building, decidedly, I hope you will take Dr. Southwood Smith and Mr. Austin into consultation. I think you would save a great deal of money by doing so, and would get good sanitary arrangements on the most efficient and simple terms.[77]

Hardwick failed to produce proper plans over the next month. In a chance meeting with Hardwick at the Athenaeum, Dickens discovered that there had been no 'deliberate preparation in black and white to discuss, and on which to compare ideas'.[78] Even though Columbia Square was technically an amateur's scheme, the project's size, large budget and number of collaborators required rigorous, formal record-keeping. Dickens was an effective administrator: he records his contributions to the project in writing, and prepares and circulates documents among the others. By contrast, he treats the absence of documentation from Hardwick as evidence that his former misgivings were correct. However, Dickens's objections to Hardwick's informality also suggest that he did not view the project as amateur.

Hardwick was subsequently replaced by Henry Darbishire[79] but Dickens's role in mediating this miscommunication is worth noting for two reasons. First, it shows how central Dickens's strategic networking was to the completed building. Indeed, his impact is traceable in its architectural structure because of his interactions with different architects. Second, it signals one reason why Burdett Coutts chose to employ male agents to assist her philanthropic works, despite her evident capability and fortune. Networking depended partly on physical spaces. The chance meeting between the men at the Athenaeum highlights the importance of male clubs within these social circles.[80] Club membership was denied even to important and wealthy women like Burdett Coutts. Even though Dickens and others treated her deferentially, then, these spaces reveal limitations to her involvement with the practical arrangement for her philanthropic works.

Other genres of text became part of the cultural mythology of the Columbia Square development, even though Dickens's role was mostly administrative and behind the scenes. Some later biographies of Burdett Coutts construct chronologies that imply a direct line of influence from Dickens's fiction to her East London schemes. In 1893, the pamphlet *Baroness Burdett-Coutts: A Sketch of Her Public Life and Work* was published as a supplement to *Woman's Mission*. Despite its focus on Burdett Coutts, the chapter describing the Columbia Square project devotes the first two pages out of five to talking about Dickens and quoting from his works: 'The gulf dividing the West from the East End of London, deep as it now is, was deeper twenty-five years ago. It was a subject on which Charles Dickens often dwelt.'[81] The pamphlet suggests that Dickens's fiction directly inspired Burdett Coutts's practical work. Similarly, in *Noble Work by Noble Women* (1900), Jennie Chappell cites the instrumentality of 'the inspiring influence of the great novelist, Charles Dickens, upon Miss Burdett-Coutts, an influence which she gratefully acknowledges, still cherishing the remembrance of his companionship and help in her work among the East End Poor'.[82] His impact on this specific project is stated even more explicitly in 1947 in Agatha Twining's 'The Story of Our Foundress':

> Charles Dickens [. . .] drew [Burdett Coutts's] attention to [the area]. There are many incidents in his various novels, especially in 'Oliver Twist' which that great Author culled from 'Nova Scotia Gardens' as that terrible place was then called, situated in Shoreditch, now Bethnal Green.[83]

Twining constructs a chronology that places Dickens's knowledge and fictional representation of the area before Burdett Coutts's choice of Nova Scotia Gardens as an appropriate site for her scheme and so, Twining suggests, Dickens's fiction is evidence of his influence on Burdett Coutts's material reforms. Each of these accounts asserts the instrumental effect of fiction. Dickens's utility as an administrator is played down as his effectiveness as a novelist is emphasised.

Burdett Coutts and Dickens's relationship was none the less seen as one of mutual benefit and influence. Although Chappell presents Dickens's fiction as an inspiration to Burdett Coutts in *Noble Work by Noble Women*, she also stresses the impact that Burdett Coutts had on Dickens's writing and career.

> Miss Coutts was one of the first to recognise the genius of the latter, and he in his turn arousing the sympathy of the heiress in the sorrows and privations of the poor, was thus the means of directing her wealth into a channel of incalculable good.[84]

Likewise, an article published in *The Lady's Realm* presents Burdett Coutts as an early advocate for the young writer, 'whose knowledge of the people [was] (then so little thought of)', as well as noting that this 'made him a helpful guide and counsellor' for her.[85] Burdett Coutts's influence is even traced into Dickens's fiction. The interviewer for *The Young Woman* in 1899 'wonder[ed] if the Master was thinking of the Baroness when he conceived those happy characters, the Brothers Cheeryble, in *Nicholas Nickleby*. Certainly he could not have had a more apt original.'[86] This is chronologically unlikely. Still, the article's assertions reflect the fact that Burdett Coutts and Dickens's relationship and collaborations were envisioned by many as one of mutual and social benefit. In such accounts, Dickens's instrumentality is based on his personal experiences, while his fiction is presented as secondary. This is surprising, given Dickens's longstanding commitment to voicing social critiques in his novels. Nevertheless, Dickens certainly questioned what genres of writing were most effective in philanthropic work.

Bleak House

The circulation of papers and texts was embedded in Dickens's role as Burdett Coutts's 'unofficial almoner'.[87] His letters frequently make references to plans enclosed, or communications he has relayed to other parties. Dickens's administrative work exposes the instrumentality of paperwork to processes of urban improvement but – particularly in moments when he mentions letters crossing, or Hardwick's failure to produce appropriate plans – his administrative roles also draw attention to the ephemerality and, often, the ineffectiveness of paperwork. The novels that Dickens produced in the 1850s, concurrently with his involvement in the Columbia Square project, explore these frustrations and bureaucracy's power either to authorise or to forestall beneficial change. The tyranny of Chancery in *Bleak House* and the Circumlocution Office in *Little Dorrit* (1855–7), and Mr Gradgrind's dehumanising reliance on Blue Books in *Hard Times* (1854) all express the inadequacy (even malevolence) of administrative processes. Dickens portrays each of these bureaucracies as impersonal, as they formalise measures that permit personal responsibility to be deferred: 'the Circumlocution Office went on mechanically, every day, keeping this wonderful, all-sufficient wheel of statesmanship, How not to do it, in motion' (*LD*, p. 120). The Circumlocution Office's 'mechanical' workings appear to defy human understanding or control; however, as Ben Kafka notes in *The Demon of Writing* and as Dickens's strategic networking reveals, bureaucracy is not impersonal. Administrative processes must be maintained by people, and this opens opportunities for individual workers to use their knowledge of the system for their own ends. The personal side of bureaucracy can enable administrators to circumvent rules in order to help others, just as it equally facilitates error and corruption.[88] Dickens's representation of philanthropy in *Bleak House* examines these tensions between the utility and futility, the materiality and immateriality, the humanity and inhumanity of paperwork.

Various models of charitable action are represented in *Bleak House*; however, none is portrayed as a viable means of effecting significant social change. Reversing gender expectations, Mr Quale is the only character to describe himself as a philanthropist. Still, Dickens's blistering satire of pseudo-professional philanthropy is fully realised in Mrs Jellyby and Mrs Pardiggle. These characters are, as John Butt and Kathleen Tillotson long since contended, representative figures for contemporary movements: Mrs Pardiggle is an attack on Puseyism, and Mrs Jellyby is based on Caroline Chisholm,[89] with whom Dickens collaborated on her Family Colonisation Society and Family Colonisation Loan Society, which helped would-be emigrants from Britain.[90] Dickens critiques these characters' 'rapacious benevolence' as self-serving and ineffective because it employs indiscriminate or ill-advised methods (*BH*, p. 124). Similar criticisms could be levelled at Mr Snagsby's casual alms-giving, which salves his own social guilt while indirectly increasing Jo's victimisation, by making him the subject of robbery rather than alleviating his suffering. Meanwhile, Lady Dedlock is ironically presented as a Lady Bountiful. She refers to her interest in Rosa as 'patronage', even though she is aware that she gains more from their relationship. 'I knew very well that if [Mr Rouncewell, who presents himself as Rosa's prospective guardian] could have had the power of seeing me as I was, he would consider the poor girl tarnished by having for a moment been, although most innocently, the subject of my great and distinguished patronage' (*BH*, p. 654). At the other end of the novel's social spectrum, working-class philanthropy is portrayed in the community aid and support that the brick-makers' wives offer each other. Local and domestic charity, realised in practical actions, is presented as the most favourable means of doing good, yet its effects are still limited. Even Esther and Mr Jarndyce often fail to achieve the results they intend. For example, their combined efforts to protect Jo in his illness – by caring for him, and writing letters on his behalf to petition for him to be admitted to hospital – do not prevent him from being turned out of Bleak House by Skimpole. Charity simply does not have the power substantially to ameliorate a society entombed in fog and subject to obstructive bureaucratic procedure.

The circulation, exchange and analysis of documents are at the heart of philanthropic activities in the text. Mrs Jellyby dictates innumerable letters about Borrioboola-Gha, and Mrs Pardiggle leaves tracts in the brick-maker's cottage. Meanwhile, writing is also a significant feature in informal charity work. Esther tries to teach Charley to read and write, for instance. The failure of these documents to communicate social change makes these actions and texts appear futile. Mrs Jellyby's letters circulate without appearing to reach anyone. The brick-makers cannot read the pamphlets that Mrs Pardiggle distributes. Charley struggles to make progress under Esther's tutelage. Nevertheless, these documents are presented as both substantial and insubstantial at once. To a degree, the materiality of the texts conveys their ideological import. Although the brick-makers and Charley cannot read, they understand the social implications embodied by the texts themselves, as the object carries connotations about class status and education. On the other hand, Mrs Jellyby's letters appear increasingly farcical as they grow in number. Indeed, the materiality of the paperwork effaces its subject. This is expressed by Caddy, whose comically outlandish wish that 'Africa was dead!' reveals how its repeated representation in writing effects a disassociation between reality and representation, making Africa an abstract and groundless sign (*BH*, p. 60). Writing, here, expresses powerlessness and frustration, both because it fails to effect its purpose and because it results in the (sometimes seemingly arbitrary) subjugation of individuals. Just as the mass of paperwork carried in at the end of the Jarndyce versus Jarndyce case is a tragi-comic realisation of its futility, the greater the volume of paperwork produced to impel philanthropic action, the more meaningless its messages become.

Paperwork is far from useless in *Bleak House*, however; it is instrumental to the plot development and affects the physical condition of the entire city. As J. Hillis Miller has argued, '*Bleak House* is a document about the interpretation of documents' and, indeed, every character in *Bleak House* is in some way concerned with paperwork.[91] The far-reaching impact of bureaucratic writing is most evident in Dickens's damning indictment of Chancery. Although Chancery itself is represented as a system that maintains outdated vested interests and is steeped in the past, it none the less has an impact in the present. Individuals (Richard Carstone, Miss Flite, Mr Grindley et al.) are frustrated, and harmed, by their inability to retrieve meaning or extricate themselves from its obstructive bureaucracy. Tom-all-Alone's is caught in Chancery and so crumbles into ruins. Meanwhile Smallweed calls in George's debt by a letter, setting in motion a chain of events that results in Tulkinghorn gaining possession of the documents that confirm the identity of Lady Dedlock's former lover. By possessing these papers, Tulkinghorn holds power over Lady Dedlock and ultimately drives her flight from Chesney Wold and subsequent death. Instances in which texts, letters and scraps of paper are useless thus contrast with other times in which documents produce perceptible effects on characters' lives and the built environment.

The danger implicit in the instrumentality of paperwork is not in the materiality of the object but its potential to be manipulated to serve individual interests. This is threatening partly because, ironically, it is unpredictable. Administration brings unlikely people into contact with sensitive documents. As Kafka notes, 'the proximity of clerks to paperwork invested them with a degree of power completely out of proportion to their social and political status'.[92] Guppy uses his professional access to legal papers to enable him to adopt the role of amateur private detective, through which he hopes to win Esther's hand. This is not to say that Guppy's role as a clerk endows him with a subversive potential to overturn Chancery bureaucracy or that he poses a significant threat to the social order. Guppy is characterised as petty, immature and unsophisticated; he is awed by people of status and is bored during the long vacation. Guppy certainly does not fully understand the system that he is trying to circumvent. While the complexity of bureaucratic structures opens them to strategic exploitation by individuals, then, their unnavigability also means that they are difficult to comprehend or master. In other words, the individual remains vulnerable to exploitation and assault, even when she or he finds loopholes to facilitate personal aims. Despite the monotony of his work and his ultimate insignificance to larger Chancery processes, however, Guppy is not alienated or subjugated by his labour but uses his administrative knowledge to pursue his own ends. Lady Dedlock certainly recognises his potential power to disrupt her life: when he first pays her a visit, she remains unsure whether Guppy is attempting to blackmail her until the end of their interview. Guppy does not ultimately achieve his first object of winning Esther, but his efforts to do so emphasise that bureaucratic writing and the administration of documents can enable social mobility or undermine the status of high-profile individuals.

The fact that the effects of paperwork tend to be negative and obstruct social change reinforces the gloomy mood of the novel; nevertheless, the questions that Dickens's representation of paperwork raises about what kinds of writing are effective or ineffective indicate a self-consciousness about how written works relate to practical philanthropy. Throughout his career, Dickens's fiction is marked by his concern to highlight various social abuses. He presents a damning portrait of debtors' prisons in the *Pickwick Papers* (1836–7), workhouses and baby farms in *Oliver Twist* (1837–9), Yorkshire schools in *Nicholas Nickleby* (1838–9), and so on. These condemnations appear as isolated episodes, included to draw public attention to specific abuses of power. Dickens's representations of contemporary evils in his earlier fiction bear little relation to other incidents in the texts, so recalling his earlier 'sketches'.[93] By the 1850s, Dickens's style had developed to portray a more integrated vision of society, which emphasises the difficulty of isolating and combating individual problems. *Bleak House* remains pointedly unresolved and thereby reinforces the view that abuses of power are enabled by wider social or environmental conditions. One might offer Jo alms like Mr Snagsby but this would not bring Tom-all-Alone's out of Chancery. To quote Hillis Miller's famous phrase, at the end of *Bleak House*, London is 'almost as dark, as mud-soaked and fog-drenched' as it is at the start.[94] The novel is not nihilistic, however, and Dickens's observations of social inequality convey anger and frustration, even if he is at a loss to suggest an adequate remedy. *Bleak House* remains caught between Dickens's desire to make his writing useful and his doubts about whether texts (fictional or bureaucratic) can effect change at all.

Dickens's involvement with the Columbia Square network influenced how he conceived the utility of fiction. As early as 1843, Dickens was inspired by Southwood Smith's *Second Report of the Parliamentary Commission on Children's Employment ('Trades and Manufactures')* and began to plan the pamphlet 'An Appeal to the People of England, on Behalf of the Poor Man's Child' to support Southwood Smith's proposals.[95] The pamphlet was rapidly abandoned but *A Christmas Carol* (1843) evolved from this earlier plan. Dickens wrote to Southwood Smith that he had conceived a scheme for a 'Sledge hammer' blow for the poor, 'with twenty times the force – twenty thousand times the force – I could exert by following out my first idea'.[96] This letter suggests that Dickens believed he could communicate a stronger sense of urgency through fiction than he could through direct political statement. Dickens uses this 'sledge hammer' metaphor again in a letter to John Forster later that same year. Writing to tell Forster about his successful petition to Burdett Coutts on behalf of the Field Lane Ragged School, Dickens mobilises the metaphor to convey how effectively his writing has inspired practical action. 'I sent Miss Coutts a sledge-hammer account of the ragged schools.'[97] A growing self-consciousness about his desire to use fiction as a 'sledge hammer' to enforce necessary reform is evident in the ways that he revised this metaphor during his involvement with Columbia Square. Dickens may have been mocking his own prior sentiments when, in an early draft of *Bleak House*, Mr Jarndyce charitably remarks:

> excellent people, you know, . . . Mrs. Pardiggle and all the rest of 'em. Excellent people! Do a deal of good, and mean to do a good deal more. But they want one pattern out of all varieties of Looms, they *must* be in extremes, they *will* knock in tin tacks with a sledge hammer, they made such a bustle and noise, and they are so confoundedly indefatigable![98]

This passage was cut from the completed manuscript. Still, Dickens's critical reappraisal of the 'sledge hammer' metaphor reflects the greater complexity of *Bleak House*'s engagement with philanthropic campaigning and an awareness of the various textual processes that underpinned the implementation of material improvements.

The period in which Dickens was involved with Burdett Coutts's network is marked by his desire to use his imaginative resources to contribute effectively to philanthropic or urban concerns. Indeed, a letter written to Henry Carey in 1854 indicates that his earlier belief in the instrumentality of writing remained consistent into the 1850s:

> To interest and affect the general mind in behalf of anything that is clearly wrong – to stimulate and rouse the public soul to a compassionate or indignant feeling that it *must not be* – without obtruding any pet theory of cause or cure, and so throwing off allies as they spring up – I believe to be one of Fiction's highest uses. And this is the use to which I try to turn it [. . .][99]

Dickens presents literature as an appropriate and effective medium for social commentary and for stimulation of public action. The letter to Carey indicates that he conceives his fiction as a social project. Conversely, the sense of hopelessness in *Bleak House* problematises his professed belief in the utility of fiction. This is further emphasised by the fact that the only character to produce fanciful writing in *Bleak House* is Skimpole, whose selfish amorality is reinforced by his squandered artistic talents. Skimpole's self-representation as an amateur author enables him to abuse charitable giving, by engaging Sir Leicester's patronage:

> Sir Leicester seemed to approve of [Skimpole's] sentiment highly.
> 'An artist, sir?'
> 'No,' returned Mr. Skimpole. 'A perfectly idle man. A mere amateur.'
> Sir Leicester seemed to approve of this even more. (*BH*, p. 682)

Skimpole adroitly recognises that Sir Leicester prefers the idea that the wealthy would patronise artists, rather than recognising the arts as a profession, and so begins to manipulate Sir Leicester's opinion of his creative works for financial gain. Skimpole's actions reveal how fanciful writing can be manipulated for personal ends in a similar way to bureaucracy. This is another reason why practical philanthropy is favourable to textual processes in *Bleak House* – both bureaucratic and fanciful writing is open to, and exposes, underlying selfish motivations that undermine its avowed social intent.

Household Words

Imaginative writing was central to Dickens's efforts to promote social and urban improvements, despite his ambivalence about the instrumentality of texts in *Bleak House*. Dickens's famous 'Preliminary Word' to the first issue of *Household Words* clearly states his ambitions to 'displace' evils that he considers a 'national reproach', while simultaneously 'cherish[ing] that light of Fancy which is inherent in the human breast'.[100] Dickens thus presents his approach to fiction as politically and socially engaged. It does not exist in the ethereal world of the imagination but is embedded in contemporary reality. Indeed, the periodical became a key platform for Dickens to air his views and he used it to launch multiple campaigns. However, *Household Words* also reinforced the instrumentality of literature more widely.

Dickens curated the impression of an integrated social project across his journalism and fiction by making explicit intertextual links between his different publications. For instance, he timed attacks on specific institutions or problems in *Household Words* so that they were published concurrently with their representation in monthly numbers of his novels. During the serialisation of *David Copperfield* (1849–50), Dickens reminds the readers of *Household Words* that '[t]he public have lately heard some trifling facts relative to Doctors' Commons, through the medium of a young gentleman who was articled, by his aunt, to a proctor there'.[101] Michael Slater has called Dickens's deliberate intertextuality 'having two shots at the same target'.[102] Enforcing his position by advertising his concerns from multiple platforms was a 'sledge hammer' approach, both because it widened his potential readerships and because it created a sense of significance and urgency through repetition. On the one hand, fictional allusions enliven serious comment in a manner amenable to the fanciful style intended in *Household Words*. On the other, references to the novels in press commentaries trade on newspaper form to imply that Dickens's fiction is engaged with current affairs, and so asks the reader to treat its representation of social issues seriously. Fiction and journalism appear to validate each other, for not only did Dickens align his critiques across his various publications, but also his practice of cross-referencing between his texts mixes fiction and non-fiction to define a style of imaginative writing that he conceives as instrumental.

Despite professing a coherent social project across Dickens's literary and periodical endeavours, *Household Words* uses very different formal devices to argue for contemporary reform from those used in his novels from the 1850s. Unlike his expansive social vision in *Bleak House*, his short-form journalism returns to the sketch style of his earlier fiction, which singled out topics for individual comment or, in Dickens's words, combined genres of imaginative writing and reportage to '[press] *facts* upon the many-headed'.[103] Written and published on a weekly basis, *Household Words* was able to respond quickly to current events or participate in ongoing debates, without needing to retain a coherent overarching narrative. For example, the periodical's commentary on the safe fencing-in of factory machinery (published alongside *Hard Times*) develops responsively over several articles, and replies directly to Harriet Martineau's criticisms of their campaign.[104] Moreover, the miscellaneous form enables different modes of address to coexist, depending on the topic. It combines, or alternates between, objective and subjective styles, which indicate that it integrates professional expertise and emotional sensitivity: the very qualifications that Dickens had used to identify ideal collaborators for the Columbia Square project. Although the 'Preliminary Word' avows that *Household Words* will never present information in a 'utilitarian spirit' and there will be 'no iron binding of the mind to grim realities', articles still refer to official reports and statistics to authenticate and support their arguments.[105] Numerical details lend the articles an authoritative air because these suggest that the contributor has done thorough research on the topic, while allusions to personal interest stories or fiction make imaginative appeals to readers. The periodical's style, and ability to respond to evolving concerns, thus helped Dickens to construct its identity as a philanthropic platform *par excellence*.

Some of Dickens's contemporaries were troubled by his attempts to turn *Household Words* into a vehicle for social reform. Martineau was particularly vocal in her opposition. She lambasted Dickens personally in her pamphlet *The Factory Controversy; A Warning Against Meddling Legislation*, in response to *Household Words*' fencing-in campaign. Just as Dickens explores the potentially dangerous consequences of inappropriate people trying to influence the course of events in *Bleak House*, so Martineau suggests that *Household Words* was promoting a stance on fencing-in grounded on 'inaccurate statements, and in a temper and by language which convey their own condemnation'.[106] She believes that Dickens's imaginative style of reportage in *Household Words* manipulates his readers' emotions but obfuscates the truth, even as it apparently presents factual information. For Martineau, fiction is not the problem. Though she notes inaccuracies in Dickens's critique of the Poor Law in *Oliver Twist*, she admits that 'there [is] the excuse that he [is] a novelist; and no one [is] eager to call to account on any matter of doctrine a very imaginative writer of fiction.'[107] The instrumentality of literature, she implies, is limited by readers' awareness of its falsity. However, Martineau is troubled by Dickens's transferral of fictional modes to newsprint because periodical form implies that it contains verifiable, up-to-date information. 'Mr. Dickens himself changed the conditions of his responsibilities and other people's judgments when he set up "Household Words" as an avowed agency of popular instruction and social reform.'[108] For Martineau, Dickens's written campaigns place him on a level with 'the pseudo-philanthropists whom he delights to ridicule', meaning that Dickens's writing was not useful to the reforms he advocated, but damaging.[109] Martineau's concerns reinforce Dickens's claim that writing could stimulate public action or material effects, as she worries about the potentially harmful impact that Dickens's fiction will have on society. Belief in the utility, and instrumentality, of writing remains constant between their opposite positions, even if they conceptualise its legacies differently.

Dickens's practical philanthropic works inform his written campaigns but his experience of writing for different publications also influenced how he supported practical initiatives. Dickens's campaigning in *Household Words* combines a clear stylistic vision with an awareness of the conditions of the periodical's publication and distribution. He applied his understanding of the material, formal and imaginative factors that influence readers' reactions to his work with Burdett Coutts. In the same letter that recommended building large houses in Columbia Square, Dickens advises Burdett Coutts about how she should organise and present her suggestion paper for the scheme to parliament:

> In the first place, it is indispensable to the Specification of the plans required, that the size and shape of the piece of ground should be accurately stated. In the second place, it seems to me very important that the request for plans should be kept altogether separate from the request

> for suggestions. I would therefore have two papers instead of one, and I would print both of them; it being very difficult to get people to read writing, or to read it without confusion if they read it at all.[110]

Dickens's letter reveals his awareness of the impact that the materiality of writing has on the ways that the content is received. He considers how its layout and length will affect readers' reactions as well as the content, and plans the paper carefully to ensure the most favourable result. Despite his mistrust of administrative processes in *Bleak House*, his continued efforts to make *Household Words* an advocate for change, and the written actions that support his practical work, show that Dickens was acutely conscious of the textual processes that accompany and impel material reforms. Dickens was not unique in his belief that writing could be instrumental in raising support for practical projects or campaigns. Although seeking to foreground women's contributions to social and material change during the nineteenth century, Burdett Coutts paid tribute to the effectiveness of writing in *Woman's Mission*: 'the cause of philanthropy [. . .] owes so much to the aid of the publicist'.[111] Dickens openly supports Burdett Coutts in the pages of *Household Words*. Even though he questions the utility of paperwork elsewhere in his fiction, then, his letters and journalism continue to attest the centrality of writing to his practical initiatives.

Dickensian Afterlives in Philanthropic Works

Some contemporaries' belief in the potential effectiveness of Dickens's fiction is revealed by rhetorical uses of Dickensian afterlives in philanthropic works. Contrary to Martineau's fears that his writing would spark inappropriate and ill-considered reactions, philanthropists appropriated and recontextualised tropes or extracts from the novels, or even claimed the novelist himself, to suit their own agendas. Mary Carpenter's treatise on *Reformatory Schools, for the Children of the Perishing and Dangerous Classes, and for Juvenile Offenders* (1851) juxtaposes extracts from his novels with transcripts of supposedly first-hand accounts. The diary of the master of a London Ragged School is placed alongside a lengthy passage from *The Haunted Man* (1848), which she admires for its chilling depiction of destitute children. Carpenter's apparent deferral to a well-known, male authority is a strategy to vindicate her own agenda. She eloquently states her case at length, but appropriates Dickens's reputation as a champion of the urban poor as a rubber stamp to convince the undecided: 'Truly says Dickens' – she says.[112] But Carpenter stops short of equating literature with eye-witness accounts. Referring to a description of desolate living conditions given in one of her case studies, she quotes a Chaplain's remark that '[i]f a writer of fiction had described such a scene as this, who could tolerate the picture'.[113] Carpenter did not interpret Dickens's fiction as realistic but as an exaggerated depiction of contemporary urban conditions. The problem, she suggests, is that reality is coming to mirror fiction, rather than the other way around.

Carpenter evokes Dickens's renowned interest in contemporary reform to confirm and reinforce her own concerns and to stimulate further interest in her cause; however, this is complicated by the fact that she links popular culture to the juvenile crime that she seeks to address. Recalling the debates about the damaging impact that adaptations of *Oliver Twist* and *Jack Sheppard* might have on London's populace, discussed in Chapters 2 and 3, Carpenter decries 'the penny theatres, where, with all the accompaniments that excite the imagination and feelings, many have learnt their first lesson in crime'.[114] She depicts popular culture as dangerous, first because it trades upon glamorous images of crime, and second because the performance venues are suitable for nefarious practices and cause children to come into contact with disreputable people. She backs up her assertions with statistics. Carpenter provides a table detailing the 'Religious Knowledge of Prisoners', which measures inmates' religious knowledge ('Knowing the Saviour's name, and able to repeat the Lord's Prayer, more or less imperfectly') against their knowledge of supposedly corrupting popular culture ('Having read, or heard read, books about Dick Turpin, and Jack Sheppard').[115] Carpenter separates Dickens's novels from other popular fiction by presenting him as a moral novelist. She thereby curates an interpretation of Dickens that buttresses her own highly religious motivations, even though his works had been previously aligned with the types of entertainments she critiques.

Octavia Hill mobilises Dickens's humanitarian reputation differently in *Homes of the London Poor*. Unlike Carpenter's appropriation of both quotations and Dickens's persona, Hill does not defer to the author or present his works as a reflection of contemporary conditions. Instead, she mines his fiction for lively rhetorical devices. Indeed, she alludes to *Hard Times* to suit two separate purposes. First, Hill repurposes tropes from the novel as a symbolic vocabulary to communicate why she believes beauty is important in improving urban living:

> The poor of London need joy and beauty in their lives. There is no more true and eternal law to be recognised about them than that which Mr. Dickens shows in 'Hard Times' – the fact that every man has an imagination which needs development and satisfaction. Mr. Sleary's speech, 'People mutht be amoothed, Thquire,' is often recalled to my mind in dealing with the poor.[116]

Hill's philosophy was realised in her social housing projects by practices like planting creepers to bring nature into these spaces.[117] However, the specific, material applicability of this afterlife is broadened in her second allusion to *Hard Times*. Widening her focus to intervene in debates about the relationship between political economy and philanthropy, Hill referred to the novel to argue why it was inappropriate to assess tenants' needs statistically:

> one is apt to forget Sissy Jupe's quick sympathetic perception that percentage signifies literally nothing to the friends of the special sufferer, who surely is not worth less than a sparrow. The individual cases, if we cared enough for it, would often give us the key to many.[118]

Case studies that name and describe the plight of an individual were frequently employed in philanthropic writings. This technique is designed to make the reader feel personally connected to the cause and can, therefore, be an effective means of engaging the reader's support. Replacing a human example with a fictional character enables Hill's intervention to have even more far-reaching applicability. Sissy is both an anti-Utilitarian symbol and an individual, sympathetic character in the novel. Repurposing Dickens's character thus allows Hill to make a case for the importance of individual charity, as opposed to applying principles of political economy to philanthropy.

Dickensian afterlives were mobilised as a means of conceptualising and articulating the individual philosophies and agendas of different philanthropists, but his novels also had tangible afterlives that stimulated support for specific causes. In 1888, a Dickens Bazaar was organised in Holborn Town Hall to raise money to pay off a debt for recent restoration works at St Peter's Church, Saffron Hill.[119] The bazaar was a lavish affair spanning three days. Prochaska notes that, as a rule,

> Considerable thought went into the opening ceremonies [of bazaars]. Speeches, songs, and royalty were *de rigueur* on grand occasions, but most bazaars had distinctive little touches. Those in aid of hospitals laid on nurses in their picturesque blue uniforms to look conspicuous. Those in aid of the welfare of children got children to perform.[120]

Such an attention to detail is evident in the programme for the Charles Dickens Bazaar. The organisers maintained the literary connection across each aspect of the event: the stalls were themed to represent different locations in Dickens's novels; the stall-holders dressed as famous characters; and celebrities connected with Dickens (Burdett Coutts and '**Henry Fielding Dickens, Esq.** (Recorder for Deal), **A Son of Charles Dickens**'[121]) were recruited to support the bazaar and participate in the opening ceremonies (Figure 4.2). There were also 'most amusing and really astonishing' Dickens-themed entertainments planned, including a 'Jarley wax-works show'.[122] Mrs George Augustus Sala mentions this bazaar in her essay for *Woman's Mission*, and remarks that at this event 'all the fair stall-holders

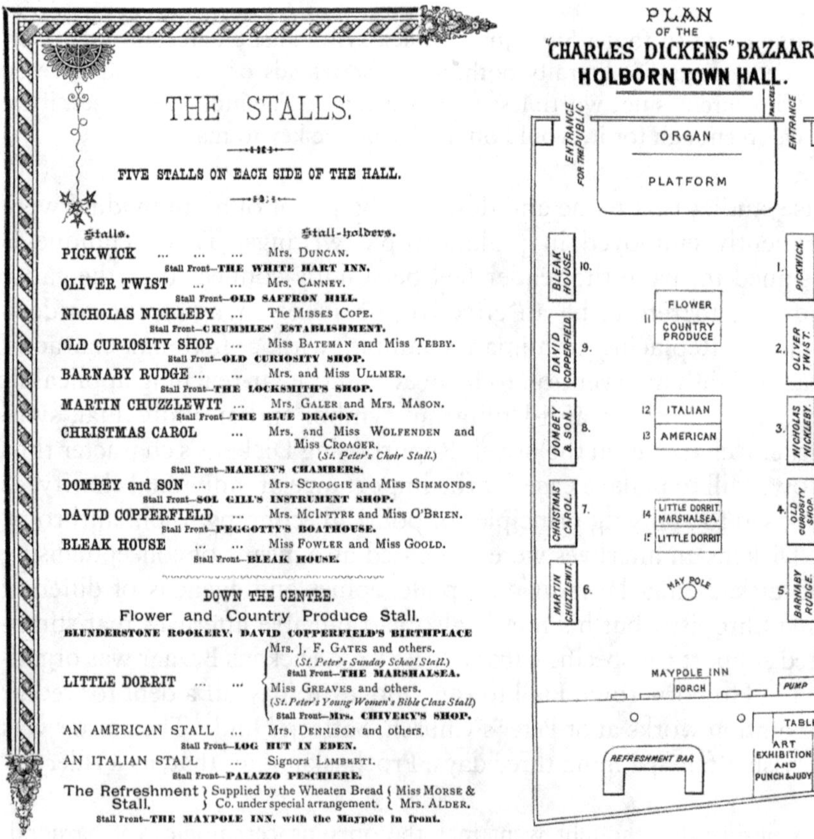

THE STALLS.

FIVE STALLS ON EACH SIDE OF THE HALL.

Stalls.	Stall-holders.
PICKWICK	Mrs. Duncan.
Stall Front—THE WHITE HART INN.	
OLIVER TWIST	Mrs. Canney.
Stall Front—OLD SAFFRON HILL.	
NICHOLAS NICKLEBY ...	The Misses Cope.
Stall Front—CRUMMLES' ESTABLISHMENT.	
OLD CURIOSITY SHOP ...	Miss Bateman and Miss Tebby.
Stall Front—OLD CURIOSITY SHOP.	
BARNABY RUDGE	Mrs. and Miss Ullmer.
Stall Front—THE LOCKSMITH'S SHOP.	
MARTIN CHUZZLEWIT ...	Mrs. Galer and Mrs. Mason.
Stall Front—THE BLUE DRAGON.	
CHRISTMAS CAROL ...	Mrs. and Miss Wolfenden and Miss Croager. (*St. Peter's Choir Stall.*)
Stall Front—MARLEY'S CHAMBERS.	
DOMBEY and SON	Mrs. Scroggie and Miss Simmonds.
Stall Front—SOL GILL'S INSTRUMENT SHOP.	
DAVID COPPERFIELD ...	Mrs. McIntyre and Miss O'Brien.
Stall Front—PEGGOTTY'S BOATHOUSE.	
BLEAK HOUSE	Miss Fowler and Miss Goold.
Stall Front—BLEAK HOUSE.	

DOWN THE CENTRE.

Flower and Country Produce Stall.

BLUNDERSTONE ROOKERY, DAVID COPPERFIELD'S BIRTHPLACE

LITTLE DORRIT	Mrs. J. F. Gates and others. (*St. Peter's Sunday School Stall.*) Stall Front—THE MARSHALSEA. Miss Greaves and others. (*St. Peter's Young Women's Bible Class Stall*) Stall Front—Mrs. CHIVERY'S SHOP.
AN AMERICAN STALL ...	Mrs. Dennison and others.
Stall Front—LOG HUT IN EDEN.	
AN ITALIAN STALL ...	Signora Lamberti.
Stall Front—PALAZZO PESCHIERE.	
The Refreshment Stall.	Supplied by the Wheaten Bread Co. under special arrangement. Miss Morse & Mrs. Alder.
Stall Front—THE MAYPOLE INN, with the Maypole in front.	

Figure 4.2 *Charles Dickens Bazaar Programme* (Source: © Camden Local Studies and Archives Centre. 41.Ho L/C/314).

dressed as some Dickens' [*sic*] character' to entice patrons.[123] Sala drew attention to the 'large sums of money' that bazaars have earned 'for good causes',[124] yet despite the considerable efforts of the organisers of the Dickens Bazaar, the event failed to raise its target amount for St Peter's restoration.[125]

The Dickens Bazaar cannot be taken as evidence that Dickensian afterlives contributed to driving or directing material change to the built environment because the bazaar was organised after the church restorations had taken place, but even if the Dickens Bazaar did not reach its fundraising target, its theme certainly created a high profile for the event, which helped to draw in a variety of volunteers. Bazaars were commonly gendered as female pursuits. In Dickens's burletta *Is She His Wife? or, Something Singular!* (1837), Mrs Lovetown complains about her failed expectations of rural married life: 'Did you not say that I should then have an ample sphere in which to exercise those charitable feelings which I have so often evinced by selling at those benevolent fancy fairs?'[126] Bazaars are presented here as frivolous activities, which enable women to construct a positive self-image while satisfying social aspirations. Conversely, an engraving advertising the Dickens Bazaar printed in *Funny Folks* indicates that this event attracted the participation of a mixed group of volunteers (Figure 4.3). It shows only one woman in the party ('Mrs. Georgina W*ld*n is going as Sairey Gamp – at least, that is her plan of Gampaign').[127] Meanwhile, the image promises potential patrons that they will see the 'Lord Chief Justice [. . .] General B**th [. . .] Mr. Joseph

Figure 4.3 'Playing the Very Dickens' (Source: © The British Library Board. PENP.NT152).

Ch*mbe*l*in [. . .] the Duke of Be*uf*rt [. . .] Mr Arthur B*lf**r [. . .] Mr. Charles B*dl**gh [and] Sir William Vernon H*rc**et' in various Dickensian outfits.[128] The humorous appeal of seeing eminent men looking ridiculous is heightened by the caption's pointedly inadequate concealment of their full names, thus indicating the amusement offered by the bazaar while making no reference to the cause it is supporting. *Funny Folks* may have misrepresented who was involved in the event, as Sala's account implies that the bazaar was organised chiefly by women. It is possible that reversing the typical gender expectation was an effort to attract a wider public to the event, yet it also says something about Dickens's appeal to a mass public. The organisers recognised that the popularity of his novels offered opportunities for capital returns and traded on Dickens to draw in a diverse range of assistants and visitors.

Unlike Carpenter or Hill, the organisers of the Dickens Bazaar openly admit that the financial benefit of an association with Dickens inspired their endeavours, even though they also pay lip service to the moral tenor of his novels. The programme directly acknowledges that the theme was chosen because the organisers 'hoped that a larger public will be interested and attracted to it than otherwise would be, and consequently that greater success will attend it'.[129] In this instance, the instrumentality of Dickens's fiction is not in its engagement with social problems, or even its portability as a symbolic vocabulary through which different issues are expressed. Instead, the potential material effectiveness of Dickens's fiction is in the promise that its mass popularity will generate financial returns. Conversely, one of the reasons why his writings were appropriate to philanthropic fundraising was still because of his humanitarian reputation. Alongside acknowledging the organisers' monetary motivations, the programme states their hope that 'In calling the Bazaar a "Charles Dickens" Bazaar, and in giving it a character [the event] shall remind all who visit it of the marvellous and high-purposed creations of that author.'[130] The diverse intentions apparently underlying the organisers' remediations of Dickens's works expose the fact that later philanthropists considered his fiction instrumental, but in various and flexible ways not necessarily derived from the texts. Particularly as the century progressed and the social abuses he detailed were reformed or evolved, his utility in charitable initiatives was increasingly indirect.

The different ways in which nineteenth-century philanthropists repurposed Dickensian afterlives indicate that his potential to affect charitable causes directly was very short-lived indeed. It is possible to track ways in which he used writing strategically to impel reform in his personal involvement with specific projects. Dickens's instrumentality to the success of the Columbia Square project uncovers his direct involvement in London's material development, and reveals the potential for individual philanthropists to affect how the built environment was improved. However, his partnership with Burdett Coutts also indirectly reveals how an individual's efforts could be limited by their connectedness, fortune and gender, or simply by the difficulties that inevitably beset any development in London. Even though the philanthropic utility of Dickens's writing could still be conceptualised as having 'opened the eyes of the many wilful blind to behold the sorrows and sufferings of their plague-stricken fellow-creatures' at the end of the nineteenth century, when the author ceased to be personally involved, and particularly after his death, the portability of his works altered its perceived or potential utility.[131]

Charity remains a part of Dickens's legacy, even though its prominence has been gradually overshadowed by the growth of a Dickens heritage industry. When the Dickens Fellowship was founded in 1902, one of its primary objectives was 'to spread the love of humanity, to campaign against those "social evils" that most concerned Dickens'.[132] However, 'charitable works have become less prominent among the Fellowship's activities' in recent years.[133] The Fellowship partly attributes this to the formalisation of philanthropy, 'the assumption by government of many of the responsibilities previously taken by charities'.[134] Instead of seeing the social interests in Dickens's work as less directly applicable than they once were, the Fellowship's website suggests that formalised administrative processes mean that these must be acted on differently or through professional channels. A public reassessment of Dickens as a heritage figure is another reason why the perceived utility of his fiction for philanthropic work has changed. As Juliet John argues, 'the price of prominence seems to have been [. . .] the fossilising of Dickens in an idea of the Victorian past'.[135] Although the flexible adjective 'Dickensian' is still regularly deployed to articulate a variety of social abuses, it is usually employed to evoke surprising or unjustifiable corollaries between Dickens's works and the modern day, rather than to express a specific continuity with a particular text or passage. None the less, analysis of Dickensian afterlives in nineteenth-century philanthropic work indicates that any instrumental impact of his fiction has almost always been effected by indirect or rhetorical allusions.

Notes

1. Urania Cottage was the 'home' for fallen women Dickens started in partnership with Angela Burdett Coutts.
2. Dickens and Burdett Coutts had a close working and personal relationship until the late 1850s, when Dickens's separation from Catherine caused a rift in their friendship. Orton notes that they saw each other 'for what may have been the last time' in April 1860, after which his work for her ceased (pp. 179–80).
3. Dickens, 'A Preliminary Word', p. 1.
4. Catherine Waters, 'Reforming Culture', in Bowen and Patten (eds), pp. 155–75, pp. 171–2.
5. Trollope, p. 154. Recording its derogatory connotations, the *Oxford English Dictionary*'s definitions of 'namby-pamby' include 'insipidly pretty, affectedly or childishly simple [. . .] lacking vigour or drive; effeminate' (*Oxford English Dictionary* <http://www.oed.com/> (last accessed 6 Oct. 2015)).
6. Anne Anderson and Elizabeth Darling, 'The Hill Sisters: Cultural Philanthropy and the Embellishment of Lives in late-Nineteenth Century England', in Darling and Whitworth (eds), pp. 33–48, p. 40.
7. Elizabeth Darling and Lesley Whitworth, 'Introduction: Making Space and Re-making History', in Darling and Whitworth (eds), pp. 1–11, p. 2.
8. Ibid., p. 2.
9. Reviewing records of the 'outdoor' relief distributed in the 1840s and 1850s, Hugh Cunningham concludes that the workhouse test was not rigidly enforced and that parishes continued to offer most help to paupers outside of the workhouse (Hugh Cunningham, 'Dickens as a Reformer', in David Paroissien (ed.), pp. 159–73, p. 164.)
10. Goodlad, p. 526.
11. Lewis, pp. 240–1 and p. 200.
12. Lewis explains, 'The dust collector who owned the site applied to the courts for time to find an alternative place of business and was allowed the maximum period of seven years. This caused a severe delay and work did not actually begin until 1859' (p. 249).
13. For example: Anon. (1873), 'Literary Gossip and Table Talk', *Illustrated Review: A Fortnightly Journal of Literature, Science and Art*, 5: 61, pp. 213–14; George Lander (1881), 'The Good Deeds of Lady Bountiful', *Time*, 4, Feb., [461]–73; London, Westminster City Archives, 420/78. Scrapbook of letters, photographs etc. about Baroness Burdett-Coutts, mainly covering the period up to her death in 1907, c. 1882 to 21 Oct. 1942. Anon., 'Death of Lady Burdett-Coutts', *The Times* (31 Dec. 1906), newspaper cutting.
14. Orton, p. 105 and p. 184.
15. Prochaska includes tables detailing the contributions made to charities by female subscribers in the appendices to *Women and Philanthropy*

in Nineteenth-century England. Although records of these institutions tend to be incomplete, Prochaska's sample includes records spanning the century. Appendix V gives the monetary value of women's contributions against the total amount of money donated. In 1853, the Colonial Missionary Society collected a total of £181, of which £25 was donated by women. In the same year, the Home Missionary Society collected a total of £349, of which £60 was given by women. Meanwhile, the Irish Evangelical Society collected £4,830, of which £1,868 was given by women. However, these statistics can be misleading about the level of female involvement in raising funds for charity. Even if women did not equal men in the amount donated, they may have actively contributed by canvassing. Moreover, married women's donations may have been given under their husband's name (p. 246).

16. Ibid., p. 30.
17. Ibid., p. 30.
18. Ibid., p. 42.
19. Angela Burdett Coutts, 'Preface', in Burdett Coutts (ed.), *Woman's Mission*, pp. ix–xxi, p. xx. *Woman's Mission* is a collection of essays by prominent, mostly wealthy female philanthropists, edited by Burdett Coutts.
20. Williams Elliott, p. 112.
21. Prochaska, p. 42.
22. *Old Bailey Proceedings Online* (www.oldbaileyonline.org, version 7.2, 18 Oct. 2015), April 1831, trial of MARY ANN LEE (t18310407-16).
23. Ibid.
24. Visiting the poor in their homes sought to forge connections across and within social classes, which were reinforced by other community-building activities, such as the regular Mothers' Meetings set up in Bristol in the 1860s and 1870s (Helen Meller, 'Gender, Citizenship and the Making of the Modern Environment', in Darling and Whitworth (eds), pp. 13–30, p. 18).
25. Prochaska, pp. 30–1.
26. Meller, 'Gender, Citizenship and the Making of the Modern Environment', p. 20.
27. Williams Elliott, p. 5.
28. Dickens, '*To* Miss Burdett Coutts, 16 March 1852', *Letters, Vol. 6*, pp. 626–7, p. 626.
29. Goodlad, p. 531.
30. Miss Louisa Twining, 'The History of Workhouse Reform', in Burdett Coutts (ed.), *Woman's Mission*, pp. 265–72.
31. Jenny Hartley gives a full history of Dickens's involvement with Urania Cottage in *Charles Dickens and the House of Fallen Women*.
32. Dickens, *Speeches*, p. 104.
33. Anon. (1867), *The Charles Dickens Dinner*, pp. 3–4.
34. Ibid., p. 6.

35. Hamlin, p. 276.
36. *Report of the Metropolitan Sanitary Association* (1850).
37. The GBH was a public health agency run out of central government, with a country-wide remit.
38. Austin was an architect and civil engineer who was secretary to the GBH over a four-year period (Fn. 4, *Letters, Vol. 6*, p. 18). He 'resigned the secretaryship of the Board of Health to become a superintending inspector. After the elimination of the board in 1854 he served as chief inspector under the Public Health Act (until 1858), and under the Local Government Act office from 1858 until his death' (Christopher Hamlin, 'Austin, Henry (1811/12–1861)', *Oxford Dictionary of National Biography* <http://www.oxforddnb.com/> (last accessed 13 Aug. 2014) (para 3 of 5)). Southwood Smith was a respected doctor and Medical Assistant of the GBH (Fn. 4, *Letters, Vol. 6*, p. 51).
39. Dickens, '*To* Thomas Southwood Smith, 1 March 1850', *Letters, Vol. 6*, p. 51.
40. Dickens, '*To* Dr James Wilson, 8 March 1851', *Letters, Vol. 6*, pp. 309–10, p. 309.
41. Dickens, '*To* Henry Austin, [23] January 1851*', *Letters, Vol. 6*, p. 265.
42. Fn. 2, *Letters, Vol. 6*, p. 40.
43. Dickens, '*To* Henry Austin, 21 February 1850*', *Letters, Vol. 6*, p. 40.
44. Dickens's first suggestion was Thornton Hunt. He wrote: 'For the life of me I can't think of anybody else who would do' (Dickens, '*To* Henry Austin, 27 February 1850*', *Letters, Vol. 6*, p. 47).
45. Anderson and Darling, 'The Hill Sisters', p. 36.
46. Shattock, p. 130.
47. Orton, p. 61.
48. Ibid., p. 87.
49. Dickens, '*To* Miss Burdett Coutts, 16 September 1843', *Letters, Vol. 3*, pp. 562–4, p. 562.
50. Dickens's remark might imply that he was attuned to the ways that other commentators had appropriated his fiction to argue for Field Lane's demolition. Alternatively, it might suggest that his fiction was absorbed in his perception of London.
51. The practice of extracting descriptive passages wholesale, as a way of representing urban conditions, is discussed further in Chapters 3 and 5.
52. WCA, 420/78. Anon. (1899), 'The Baroness Burdett-Coutts', *The Young Woman*, Apr., pp. 252–7, p. 255, periodical cutting.
53. WCA, 420/78. Anon. (1896), 'The Baroness Burdett-Coutts', *Lloyd's Weekly Newspaper*, 14 Jun., newspaper cutting.
54. Orton, p. 155.
55. Lewis, p. 243.
56. Ibid., pp. 244–5.

57. Lewis draws attention to 'the large amount of control which Burdett Coutts exercised on the design of [St Stephen's] church' prior to the construction of these model dwellings. Her role in the development of Columbia Square may thus be interpreted as a continuation of established practices (ibid., p. 199).
58. London, Westminster City Archives, 420/61. *Account for Making the Chancel Carpet and Other Church Furnishings for St Stephen's Submitted to Miss Burdett Coutts by Elizabeth Besserier, Embroideress, of 9 Judd Street, Brunswick Square* (n.d. [1850]), accounts, unpaginated.
59. Ibid., n.p.
60. Ibid., n.p.
61. Orton, p. 155.
62. The editors of the Pilgrim *Letters* note that 'CD has changed his view since commending the Bagnigge Wells houses (see To Miss Coutts, 3 Mar and fnn) as a model – perhaps through discussion with Austin' (Fn. 2, *Letters, Vol. 6*, p. 644).
63. Dickens, '*To* Miss Burdett Coutts, 18 April 1852', *Letters, Vol. 6*, pp. 644–6, p. 644.
64. London, Westminster City Archives, 1184/37. Anon. [1947], 'A Goodly Heritage'. Typed play script [Westminster City Archives also holds a copy of this script under the reference number 420/78].
65. Orton, p. 221.
66. Fn. 1, *Letters, Vol. 6*, p. 645.
67. Dickens, '*To* Dr William Brown, 17 November 1851*', *Letters, Vol. 6*, p. 539.
68. Dickens, '*To* Miss Burdett Coutts, 19 February 1852', *Letters, Vol. 6*, p. 605.
69. Jenny Hartley explores Dickens's high-level of involvement with Urania Cottage in *Charles Dickens and the House of Fallen Women*; however, a letter written to Burdett Coutts on 10 January 1850 reveals the control and influence that Burdett Coutts continued to exert over the running of the institution. Outlining his response to a request from Elizabeth Gaskell, who had proposed a new candidate for the 'Home', Dickens states that he has been conscious of respecting Coutts's sensibilities in his replies: 'What you suggest to me to say to Mrs. Gaskell about the girls and the passage, I wrote to her yesterday. All the rest that you so kindly write, I will make known to her tonight' (*Letters, Vol. 6*, p. 7; see also p. 6, fn. 4).
70. Dickens, '*To* Miss Burdett Coutts, 18 April 1852', p. 645.
71. Anon., *Baroness Burdett-Coutts*, p. 109.
72. Dickens, '*To* Miss Burdett Coutts, 1 August 1850', *Letters, Vol. 6*, pp. 141–2, p. 142.
73. Dickens, '*To* Miss Burdett Coutts, 13 January 1853', *Letters, Vol. 6*, pp. 573–4, p. 573.
74. Ibid., pp. 573–4.

75. For example, Columbia Square has large windows, as the absence of light was seen to worsen sanitary conditions in the mid-nineteenth century. In 1851, Dickens was at work with Austin, campaigning to have the Window Tax removed on sanitary considerations. Dickens wrote to ask Austin, 'Have you any printed particulars in any Reports, concerning the more obvious absurdities & evils of the Window Tax? If you have, and can send them up to me (in Devonshire Terrace) *in the course of tomorrow forenoon*, I think I can do great service to the Repale [*sic*] cause' ('*To* Henry Austin, [23] January 1851*', p. 265, italics in original).
76. Dickens, '*To* Miss Burdett Coutts, 16 March 1852', *Letters, Vol. 6*, pp. 626–7, p. 626.
77. Ibid., p. 626.
78. Dickens, '*To* Miss Burdett Coutts', *Letters, Vol. 6*, p. 651.
79. Lewis, p. 250.
80. Mary Shannon and Joanne Shattock have drawn attention to the impact that the arrangement and occupancy of built space have on personal networks.
81. Anon., *Baroness Burdett-Coutts*, p. 105.
82. Chappell, p. 16.
83. London, Westminster City Archives, 420/80. Agatha G. Twining, 'The Story of Our Foundress' ([1947]), hand-written manuscript, pp. 19a–20.
84. Chappell, p. 14.
85. WCA, 420/78. Anon. (n.d.), 'The Baroness Burdett-Coutts', *The Lady's Realm*, pp. 542–48, p. 547, periodical cutting.
86. WCA, 420/78. Anon. (1899), 'The Baroness Burdett-Coutts', *The Young Woman*, p. 255, periodical cutting.
87. Orton, p. 87.
88. Ben Kafka relates the story of an administrator at the Committee of Public Safety during the 1789 French Revolution called Charles-Hippolyte Labussière, who risked his life to save individuals destined for execution by destroying official documents. 'The clerk "went to the baths, soaked all of the documents until they were almost reduced to paste, and then launched them, in small pellets, through the window of the bathing room into the river"' (p. 51).
89. Butt and Tillotson, p. 194.
90. Joanna Bogle, 'Chisholm [*née* Jones], Caroline (1808–1877)', *Oxford Dictionary of National Biography* <http://www.oxforddnb.com/view/article/5321?docPos=1> (last accessed 27 Jun. 2017) (para 5 of 7).
91. J. Hillis Miller, *Victorian Subjects*, p. 179.
92. Kafka, p. 81.
93. Butt and Tillotson, p. 177.
94. J. Hillis Miller, *Victorian Subjects*, p. 188.
95. Slater, *Charles Dickens*, p. 213.

96. Dickens, '*To* Dr Southwood Smith, 10 March 1843', *Letters, Vol. 3*, p. 461.
97. Dickens, '*To* John Forster, [24 September 1843], *Letters, Vol. 3*, pp. 572–3, p. 572. Dickens continued to campaign on behalf of the Field Lane Ragged School and wrote an article in 1846: *Daily News*, 13, 4 Feb., p. 4. This was subsequently reprinted: (1846), *Leicester Chronicle*, 1840, 7 Mar., p. 4.
98. Charles Dickens, qtd in Butt and Tillotson, p. 193.
99. Dickens, '*To* Henry Carey, 24 August 1854*', *Letters, Vol. 7*, pp. 404–5, p. 405. Italics in original.
100. Dickens, 'A Preliminary Word', pp. 1–2.
101. Dickens and Wills, p. 2.
102. Slater, *Charles Dickens*, p. 308.
103. Dickens, '*To* Henry Austin, 29 January 1850*', *Letters, Vol. 6*, pp. 18–19, p. 19.
104. *Household Words* participated in campaigning for the safe fencing-in of machinery in factories, to minimise workers' risk of injury. A series of articles on the subject appeared between 1854 and 1856, written by Dickens's chief contributor, Henry Morley: 'Ground in the Mill', 'Fencing with Humanity', 'Death's Cyphering-Book', 'More Grist to the Mill', 'Two Shillings per Horse-Power' and 'Our Wicked Mis-Statements'. Harriet Martineau, however, believed that their arguments revealed a sparse understanding of the conditions and dangers of actually working in factories.
105. Dickens, 'A Preliminary Word', p. 1.
106. Martineau, p. v.
107. Ibid., p. 36.
108. Ibid., p. 36.
109. Ibid., p. 44.
110. Dickens, '*To* Miss Burdett Coutts, 18 April 1852', p. 644.
111. Burdett Coutts, 'Preface', in *Woman's Mission*, p. xii.
112. Carpenter, p. 59.
113. Ibid., p. 67.
114. Ibid., p. 73.
115. Ibid., p. 23.
116. Hill, *Homes of the London Poor*, pp. 46–7.
117. Anderson and Darling, 'The Hill Sisters', p. 40.
118. Hill, *Homes of the London Poor*, p. 63.
119. The bazaar programme details that 'The purpose of the Bazaar is to raise sufficient money to pay off a debt of about £400, remaining after the Restoration of the interior of St. Peter's Church, Saffron Hill, and to meet the expense of urgent repairs to the exterior of the Church, which are estimated to cost £400; the amount required, therefore, is £800' (London, Camden Local Studies and Archives Centre, Holborn Library, 41.Ho L/C/314. *Charles Dickens Bazaar programme* (1888), programme, n.p.).

120. Prochaska, p. 61.
121. CLSAC, *Charles Dickens Bazaar programme*, programme, n.p. Bold in original.
122. London, Camden Local Studies and Archives Centre, Holborn Library, 41.Ho L/C/314. *Charles Dickens Bazaar programme* (1888), newspaper cutting, n.p.
123. Mrs George Augustus Sala, 'Working Guilds and Work Societies', in Burdett Coutts (ed.), *Woman's Mission*, pp. 72–8, p. 78.
124. Ibid., p. 78.
125. CLSAC, *Charles Dickens Bazaar programme*, newspaper cutting, n.p.
126. Dickens, *Is She His Wife?*, p. 3.
127. Anon. (1888), 'Playing the Very Dickens', *Funny Folks*, 708, 16 Jun., pp. 188–9.
128. Ibid., pp. 188–9.
129. CLSAC, *Charles Dickens Bazaar programme*, programme, n.p.
130. Ibid., n.p.
131. Anon. (1894), 'Writing in the Strand on the Baroness Burdett Coutts, Miss Mary Spencer Warren says', *Woman's Signal*, 18, 3 May, p. 293.
132. Dickens Fellowship (para 2 of 6).
133. Ibid. (para 6 of 6).
134. Ibid. (para 6 of 6).
135. John, *Dickens and Mass Culture*, p. 273.

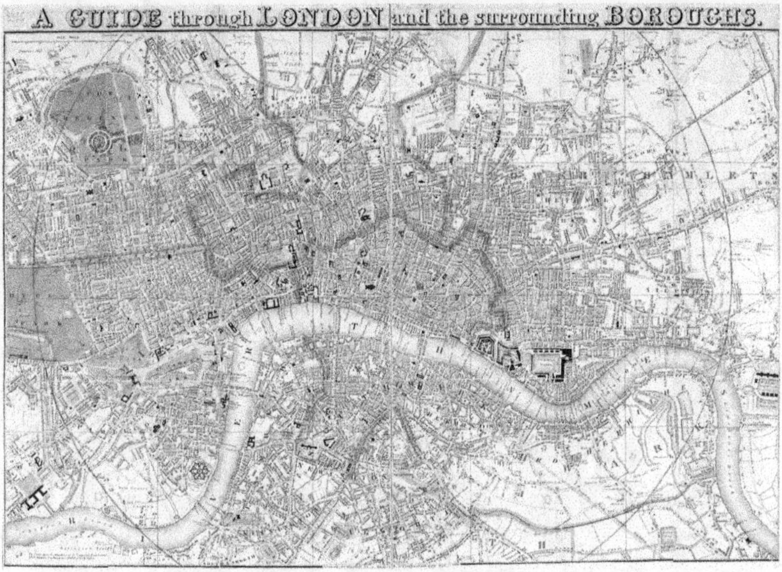

Plate 1. *A Guide through London and the Surrounding Boroughs ([With] A Guide to the Streets and Buildings . . . Being a Sequel to Russell's Map of London. By J. Gilberts)*, 1836 (Source: © The British Library Board. Maps 3480 (114)).

Plate 2. *Cruchley's New Plan of London and Its Environs / Engraved by Cruchley*, 1847 (Source: © The British Library Board. Maps Crace Port 7.253).

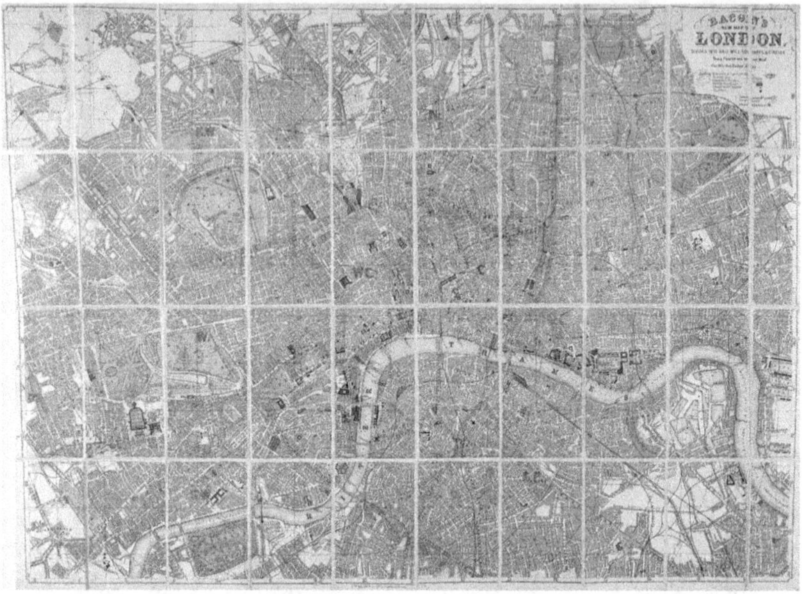

Plate 3. *Bacon's New Map of London, Divided into Half-mile Squares & Circles. Scale, four inches to the mile*, 1876 (Source: © The British Library Board. Maps 24.aa.19).

Plate 4. 'Print of Sadler's Wells Theatre, Drawn and Engraved by Rowlandson & Pugin, Aquatinted by Bluck, Published by Ackermann' (Source: © Victoria and Albert Museum. 2015HV0511-01).

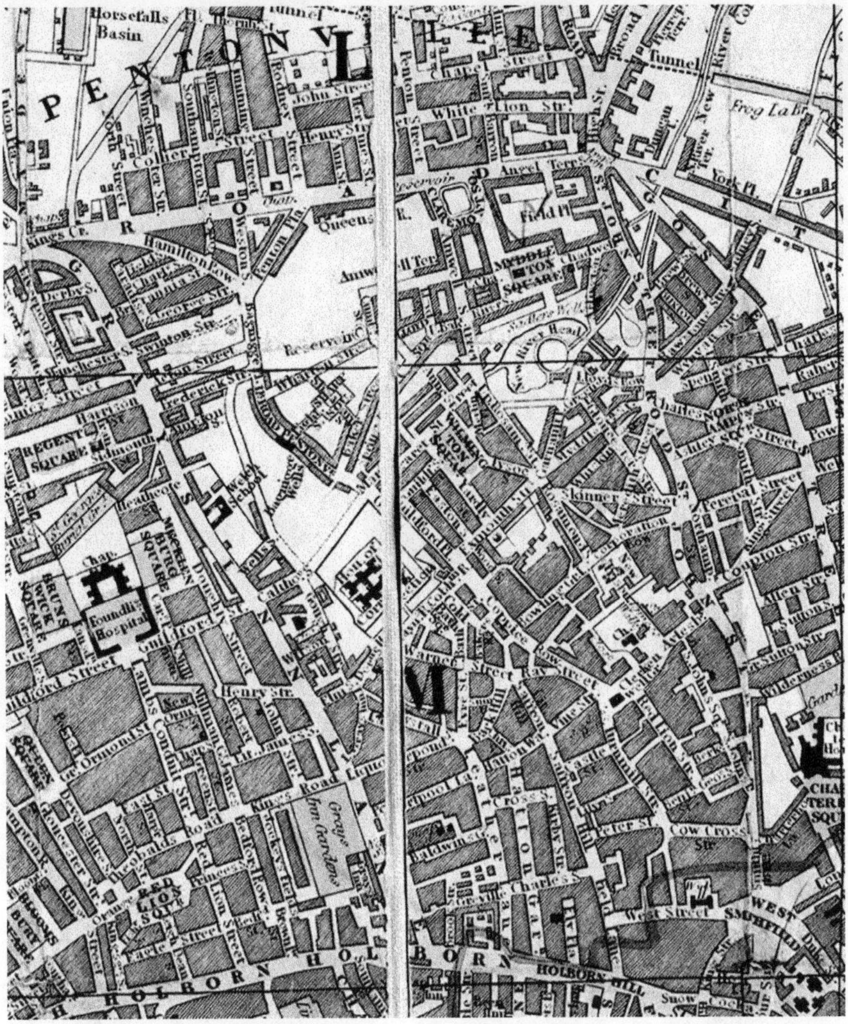

Plate 5. *Cruchley's New Plan of London* (detail), 1838 (Source: © Islington Local History Centre. FBAR3/CAB3).

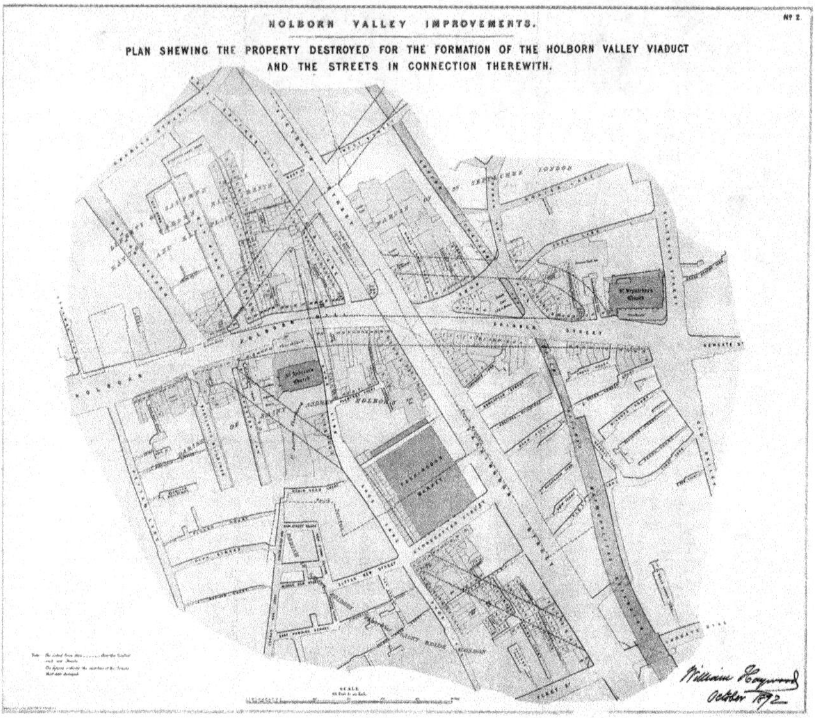

Plate 6. *Holborn Valley Improvements* (Source: © Camden Local Studies and Archives Centre. 85.23).

Plate 7. *Jacob's Island, Rotherhithe* (Source: © Museum of London. 53.130).

Chapter 5

From Sanitary Reform to Cultural Memory: The Case of Jacob's Island

Repurposed nineteenth-century warehouses, mid-twentieth-century social housing and twenty-first-century flats and offices now occupy Jacob's Island: the site that Charles Dickens describes in *Oliver Twist* (1837–9) as 'the filthiest, the strangest, the most extraordinary of the many localities that are hidden in London' (*OT*, p. 416). Even the topography has changed. The tidal waterways that previously surrounded the district have been filled in (Figure 5.1).[1] One accessed the site by crossing rickety wooden bridges, and, once

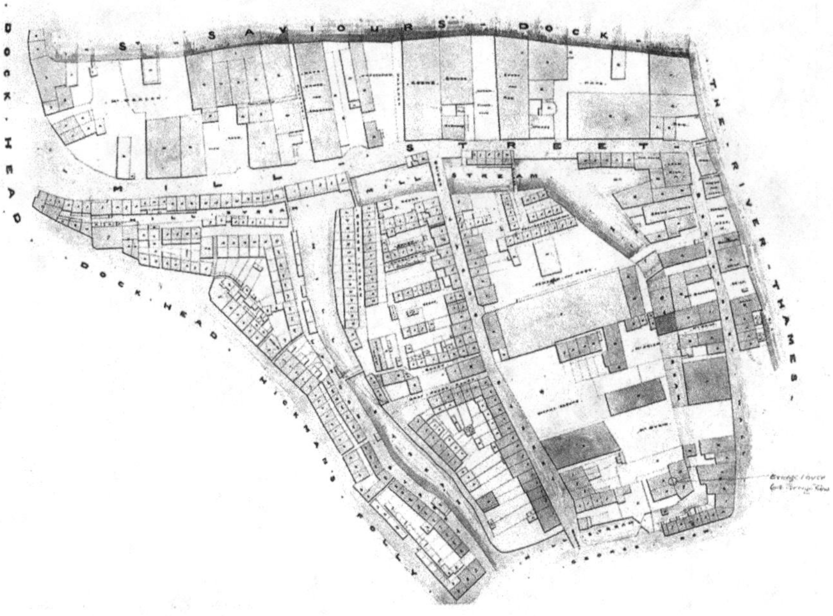

Figure 5.1 *Valuation Plans for the Parish of St Mary Magdalen, Bermondsey* (Source: © Southwark Local History Library and Archive, 912StMM).

inside, streams and canals further cross-sectioned this 'small but densely populated place'.[2] The inlets from the Thames formerly served an industry of water mills, but by the time that Dickens made Jacob's Island the setting for Bill Sikes's death these waterways had become open sewers that received the inhabitants' household waste and effluvia.[3] It is also likely that the water would have been contaminated by adjacent tanneries (Figure 5.2). The use of manure during the manufacture of leather would have at least exacerbated its already malodorous conditions. Off the beaten track, and long

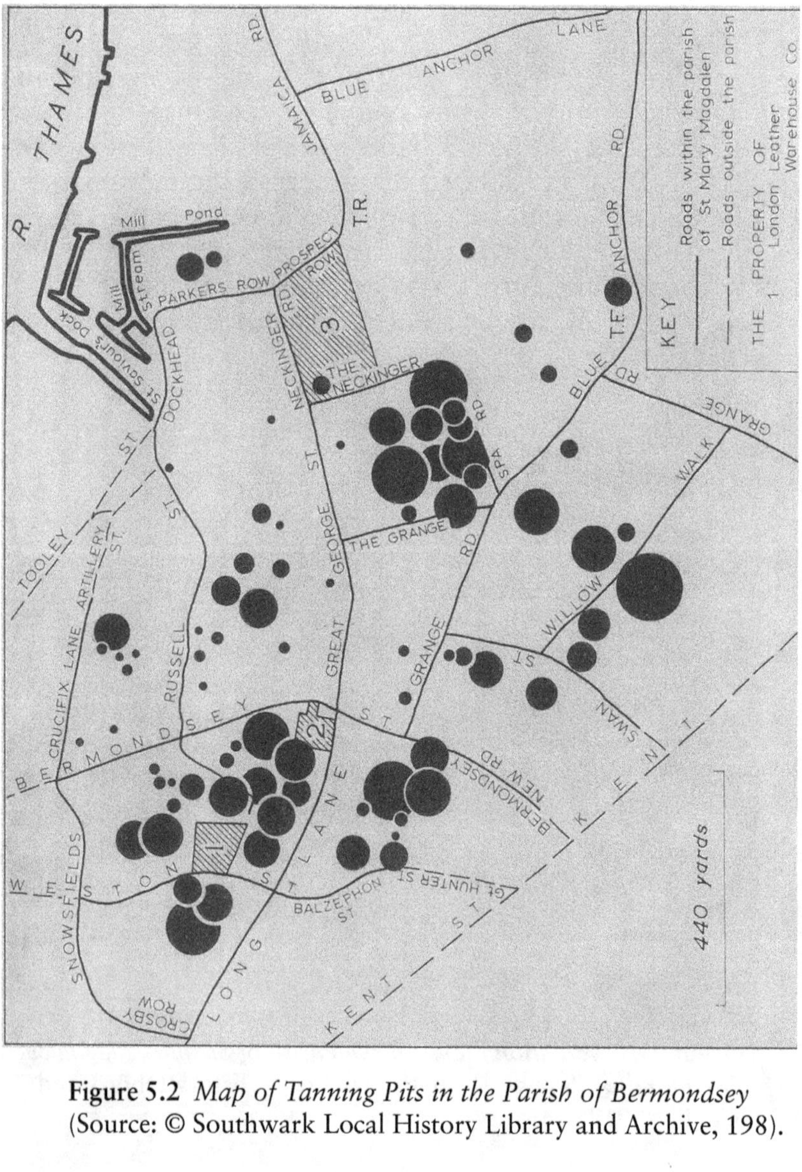

Figure 5.2 *Map of Tanning Pits in the Parish of Bermondsey* (Source: © Southwark Local History Library and Archive, 198).

neglected by civic bodies, Dickens even claims that Jacob's Island is 'wholly unknown, even by name, to the great mass of [London's] inhabitants' (*OT*, p. 416).

Jacob's Island was far from obscure by the mid-nineteenth century, however. During the 1840s the district was repeatedly investigated by social explorers, and by the 1850s it had adopted an almost symbolic significance in parliamentary and committee debates about metropolitan sanitary reform. Lord Ashley (later Shaftsbury) singled out Jacob's Island in a discussion about the 'Sanitary State of the Metropolis' in 1852, for instance, calling it a 'famous place [. . .] of a most disgusting description'.[4] In the popular press, too, references to Jacob's Island connoted dangerously insanitary conditions. For, having been linked to outbreaks of cholera in 1832 and 1848, and named 'the very capital of cholera' by Henry Mayhew,[5] Jacob's Island represented a threat to London as a whole. Although how disease spread was still improperly understood, leading sanitary reformers, such as Edwin Chadwick, stressed that improvement of living conditions was vital to combating public health issues associated with poor sanitation and contaminated water successfully. It is easy to see why Dickens's description of Jacob's Island was pertinent to such concerns. *Oliver Twist* anticipates the currents of the mid-century sanitary movement in its stress on the area's 'confined' living quarters, 'tainted' air, and the 'muddy ditch[es]' from which the inhabitants 'haul the[ir] water up' (*OT*, p. 417). The site's notoriety was thus reinforced by fiction and non-fiction alike, and campaigns for its reform frequently comingle references to both creative and apparently factual writing.

Living conditions in Jacob's Island were awful, as the sanitary problems caused by its dilapidated and overcrowded built environment were aggravated by stagnant water. The tidal inlets were supposed to be refreshed by so-called 'fresh' water from the heavily polluted Thames, but the sluice gates – which controlled when water could enter or exit – were opened infrequently.[6] An interview with an inhabitant featured in Angus B. Reach's investigative study *London Penetralia* (1846) explains that

> the sluices is private property, and the man as owns them 'ill only open them when he likes – not when we like. The place where them sluices is, was a mill in the old times, and worked by tide – but it don't go now.[7]

Whether this statement was faithfully transcribed by Reach or not, the Bermondsey Improvement Commission's *Committee of Health Minute Book* proves that it reflects very real neglect.[8] On 28 November 1853 it was noted that:

> The Clerks were also directed to write to the Commissioners of Sewers that they are informed that 150 houses are allowed to Drain into the open Mill Pond in the Parish of Rotherhithe and that many of the poor Inhabitants near thereto were obliged to take the supply of Water from such Ponds which was considered very prejudicial.[9]

Although the minutes from this meeting present sanitary reform as both a necessary measure to protect the health of the area's inhabitants and a moral duty to the poor, the Bermondsey Improvement Commission's efforts came only after cholera had focused public scrutiny on the area. Indeed, the minutes prove that five years after the 1848 cholera epidemic there was still no distinction between the water that acted as a drain and that used for drinking, cooking and washing.

The human cost of poor sanitation was obviously one reason why sanitary reform was hotly debated in the mid-nineteenth century but it was also significant to changing administrative contexts. As Lauren Goodlad explains,

> mid-century sanitary reforms stalled because of hardened divisions over technology, finance, ideology, and politics. The crux of the debate was rarely the need for action, but the far more difficult question of in whom and how to vest the authority to act.[10]

London was excluded from the remit of the 1848 Public Health Act, which centralised public health administration for the rest of the country. Consequently, metropolitan sanitation continued to be planned and regulated by local boards into the early 1850s. In part, this was because there was strong opposition to centralised administration among members of London's local government. However, the progress made by vestries was limited and slow. Although the Bermondsey Improvement Commission's minute book shows that it took some minor action to improve Jacob's Island, its interventions were piecemeal and often ineffective. In October 1853, we see the committee make repeated efforts to compel 'the Owner of 7 houses in Metcalf Court' to 'remove the Soil' – otherwise, human faeces – from 'the Cellars' of his properties.[11] The committee had limited powers to force private landlords to maintain their properties and ended up paying to clean the cellars in Metcalf Court themselves. Anthony Wohl notes that, 'apart from any consideration of self-interest', the powers of vestry administrations were inadequate because they were 'essentially amateur' committees, 'often chaired by the local vicar, and constituted by ever changing personnel'.[12] Their inability to drive sufficient sanitary reform consequently inspired campaign groups to agitate for changes to public health policy in London.

Britain's liberal governance was seen as a positive alternative to European bureaucracy by those opposed to centralised administration, but the failure of this system to combat epidemic disease led to increased pressure from committees who favoured centralisation. In 1850, the Metropolitan Sanitary Association (MSA) was formed in response to London's exclusion 'from the provisions of the Public Health Act, [. . .] with the view', in Dickens's words, 'of remedying this grievous mistake'.[13] Dickens was a member of the MSA and favoured centralisation over 'Vestrylization'.[14] He believed localised administration stood in the way of social and urban progress because its priority was to protect vested interests. In 1855, the Metropolitan Board of Works (MBW) was established to oversee all London improvements, with a particular emphasis on the urgency of constructing an interconnected sewerage system. The MBW faced similar criticisms to those that had formerly been levelled at local boards. It was again an unelected body, and its larger remit did not mean that vested interests were not protected.[15] Nevertheless, by consolidating and overriding multiple smaller authorities, it was able to effect larger changes and with greater speed.[16] Dickens praised these developments in a letter to his Swiss friend, William De Cerjat, in 1865; he admired the MBW's Thames Embankment and sewerage network, not only because they were 'really fine' works but also, strikingly, because they were 'really getting on'.[17] The urgency of sanitary reforms thus impelled larger administrative changes, which challenged prior structures of power, and ways of conceiving and regulating metropolitan space.

As we have seen, Jacob's Island exemplified poor urban sanitation in mid-century debates. It symbolised the potentially fatal consequences of unhealthy living conditions, but later users still frequently appropriated Dickens's representation of the site in *Oliver Twist* to reinforce the urgency of sanitary reform, both in Jacob's Island and in the capital at large. In 1842, for instance, George Dodd quoted from *Oliver Twist* at length, and asserted that 'the features which this spot presents are described so vividly, and with such close accuracy, that we cannot do better than quote the passage'.[18] As I will go on to explore, Dodd evoked Dickens's account as a means of substantiating and emphasising his own criticisms of the area's insanitary state. Dickens's impact on the perceived identity of Jacob's Island was considerable. The Rev. W. Lees Bell's later *History of Bermondsey* (1880) even opined that *Oliver Twist* had spurred a groundswell of concern that drove the site's redevelopment to almost as significant a degree as the cholera outbreak: 'what popular writers and newspaper articles could not do the Cholera did, and in 1850 the crazy houses were pulled down, the ditches or canals filled up, and the Mill Stream and Neckinger arched over'.[19] Lees Bell is right to note that the version of this area 'so powerfully pictured in Dickens's novel of *Oliver Twist*' dominated the site's popular representation both prior to initial improvements made in 1850 and after its demolition.[20] Sanitary reforms were made in Jacob's Island in a piecemeal fashion: the tidal ditches were gradually filled in, and dilapidated housing was eventually torn down and replaced by warehouses. Even as the city changed, however, the same passage from *Oliver Twist* was quoted repeatedly in subsequent descriptions. These afterlives reveal ongoing intersections between its representation in writing and urban redevelopment, as both Dickens's novel and other writers' accounts (especially Mayhew's famous *exposé* for the *Morning Chronicle*) were recalled and reprinted throughout the process of the area's improvement.

Dickens participated in, and attempted to direct, how the afterlives of his fiction were repurposed in contemporary debates about London's sanitary improvement. He returned to the now famous Jacob's Island passage in his earlier novel to support his campaigns for sanitary reform in the 1850s, while he was a member of the MSA.[21] Even though he did not alter its melodramatic rendering in the text, he produced afterlives that reframed *Oliver Twist* in line with his updated social concerns. Through this, he presented the novel as part of a broader social project, as he constructed links between this description, his later novels and his campaigns for material change. Nevertheless, Dickens did not have the final say about how the scene should be interpreted. As early as the 1870s, press commentators responded to the area's physical alteration and evoked *Oliver Twist* as a record of a bygone city. By the 1880s, artists and writers nostalgically reimagined Dickens's account of the site in an urban picturesque aesthetic. Then, in the twentieth century, another mass redevelopment of the area triggered more wistful yearning for Dickens's London. Consequently, as this chapter will argue, we can track Dickensian afterlives in both the cultural processes by which the history of Jacob's Island has been constructed, and the processes that drove its material destruction earlier in the nineteenth century.

Tracing Dickensian afterlives makes it possible to see processes through which cultural memories about Jacob's Island are constructed.

The concept of cultural memory is a means of analysing how stories about the past are created, disseminated and accepted as a shared heritage. We discern the significance of *Oliver Twist* to cultural memories of Jacob's Island because it was repeatedly evoked as a representation of the area's past across multiple media and fora. None the less, while literary afterlives are frequently used to implant a sense of a common history or cultural heritage, the different ways that texts are reimagined in multiple media mean that literary afterlives simultaneously reveal that these cultural memories are far from stable. As Anne Rigney puts it, '[t]hese memory sites are not fixed entities or finished products, [. . .] but rather imaginative resources for generating new meanings and contesting old ones'.[22] The different ways in which the same passage from *Oliver Twist* was reimagined to portray a specific place gives textual form to these processes. Conversely, the fact that the novel was also frequently evoked in arguments for its material improvement earlier in the nineteenth century changes the stakes in its later historicisation. In fact, the tracking of Dickensian afterlives reveals how literary narratives have been used to obscure the social impact of urban developments both during and after its improvement.

Dickens's writing was central to the reappraisal of Jacob's Island as a lost relic of a former time, just as it had been to arguments for the site's demolition. Indeed, its identity was reimagined so rapidly that there were temporal and imaginative overlaps between appropriations that used *Oliver Twist* to argue for contemporary urban reforms and those that evoked the same passage as a historical reference point. Moreover, imaginative reappraisals of Jacob's Island as a historical relic were published before its material redevelopment was complete. In locating and analysing Dickensian afterlives at each stage of the area's progress – from being defined as a contemporary problem site to one that inspired nostalgic sentiment – this chapter explores the role of literature in negotiating contemporary social anxieties connected with slums, but then moves on to examine its part in narrating, manipulating and eclipsing the cultural and social histories of Jacob's Island and its communities. Where demolished sites that have been (and still are) commonly associated with, and represented through, Dickens's works – like Jacob's Island – Dickensian simulacra have come to stand for their cultural history. It is difficult to find traces of the actual people who lived in these slum areas but Dickensian afterlives survive in abundance. Despite Dickens's reputation as *the* champion of the urban poor, the way that Dickensian afterlives have been used to campaign for and historicise urban change implicate his work first in displacing members of London's poor population (when the areas they lived in were redeveloped), and then in obscuring these people from view, as their living memories are veiled by literary characters and imagery. The material and social afterlives of Dickens's fiction in the case of Jacob's Island are thus opposite to his vision for greater social equality in London.

The 1840s: Exploring Jacob's Island

From the early 1840s on, Dickens was widely credited with alerting the reading public to the existence of Jacob's Island. Other writers regularly quote and allude to *Oliver Twist* in their accounts of the district. Dodd even remarks on the significance of Dickens's description to public images of the area:

> All Londoners have heard of the 'Rookery', or, more irreverently, the 'Holy Land' of St. Giles's; [but] far less is known of 'Jacob's Island' in Bermondsey, though it has been rendered familiar to many by the most successful of living novelists.[23]

Dickens's representation of Jacob's Island was certainly well known by the time Dodd published his article 'Modern Bermondsey' in 1842, but *Oliver Twist* was in fact preceded by Robert Wilkinson's *Londina Illustrata* (1819). Wilkinson's book offers an engraving showing a 'South View of London Street, Dockhead, in the Water Side Division of the Parish of St Mary Magdalen Bermondsey. SURREY', alongside a map of the district.[24] The scene is dilapidated and follows an illustration of buildings that were about to be demolished in the Strand. The condition of Jacob's Island and its position in the volume thus indicate that similar destruction is predicted in London Street. In juxtaposing these images, Wilkinson presents both scenes as records of London's past. As early as 1819, therefore, the place was interpreted as a relic of Old London, and drawn in a style that anticipates the *Illustrated London News*'s picturesque representation of urban demolitions in the 1850s and 1860s.[25] However, the impact that *Londina Illustrata* had on how Jacob's Island was popularly perceived appears to have been limited. The book is a hefty, richly illustrated tome, beyond the means of many readers. *Oliver Twist* was a more useful point of reference for mid-century social explorers. Aside from the novel's popular appeal, which allowed later users to mine the story for widely recognisable representational tools, its pertinence to current sanitary concerns in the 1840s meant that it was evoked as commentary on contemporary London, rather than as a record of its past.

Dodd presents *Oliver Twist* as evidence that supports his call for sanitary reform in Jacob's Island. His narrative is framed as a walk around Bermondsey and details his route by recounting street names and landmarks. Titled 'Modern Bermondsey', Dodd celebrates the area's industrial progress by describing the variety and vitality of trades and manufactures based in the district. His criticism of Jacob's Island is thereby accentuated because its degenerated conditions are in close proximity to thriving industries. Dodd's meticulously observed portrayal is purportedly taken from the objective standpoint of a strolling visitor to the district. He affects a disinterested tone, and foregrounds his critical praxis by evaluating the conclusions he draws from first-hand observation with secondary sources. One of these is *Oliver Twist*. Reading Dickens is presented as part of Dodd's wider research, and so the novel is presented as giving a faithful and realistic depiction of contemporary London. 'This is the scene', he attests, in between quoting long extracts from *Oliver Twist*.[26] Dodd's self-representation as a first-hand observer indicates that quoting from the novel was less an attempt to enliven his own writing, than to corroborate his claims. The novel is represented as urban reportage – an interpretation that Dodd substantiates by comparing it to other accounts. He notes its similarity to the 'view of this spot' given in *Londina Illustrata*, for example: 'the interval of time does not seem to have produced much change in the appearance of the scene'.[27] In fact, Wilkinson's antiquarianism is distinct from Dodd's and Dickens's portrayal of Jacob's Island as a modern problem site. Nevertheless, reference to multiple texts allows Dodd to cast *Oliver Twist* as part of his wider critical analysis of the district, so justifying its significance to his investigations.

In 1846, Reach affected a similarly analytical approach in *London Penetralia*, but aligned *Oliver Twist* even more explicitly with contemporary arguments for sanitary reform than Dodd had done four years earlier. Reach vociferously criticises the fact that local government bodies tolerate the insanitary conditions in Jacob's Island. In particular, he draws the reader's attention to the dangerously polluted water that inhabitants are forced to drink: 'It required a little screwing up, but we tasted the loathsome fluid. Earthy, nauseously mawkish, its savour was of the sepulchre.'[28] Reach's ingestion of the water has a shocking and repulsive effect, as it prompts the reader to imagine what other substances are dissolved in the liquid. Yet despite his avowed commitment to first-hand research and an evident desire to shock, Reach still supports his claims by quoting long extracts from *Oliver Twist*. Perhaps he was merely attempting to ride on Dickens's coattails by associating his writing with such a popular author. Although Dodd was a reasonably successful journeyman writer,[29] Reach struggled to make a living despite working 'sixteen hours a day as a shorthand reporter, comic writer, and novelist'.[30] Nevertheless, Reach's self-construction as a social explorer in turn presents *London Penetralia* as a critique of contemporary metropolitan conditions. Dickens's writing was thus repeatedly re-presented as urban reportage, to supplement and authenticate later writers' apparently first-hand research.

In *Oliver Twist*, Dickens layers topographic and social description with sensational details that heighten the narrative tension of this climactic scene. Jacob's Island is the setting for Sikes's attempted escape. It is portrayed as a pestiferous slum, and so is dangerous both because of its insanitary conditions and because it shelters a community of desperate criminals: 'They must have powerful motives for a secret residence, or be reduced to a destitute condition indeed, who seek a refuge in Jacob's Island' (*OT*, p. 418). The distance between Jacob's Island and wealthier areas in London is thereby presented as both geographic and cultural. 'To reach this place,' Dickens's narrator explains, 'the visitor has to penetrate through a maze of close, narrow, and muddy streets, thronged by the roughest and poorest of water-side people, and devoted to the traffic they may be supposed to occasion' (*OT*, p. 416). The terrain and its populace appear to obstruct easy access. Sikes's retreat to Jacob's Island makes his capture more unlikely, and so increases the reader's sense of danger and suspense. Dickens further emphasises the site's difference to other urban spaces by amassing negative superlative adjectives in his account. In the first paragraph alone, Jacob's Island is labelled the 'dirtiest', 'blackest', 'filthiest', 'strangest' and 'most extraordinary' of London's 'hidden' localities (*OT*, p. 416). While *Oliver Twist* certainly presents a vivid portrayal of the site's insanitary conditions, therefore, the topography of Jacob's Island also contributes to building narrative tension – something which Dodd and Reach downplay.

In representing *Oliver Twist* as a detailed exploration of contemporary slum conditions, Dodd and Reach construct Dickens's identity as an expert on contemporary London: a persona pertinent to the mid-century public health movement. As Goodlad argues, in the early stages of the sanitary movement, a version of the public servant emerged that was 'part hero, part expert', whose 'credentials were predicated on zealous dedication to a social cause and, consequently, on unique and hard-won expertise'.[31] These figures were quickly superseded by 'the public school and Oxbridge educated professional'; however, Dickens's characterisation as a specialist by the social explorers of the 1840s overlaps with the period in which such men were influential drivers of large-scale urban improvements.[32] Aside from outbreaks of epidemic diseases, Edwin Chadwick's 1842 *Report on the Sanitary Condition of the Labouring Population of Great Britain* was another significant factor in focusing public attention on sanitary reform in the 1840s. Chadwick was both a public servant and an indefatigable advocate of sanitary reform, who made recommendations based on substantial research. The *Report* envisions systematic assaults on public health problems through practical measures, such as a mass sewerage system to remove noxious waste.[33] Metropolitan sewage disposal was not centralised until after the MBW was established in 1855, but Chadwick's report contributed to changing public policy about who should be given the authority to plan and implement such measures. The professionalism that social explorers attribute to Dickens suggestively positions imaginative writing in dialogue with official reports that investigated the modern city and made authoritative recommendations for its improvement. Reach even went so far as to say that Jacob's Island was unknown to many Londoners prior to Dickens's account. 'It's [*sic*] name is not even laid down in London maps. Until the appearance of a work of fiction some years ago, probably not one Londoner in ten thousand had ever read or heard of Jacob's Island.'[34] Reach's assertion that *Oliver Twist* had been useful in mapping modern London aligns Dickens's novel with non-fiction documents that sought to measure and account for contemporary conditions through statistics or cartography.[35] Nevertheless, even though Reach reinforces his critiques of urban conditions by allying his work with Dickens's supposedly expert insight, the name *London Penetralia* – meaning London's 'secret parts' or 'mysteries' – simultaneously evokes a titillating affect.[36] Similarly to Dickens himself, these social investigators explored the pleasures that slum tourism generates for wealthier readers, as well as exposing social injustice.

As in *Oliver Twist*, Dodd's and Reach's accounts layer apparently objective and sensational details. While both quote from the novel as a faithful portrayal of the district, they also take cues from Dickens's emotive vocabulary. In addition to republishing long extracts, Dodd's own commentary patterns Dickens's dramatic model of urban description. Depicting Jacob's Island 'in all its ragged glory', Dodd draws readers' attention to 'mean and dilapidated houses' and 'small, crazy, and very primitive wooden bridges'.[37] This reinforces the details given in the novel. *Oliver Twist* also emphasises the cramped, dirty and dilapidated condition of the built environment: 'rooms so small, so filthy, so confined, [. . .] dirt-besmeared walls and decaying foundations' (*OT*, p. 417). Dodd even directly mimics some of Dickens's more emphatic adjectival choices. For example, Dodd's use of the word 'crazy' to describe the ramshackle wooden bridges follows Dickens's description of '[c]razy wooden galleries' (*OT*, p. 417). In contrast to the formal tone and careful diction Dodd employs to describe Bermondsey's industries, his account adopts a sensational tenor when he enters Jacob's Island. Consequently, he presents the site's obscurity as intriguing as well as dangerous. Reach also draws on the novel by employing comparable diction ('crazy' features again) and laying emphasis on similar features of the scene:

> Crazy wooden galleries common to the backs of half-a-dozen houses, with holes from which to look upon the slime beneath; [. . .] wooden chambers thrusting themselves out above the mud and threatening to fall into it – as some have done [. . .] (*OT*, p. 417)

> Imagine this pestilential ditch bounded, and its reeking banks formed by a long succession of picturesque wooden dwellings, old, crazy, crumbling, in some places leaning heavily over the mud, in others settling down bodily into it. (*London Penetralia*, p. 12)

Dodd and Reach give a low profile to the topography's narrative role when they refer to Dickens's novel as a form of urban investigative journalism. However, corollaries between their accounts and Dickens's description reveal that these later social explorers still sought to satisfy readers' tastes for sensational criminal scenes, at the same time as providing hard-hitting information about contemporary conditions.

In contrast to Dodd's and Reach's earlier studies, Dickens is notably absent from Henry Mayhew's famous report for the *Morning Chronicle* (1849).[38] Unlike previous social explorers, Mayhew's decision not to refer to *Oliver Twist* presents his report as a different kind of urban investigation, unmediated by fiction. This is not to say that Mayhew pretended not to have textual predecessors, but rather that he constructed a different literary genealogy to Dodd and Reach. Instead of extracting passages from Dickens's novel to support and inform his representation of Jacob's Island, Mayhew only alludes to reports that were supposedly based on fact. Mayhew quotes from *London Penetralia*, which, like the *Morning Chronicle* article, argues for contemporary sanitary reform based on personal examinations of the area.[39] Still, Dickens is indirectly present in Mayhew's account because Reach's representation of Jacob's Island was informed by *Oliver Twist*. Dickensian afterlives in 1840s social exploration thus meant that the novel still shadows the *Morning Chronicle* article.

Fictional and investigative writing had a greater impact on how Jacob's Island was popularly perceived than official reports. Although ultimately the site's redevelopment was triggered by the 1848–9 cholera epidemic, the 'Report of the General Board of Health on the Epidemic Cholera of 1848 & 1849' (1850) deals with the area south of the river more broadly than the social explorers writing in the 1840s.

> Thus estimating the intensity of the epidemic force by the amount of mortality from cholera and diarrhœa, proportionably [*sic*] to every 1,000 living, it appears that Rotherhithe, which was the first in the order of mortality in the late, was only the ninth in the former epidemic; Bermondsey, the second in the late, was the fourth in the former; Southwark, the third in the late, was the first in the former; and Newington, the fourth in the late, was the sixth in the former epidemic, and so on.[40]

Mayhew's famous article, 'A Visit to the Cholera Districts of Bermondsey', is different to the General Board of Health's report in that it specifically identifies Jacob's Island as 'the very capital of cholera'.[41] Conversely, the report indicates that Bermondsey did not have the highest mortality rate during the 1848–9 epidemic. While the report corroborates Mayhew's claim that death tolls in the area were high, Jacob's Island was not the centre point of the cholera outbreak that he suggests. Nevertheless, his article, and those of other social explorers from whom Mayhew quoted, certainly contributed to calls for sanitary reform in the district at a time when public anxieties were focused by fears about cholera and other deadly diseases. This is measurable in the fact that, by the 1850s, Jacob's Island was repeatedly evoked in parliament to advocate public health measures, such as the Metropolis Water Act (1852), which legislated for the increased provision of clean water in London.[42] Jacob's Island remained an exemplar of poor sanitation even after material reforms began in 1850.

The 1850s: Dickens's Interventions

The speech Dickens gave at the first meeting of the MSA on 6 February 1850 marks the beginning of his concerted efforts to direct how *Oliver Twist* was repurposed in mid-century sanitary debates. Sanitary reform was one of Dickens's major social concerns,[43] and the relevance of Jacob's Island to public anxieties about cholera, unclean water and sewage disposal offered him opportunities to reframe his earlier novel in line with contemporary debates. Dickens responded to recent improvements in Jacob's Island when he alluded to *Oliver Twist* in his speech to the MSA in 1850. Unlike the social explorers writing in the 1840s, whose appropriations of *Oliver Twist* in their campaigns preceded the site's material change, Dickens evokes his description as an illustration of its successful improvement:

> nothing was cheaper than good sanitary improvement, as they knew in the case of 'Jacob's Island', which he had described in a work of fiction some ten or eleven years ago, and where the improvements had been made at a cost of less than the price of a pint of porter or two glasses of gin a week to each inhabitant. [*Hear, hear.*][44]

Dickens presents *Oliver Twist* as a record of the site's conditions in the late 1830s, so, he suggests, the novel elucidates the scale and success of its material change by providing a stable point of comparison. However, the afterlives Dickens produced in the 1850s did not simply recall his novel as a representative tool; he also mobilised *Oliver Twist* for political commentary. Dickens evoked the contrast between present-day Jacob's Island and its literary representation to attack larger, ongoing social problems and London's fragmented governance. In his first speech to the MSA, he presents the vestry that had implemented its sanitary reform as a special case. This vestry is notable because of its difference to the conscious neglect of other local government committees, which he says are made up of 'the small owners of small tenements, who pushed themselves forward on boards of guardians and parish vestries, and were clamorous about the ratings of their property'.[45] Dickens's statement reinforces a widespread popular opinion that local government bodies were generally corrupt, and so supports his case that London's administrative systems had to be reformed, as well as its dilapidated topography. The Bishop of London echoed Dickens's remarks and his references to *Oliver Twist*. Conversely, unlike Dickens's speech, the novel is not concerned with centralisation. This afterlife reframes the novel for an updated context, by investing it with political resonances that are not traceable in the text.

Rather than directly rebutting Dickens's contentious advocacy of centralisation, representatives of London vestries responded to his speech by attacking his rhetorical use of *Oliver Twist*. One such objector was Sir Peter Laurie, an alderman in the Marylebone vestry, who had previously served as Lord Mayor of London.[46] Laurie was not renowned for his sympathy with the poor. Indeed, he was the model for Alderman Cute in *The Chimes* (1844), whose catch-phrase assertion that he will 'Put Down' the 'nonsense talked about Want'[47] was based on Laurie's 'campaign to "put down" suicide among the poor by inflicting prison sentences on all those brought before him charged with attempting the offence'.[48] Laurie and Dickens clashed publicly again when Laurie responded to Dickens's call for sanitary improvement in a heartless and ill-informed manner.

Laurie and other vestryman rejected the idea that Dickens's fiction could be used to argue for London improvements, and instead evoked *Oliver Twist* to attack the MSA:

> To illustrate how misguided and misinformed reformers of all kinds could be, [Laurie] begged their permission to read out a passage from the recent speech by the Bishop of London about Jacob's Island: 'The Bishop of London, poor soul', said Sir Peter, 'in his simplicity, thought there really was such a place . . . whereas it turned out that it only existed in a work of fiction, written by Mr. Charles Dickens ten years ago [*roars of laughter*]. The fact was admitted by Mr. Charles Dickens himself at the meeting . . . Mr. Dickens said ". . . nothing was cheaper than good sanitary improvements, as they knew in this case of 'Jacob's Island' [*laughter*], which he had described in a work of fiction some 10 or 11 years ago".'
>
> The vestry was delighted. Another member agreed that 'It was all very well to listen to the rubbish of Mr. Charles Dickens who sold his work at a very high price, and got a good living out of it . . . All that was cant and humbug.'[49]

Laurie mocks the Bishop of London by presenting his concerns as a foolish consequence of holy innocence. Dickens is critiqued more virulently. Laurie portrays his literary representation of Jacob's Island as consciously manipulative and self-interested. The social role of authors was examined in the 'Dignity of Literature' debates of the 1850s, which analysed the professionalisation of authorship alongside fictional representations of contemporary social issues. Intervening in these debates, Laurie's speech opines that literature should play no role in public matters. Conversely, advocates for its societal value contended that fiction had the potential to have a practical impact in society because it could disseminate social and moral critiques.[50] On the one hand, professionalising writing carried the possibility of objectivity, as authors were severed from their prior class status or the necessity of pleasing patrons.[51] On the other, this financial interest was often seen to vulgarise and discredit their work. Laurie and the other vestryman represent the latter belief, and counter Dickens's efforts to reframe *Oliver Twist* for social comment by reinforcing the fictional genesis for his remarks. Of course, Laurie's attack did not discredit Dickens but had the opposite effect. Laurie was shamed as members of the press rushed to Dickens's defence and critiqued Laurie's outrageous want of sympathy or knowledge about living conditions in slum areas. Meanwhile, Dickens continued to mobilise his fiction frequently when he participated in contemporary debates.

How Dickens reframed *Oliver Twist* to comment on mid-century sanitary reforms shifted dynamically in response to Laurie's attack. Following Laurie's attempts to discredit him, Dickens replied by inserting a new preface into the new Cheap Edition of *Oliver Twist*, which denounced Laurie publicly. In the month following their dispute, Dickens wrote to his brother-in-law, Henry Austin:

> I will shew you tomorrow a few lines of Sanitary Preface I have done, to the cheap Oliver. I have gone to the expence [*sic*] of printing it to 'sew up' with Copperfield at the end of the month – with the patriotic view of 'sewing up' at the same time, Sir Peter Laurie [. . .][52]

His tactics were aggressive. Michael Slater explains that

> [t]o give the widest possible publicity to this devastating counter-attack, as well as to advertise the Cheap Edition, Dickens caused a two-page insert carrying the new *Oliver* preface to be included in all copies of *Copperfield XII*, immediately after the text of the instalment and preceding the end adverts.[53]

Therefore, while Laurie questioned the utility of fiction, Dickens chose it as the most appropriate and powerful weapon through which he could respond to Laurie's criticisms. *David Copperfield*'s circulation ensured that Dickens's opinions were widely disseminated. Moreover, Dickens reinforced his satirical criticism of Laurie as emphasised by intertextual references to *The Chimes*: 'SIR PETER LAURIE having been himself described in a book (as I understand he was, one Christmas time, for his conduct on the seat of Justice), it is but too clear that there CAN be no such man!'[54] The preface mercilessly ridicules Laurie's remark that Jacob's Island is fictional and names him repeatedly in bold capital letters. Dickens thus utilises the popularity and humour of his novels to garner public support for his position and condemn his opponent. None the less, Laurie's and Dickens's allusions to *Oliver Twist* prove that the same passage could be repurposed to advocate opposed positions in debates about London's sanitary improvement, and that the novel's afterlives evolved in dialogue with current debates.

The preface to the 1850 Cheap Edition of *Oliver Twist* is Dickens's personal riposte to Laurie's attack, but it also directs readers to interpret the text with an awareness of its relevance to mid-century sanitary debates. The reader's attention is immediately drawn to Jacob's Island, instead of any other incident or location portrayed in the novel:

> Eleven or twelve years have elapsed, since the description was first published. I was as well convinced then, as I am now, that nothing effectual can be done for the elevation of the poor in England, until their dwelling-places are made decent and wholesome.[55]

In contrast to his satirical representation of Laurie, Dickens adopts a business-like tone to discuss Jacob's Island and the fact that the site 'had lately attracted the attention of the Board of Health, in consequence of its having been ravaged by cholera'.[56] His description can certainly be read as an *exposé* of the area's conditions. Indeed, Dickens was following the lead of the social explorers who referred to *Oliver Twist* in such terms in the 1840s. Nevertheless, the sober diction Dickens employs to talk about Jacob's Island in the preface contrasts with the extreme tone of his description in the novel.

Rather than changing his fiction to make his sanitary message more explicit, Dickens used paratextual material to reframe *Oliver Twist* in line with updated contexts. Dickens's preface suggests that the novel's representation is sympathetic because the preface presents the poor as victims of ongoing injustice. As we have already seen, however, Dickens's representation of Jacob's Island in the novel itself is ambivalent. Sikes chooses this 'secret residence' because the topography facilitates the activities of murderers and criminals, by providing adequate cover for their illicit activities (*OT*, p. 418). By asking the reader to treat the passage as a realistic depiction that is still relevant to current contexts of reform, Dickens re-presents *Oliver Twist* selectively. No mention is made of the novel's central criticism of the New Poor Law. Instead, the description of Jacob's Island is alone evoked to portray *Oliver Twist* as part of Dickens's ongoing campaign for sanitary reform. Reframing *Oliver Twist* thus allows Dickens to alter and extend the novel's applicability to contemporary contexts, even though his interventions ironically suggest that the novel transcends temporal parameters, as it appears to depart from the social concerns professed most loudly at its original publication.

Reframing *Oliver Twist* with new paratextual material enables Dickens to claim his earlier novel as part of a coherent social project across his œuvre. The 1850 *Oliver Twist* preface was not the only occasion where he used paratextual material to reframe previous novels to suit updated social concerns. In the 1850 preface to the Cheap Edition of *Martin Chuzzlewit* (1843–4), Dickens argues that driving sanitary reforms was always central to his creative process: 'in all my writings, I hope I have taken every possible opportunity of showing the want of sanitary improvements in the neglected dwellings of the poor'.[57] Dickens's interventionist ambitions are certainly evident in his novels. Concurrently with his involvement with the MSA, Dickens drew readers' attention to the danger posed by insanitary conditions by linking vivid descriptions of London slum areas with the threat of disease. In *David Copperfield* (1849–50), the scene of Martha's near-suicide in the Thames is set in a 'dreary' neighbourhood: 'There was a story that one of the pits dug for the dead in the time of the Great Plague was hereabout; and a blighting influence seemed to have proceeded from it over the whole place' (*DC*, p. 686). The connection between urban sanitation and disease is even more explicit in *Bleak House* (1852–3), as the infection that issues from the dilapidated slum Tom-All-Alone's threatens the entire city: 'There is not an atom of Tom's slime [. . .] but shall work its retribution, through every order of society, up to the proudest of the proud, and to the highest of the high' (*BH*, p. 710). However, Dickens's attempts to retroactively influence how his earlier fiction was interpreted perhaps reflects an awareness that the afterlives of his novels were difficult to control. There was no guarantee that later users would focus on the concerns voiced in the text. Paradoxically, Dickens also contributed to this instability by participating in rhetorical reuses of his works, and by repeatedly reframing his novels in response to evolving social and material contexts.[58]

Dickens and Laurie's exchange reveals how multiple temporalities intersect and overlap in Dickensian afterlives, even when they refer to the same passage, place and debate. Dickensian afterlives were unfixed, even when Dickens encouraged readers to apply his fiction to contemporary contexts himself. In his first speech to the MSA in 1850, he refers to *Oliver Twist* as a record of what Jacob's Island used to look like. In so doing, Dickens simultaneously evokes the area's past and present in dialogue with his fiction. However, after Laurie denounced Dickens's words and claimed that Jacob's Island existed only in fiction, members of the press leapt to Dickens's defence:

> Mr. Dickens himself is above suspicion, as well as above reproach on the score of veracity. To doubt, still more to deny, that Jacob's Island has 'a local habitation and a name' in the huge circumscription, popularly denominated London, is 'therefore' an offensive absurdity.[59]

This vindication argues that Dickens's fictional account is verifiable, and that the way he portrays Jacob's Island in *Oliver Twist* still accurately reflects London's contemporary built environment. The journalist's defence thus recalls Dodd's and Reach's approach, and presents Dickens's description as evidence of urgently needed sanitary reform. Paradoxically, however, the journalist is responding directly to Dickens's assertion that the space was undergoing physical transformation, meaning that the site could not look the same. Multiple historical temporalities intersect with the extra-temporal realm of fiction in this dialogue, as London's past and present are conceived through, and comingled with, literary representation.

Dickens evoked Jacob's Island differently again the following year in a second speech to the MSA. While his 1850 address presents his description of Jacob's Island as a representation of the district prior to positive alterations, his 1851 speech emphasises the site's ongoing neglect. Recalling listeners' memories of his prior dispute, Dickens casts Laurie as an antagonist in his campaign for London's sanitary reform and centralisation:

> I have the honour – of which I am very sensible – to be one of the constituent body of the amazing Vestry of Marylebone [*laughter*]; and if you chance to remember (as you very likely do) [. . .] what my vestry *said*, you will probably agree with me that between this so-called Centralization, and this Vestrylization, the former is by far the best thing to stand by in an emergency. My vestry even took the high ground of denying the existence of cholera in any unusual degree. [*Laughter.*] And though that denial had no greater effect upon the disease than my vestry's denial of the existence of Jacob's Island had upon the Earth about Bermondsey, the circumstance may be suggestive to you in considering what Vestrylization is [. . .][60]

Rather than focusing on Jacob's Island's improvement, this time Dickens chooses to remind his listeners of its link to the cholera epidemic to reinforce his argument for centralisation. Laurie personifies the bad practice of local vestries in this speech, and Dickens presents the cholera outbreak in Jacob's Island as the inevitable consequence of such incompetence and corruption. Dickens's speech also serves his own interests, however. In positioning himself as Laurie's opponent, Dickens asserts his own credibility as a social commentator – an identity that, as Chapter 4 explored, he consciously cultivated in the 1850s.

Oliver Twist's pertinence to the sanitary debates of the late 1840s and early 1850s was conceived because of the specific location it describes, rather than because it represents a particularly outspoken critique of London's sanitary conditions. In fact, it is ironic that the attention Jacob's Island received following the 1848 cholera epidemic made *Oliver Twist* appear newly relevant to sanitary debates. Chadwick's 1842 *Report* laid the foundation for 'the Sanatory [*sic*] cause' that Dickens supported so enthusiastically.[61] Nevertheless, Chadwick had also played an instrumental role in the Poor Law Commission, and so had been deeply involved with the implementation of the workhouse test under the New Poor Law.[62] Dickens was profoundly committed to the anti-Poor Law campaign. He presents damning depictions of its abuses throughout his career – from his portrayal of the cruelties institutionalised in the workhouse in *Oliver Twist* to Betty Higden's desperate flight from that system in *Our Mutual Friend* (1864–5). Although Kathleen Blake contends in *Pleasures of Benthamism* that Dickens was not as anti-Utilitarian as has previously been supposed, and that he in fact gave positive presentations of the virtues that accord with Bentham's thinking, *Oliver Twist* was clearly written in opposition to the New Poor Law. The fact that Dickens's most virulent anti-Poor Law novel was used to support social reforms of which Chadwick was the main author is remarkable.

Metropolitan reforms produced unlikely coalitions, and Dickens became deeply involved with Chadwick's network of Benthamite reformers. Chadwick headed the General Board of Health (GBH), which Christopher Hamlin has called 'the first modern public health agency'.[63] With the exception of London, the GBH was a country-wide authority that pursued measures largely directed by Chadwick's research. As Chapter 4 explained, Dickens was connected to the GBH's individual members, as a colleague, friend or relation. Dickens was acquainted with Chadwick, brother-in-law to Henry Austin (an architect and civil engineer who was secretary to the GBH over a four-year period[64]), and friendly with Dr Thomas Southwood Smith (a respected doctor and Medical Assistant of the GBH[65]). Dickens's involvement with this network reinforced his desire to promote sanitary reform in London, and he also used his contacts to facilitate his own campaigns. Dickens regularly prevailed on Austin to check facts for *Household Words* and commissioned him to write articles for the periodical: 'I should be very glad indeed, if you could find leisure to write or suggest anything (the former, the better) tending to promote the Sanitary cause, for the H. W.'[66] Moreover, their close relationship, and mutual respect, meant that Austin gave Dickens early access to new reports produced by the GBH so that he could publish responses to them in his periodicals.[67] Dickens was willing to work with Chadwick to promote metropolitan sanitary reforms but this should not be taken as a signal of a radical change in his beliefs. Instead, it exposes the possibilities for collaboration between representatives from different political backgrounds in this era, and reveals that the belief in the socially ameliorative power of improvements was supported by people from alternative political backgrounds.

Sanitary and topographic reform began in Jacob's Island in 1850 but it did not happen all at once. The area remained a cause for concern in the 1850s, and calls for its demolition indicate that its redevelopment was slow and disjointed. In 1852, for example, Thomas Beames argued, 'Let us [. . .] repair the injuries which the poor sustain – let us wipe away the blot which all may witness, and write at once the death-warrant of Jacob's Island.'[68] Again in 1853, Dickens opined in a letter to Angela Burdett Coutts that the area around Jacob's Island was so bad that '[a]n act of parliament would be necessary to clear the place'.[69] The district was ravaged by fire in 1861, impelling widespread demolitions that replaced a previously piecemeal approach to sanitary reform in the area.[70] The place was transformed and its remaining inhabitants were displaced. By the time that *Oliver Twist* was republished with a new preface in 1867, therefore, the site's topography and social makeup, and the contexts of urban improvement, had changed. London's sanitation had been brought under the control of a centralised body, the MBW, and Jacob's Island had been altered extensively by fire and demolitions. However, Dickens continued to reframe *Oliver Twist* to comment on contemporary sanitary issues and to attempt to manage the novel's legacy.

> In the year one thousand eight hundred and fifty, it was publicly declared in London by an amazing Alderman, that Jacob's Island did not exist, and never had existed. Jacob's Island continues to exist (like an ill-bred place as it is) in the year one thousand eight hundred and sixty-seven, though improved and much changed.[71]

After Dickens

The role that Dickensian afterlives performed in later representations of Jacob's Island changed when the sanitary issues associated with the place were less pressing, and Dickens could no longer play a curatorial role. Prior to the 1870s, Dickens's description of Jacob's Island had been repurposed as evidence of urgently needed sanitary improvements, and as a rhetorical yardstick against which its subsequent material change could be judged. As we have seen, afterlives that alluded to *Oliver Twist* as a representation of a contemporary problem site, and as a record of London's past, were produced concurrently in Dickens's lifetime. After his death in 1870, however, Dickens's London was reimagined as a version of a bygone city with astonishing rapidity, and while the material redevelopment of Jacob's Island was still incomplete.

The speed with which Dickens's London was reconceived is revealed by the fact that, in the early 1870s, afterlives that asserted *Oliver Twist*'s contemporary applicability to sanitary reform interacted, even overlapped, with appropriations of the text as a historical record. In 1872, only two years after Dickens's death, the *Ragged School Union* magazine published an article in which his description of Jacob's Island was used to evoke its past, earlier redevelopment and current conditions, within the same piece. Describing the changes that had occurred in the area over the past two decades, the article states that:

> The foul ditch, a creek of the Thames, has been filled up, and no longer pollutes soul and body. Huge warehouses have replaced the hovels of burglars; [. . .] The poor no longer drink the filthy, unfiltered creek-water, for most houses have the water laid on; though the less that is said about the state of the water butts the better. As might have been expected, the moral aspect of Jacob's Island has so changed that the Bill Sikeses would scarcely choose it now for a place of refuge.[72]

In reprinting Dickens's description as a historical account, the *Ragged School Union* draws readers' attention to material changes to Jacob's Island. The novel has historical value, according to the article, because of its dissimilarity to the current physical space. *Oliver Twist* thus allows the writer to construct a legible representation of the site's transformation by measuring the scale and success of the area's redevelopment in comparison to Dickens's fictionalised portrayal. The modern built environment is conceived alongside and through the simultaneous evocation of its past and its fictionalisation. However, Dickensian afterlives also serve a symbolic function and defy the specific spatial and temporal parameters implied by the article's representation of the changing built environment. The plural 'Sikeses' in the above quotation suggests, for example, that Dickens's characters personify wider social problems. In this, characters are severed from the specific historicisation against which, the article proposes, readers should interpret Dickens's descriptions of London places.

Multiple temporalities and fiction intersect and overlap in the *Ragged School Union*'s portrayal of Jacob's Island, but the article goes so far as to suggest that there are also reciprocal pathways of exchange between fictional representation and material change. Similarly to earlier commentators, the writer credits Dickens with alerting the public to Jacob's Island's very existence:

> About a quarter of a century ago society was startled by Charles Dickens's sketch of a London 'crime garden'. So little was then known of the haunts of crime, that many believed the fact to be exaggerated, whilst a City magistrate denied on the bench that there was even such a place as 'Jacob's Island'.[73]

The link between Dickens's fiction and localised improvements is conceived as both imaginative and practical. Noting that *Oliver Twist* had provoked and facilitated further investigations and comment, the writer traces how the fictional depiction of Jacob's Island and its significance to later sanitary campaigns culminated in material change. Recounting Dickens's dispute with Laurie, for instance, the *Ragged School Union* claims that this disagreement about the reliability of *Oliver Twist*'s representation prompted philanthropists to establish the Jacob's Island Ragged School in 1855. Yet not only is the novel used to tell the story of how the Ragged School was founded, but its location in the contemporary city is also mapped in relation to the novel. The 'Ragged School', we are told, was opened 'a few yards from Bill Sikes's house'.[74] The location of Sikes's retreat is not named in *Oliver Twist*. In constructing a representation that comingles fiction with the physical space, the writer consciously embellishes her or his reading of Dickens's account to establish further connections between the novel and the modern city. The effect is that the article implies temporal and spatial continuity and development between Dickens's description and the present day, and so reinforces the assertion of *Oliver Twist*'s significance to the area's redevelopment and the Ragged School's philanthropic activities.

Alluding to *Oliver Twist* allows the *Ragged School Union*'s writer to justify and explain material improvements in positive terms. She or he evokes *Oliver Twist* as a record of a dark and dangerous past, and as a symbolic vocabulary for certain social problems. The interventions of philanthropists and urban developers can thus be conceived as assaults upon urban disorder and disease – a narrative that obscures the negative social effects of improvement. For the former inhabitants of slum areas, demolition meant displacement. Tenants were given scant, if any, compensation, and little appropriate housing was built to accommodate the people who were forced from their homes. Even though slum clearances were commonly conceived as part of a creative process of necessary urban amelioration, given the inadequate supply of affordable housing for the poor, in reality slum-dwellers were forced to pack even more closely into remaining tenements, and at higher rents driven by increased demand. Contrary to Dickens's reputation as champion of the urban poor, the *Ragged School Union* borrows Dickens's supposed authority as an urban commentator to argue for the benefits of demolishing Jacob's Island. Indeed, as in its claims that *Oliver Twist* inspired the Ragged School's work in the area, the article states that *Oliver Twist* is partially responsible for its wider topographic reform: 'Such a picture could not but lead to some improvement in the sanitary condition of Jacob's Island.'[75] Written only two years after obituaries had lauded and memorialised Dickens as both a reformer and a writer, the *Ragged School Union*'s assertion that he had an instrumental impact on changing the material and social conditions of London was not unique. For instance, in the same year that this article was published, John Forster's biography similarly claimed that 'with only the light arms of humour and laughter, and the gentle ones of pathos and sadness, he carried cleansing and reform into [. . .] Augean stables'.[76]

Throughout the course of its redevelopment, Dickensian afterlives influenced the perceived social identity of Jacob's Island by hiding its real inhabitants from view. The census that was taken closest to its initial improvements suggests that Dickens's characterisation of Jacob's Island's population as transient and nefarious was not representative. The results of the 1851 census reveal a population deeply rooted in the area. In Metcalf Court – which a later writer (H. W. Jackson) believed was the location of Sikes's death – most of the dwellings were arranged into family units and almost all the men were employed.[77] Jacob's Island was not a waste-ground for human 'refuse', but was inhabited by the labourers and mariners of local waterside industries and their families (*OT*, p. 417). Apart from

Frances Price from Sussex, David Davis from South Wales and his wife, Jane Davis, from Kent, all the inhabitants of the court were born in Bermondsey or its neighbouring parishes. There was also a wide discrepancy in the ages of the inhabitants. The youngest named was just one year old and the oldest was seventy-seven; she was not the only septuagenarian.[78] As unhealthy as this district undoubtedly was, then, Dickens none the less seems to have described its social identity as largely criminal for dramatic effect. His misrepresentation had an impact on the population, however, as his sensational reimagining of the place was later mobilised by other commentators to argue for its improvement.

As Chapter 1 explained, Dickens critiques the damaging consequences that creative destruction had on the poor elsewhere in his fiction and journalism, and yet, contrary to his awareness of social injustices caused by demolitions, the ways that *Oliver Twist* was mobilised to argue for improvement show that Dickensian afterlives played a role in driving, or excusing, its effects. The popular images of the site that were circulated in the press and in debates about the area's conditions were constructed and mediated by people without experience of living in the district, who would almost always have been members of middle-class or wealthy social groups. In contrast, no evidence remains to suggest how the population living in Jacob's Island would have represented the district or themselves, or reacted to its improvement. Instead, these people are frequently replaced by fictional figures in later representations, which are deployed to reinforce the area's perceived criminal and destitute identity – as in the *Ragged School Union*'s reference to the 'Bill Sikeses' who had previously sought refuge there. However, this not only appears to justify the necessity of demolitions, but also disassociates their social impact from real people.

The very recently displaced residents of Jacob's Island were further dislocated from social participation or cultural history when *Oliver Twist* was reimagined as a representation of London's past and evoked as a carrier of cultural memories in public fora. 'Sites of memory [. . .] always point to the absence of living memory,' notes Astrid Erll in *Memory in Culture*.[79] Indeed, analysis of how Jacob's Island was reimagined through Dickens's description and characters provides a telling example of how cultural memories can efface and eclipse certain social groups. Whether by using characters to define certain communities as Other to a magazine's target readership, or by evoking descriptive passages as exemplary accounts of a shared historical past, a Dickensian vocabulary appealed to, and helped to construct, versions of collective identity. These were established by the popular dissemination of Dickens's works across multiple media, as much as by the fact that reference to Dickens aligns individual reading experiences with those of a wider public. Appropriations of Dickens in such contexts thus build on the assumption that readers already recognise him as a common cultural reference point. In so doing, however, users foreground the selectiveness of such imagined communities, as the social groups included in such imagined collectives were entirely separate from the slum residents represented through Dickensian imagery and characters.

Fiction effaces living memories. There can be no living memory of Dickens's London because it is fictional. Consequently, the articulation of Jacob's Island through Dickensian afterlives effects the deliberate removal of certain social histories. It is a critical truism to say that cultural memories are as dependent on forgetting as remembering: 'In processing our experience of reality, forgetting is the rule and remembering the exception.'[80] In the case of Jacob's Island, Dickensian afterlives are this exception; however, their fictional genesis signals a fracture between representations of space and lived space. This is reinforced by the fact that later commentators frequently deployed afterlives to illustrate a contrast between the site's past and present. Literary allusion marks a break with the possibility of preserving a 'true picture of the past' – which Walter Benjamin conceives as 'flashes' that bid their 'final farewell in the moment of its recognisability' – rather than a means of conceptualising a historical continuum.[81]

The cultural memories produced by Dickensian afterlives changed as further alterations to the built environment permitted Dickens's London to be nostalgically reimagined as a version of Old London. As early as the 1880s, Dickensian afterlives were produced that reconceived his portrayal of Jacob's Island in a picturesque style that emphasised its disconnectedness from modern London. In 1887, less than two decades after the writer's death, James Lawson Stewart produced a series of watercolour scenes from Dickens's novels in an urban picturesque mode. Stewart's representation of Jacob's Island both clings to, and departs from, Dickens's text (Plate 7). Some of the details of the scene are reasonably coherent with those in Dickens's description: 'Crazy wooden galleries common to the backs of half-a-dozen houses' line a waterway faced by 'windows broken and patched' (*OT*, p. 417). Stewart's painting preserves the dilapidation in Dickens's account; conversely, it is drawn in a comfortably picturesque rather than a threateningly noxious style. Depicting scenes characterised by 'contrast rather than [. . .] unity, [. . .] irregularity rather than [. . .] continuity, and [. . .] the fragment rather than [. . .] the whole', Stewart's urban aesthetic follows eighteenth-century picturesque art.[82] The jumbled houses are pleasantly irregular, the sepia tones are easy on the eye and the vanishing point is positioned off-centre, giving a piquant unpredictability to the environment portrayed. In contrast to Dickens's account, there is no indication that the area is dangerously polluted. Strollers cross the bridge in apparently amicable conversation while another person purposefully carries goods in a basket on her head. There is even a duck swimming on the waterway. If anything, it is the duck that signals the greatest single departure from Dickens's disgust at Jacob's Island's insanitary conditions and the 'slime' and 'mud' of Folly Ditch (*OT*, p. 417). Stewart's representation encourages the viewer to enjoy the scene, indicating a desire to linger in Dickens's London, like the strollers crossing the bridge in the painting.

Stewart's nostalgia conveys a sanitised vision of Old London, which eschews the dangerous connotations associated with dilapidated urban areas earlier in the nineteenth century. His reimagining of Dickens's scene was thereby permitted, in part, because the description in *Oliver Twist* no longer had a material counterpart. Like the ruins that were frequently the subject of picturesque art, the pleasure of viewing these images had to be 'at one remove' from the present, and 'softened by art'.[83] In other words, the viewer's aesthetic pleasure in dilapidated urban scenes would surely have been dampened if it could be seen to threaten another cholera outbreak. By the late 1880s, Stewart had no need to continue to agitate for topographic or sanitary reform. The social and environmental implications of *Oliver Twist*, and of its afterlives up to the 1870s, were effaced concurrently with the demolition of Jacob's Island. Stewart's nostalgic retrospective of the site and Dickens's fiction was therefore enabled by its material redevelopment.

The role Dickensian afterlives played in the construction of cultural memories was again reconceived when Jacob's Island was demolished wholesale in the early twentieth century. In the 1920s, three and a half acres of south London, including Jacob's Island, were destroyed. Instead of sparking positive narratives about the site's material progress, however, linked Dickensian afterlives popularised a perceived cultural identity founded on literary tourism. Newspaper reports detailing the 1920s redevelopment constantly refer to Dickens in their headlines: 'London to Lose Link with Dickens', 'Dickens' "Jacob's Island" To Go', 'Where Bill Sikes Died.

House to be Removed by L.C.C. Scheme of Demolition'.[84] Again obscuring the area's population and industries from view, these afterlives show that the imaginative association between *Oliver Twist* and Jacob's Island endured throughout numerous processes of material change in the district. Moreover, the impact that *Oliver Twist* had on how improvements were conceived is proven by the proliferation of Dickensian afterlives across multiple media and official and unofficial documents. An article in the *Southwark and Bermondsey Recorder* even states that Dickens's fiction was included in cartographic plans:

> Some doubt has hitherto existed as to the precise position of the house where Sikes died, but all doubts have been set at rest by Mr. G. W. Mitchell, a clerk, at Bermondsey Town Hall, who, when engaged on revising drainage plans at the offices of the London County Council, discovered one dated April 5th, 1855, on which was marked the house – one of the many 'cribs,' where Fagan [*sic*], the Jew, Bill Sikes, the robber, and their evil associates often met. [. . .] The house was at the back of what is now No. 18, Eckett-street, then known as Edward-street, in a court named Metcalf Court, which has been swept away, and is now occupied by the stables and yard of Messrs. R. Chambers and Co., Carmen contractors.[85]

Rediscovered during the planning of the 1920s demolitions, these drainage plans were found serendipitously but not randomly. Unfortunately, I have been unable to locate the documents within the course of my research; nevertheless, the discovery was reported in several newspapers, including *The Times*.[86] The remediation of *Oliver Twist* across these numerous contexts and channels shows that fiction was enmeshed in dialectical relations with how the city was conceived. Given that the exact location of Sikes's death is not named in the novel, Dickensian afterlives extend what details are made available in the text, and so continue to revise these relations between the material and the literary.

Even when afterlives selectively appropriate or alter the text, its various incarnations reveal that *Oliver Twist* has lingered in Jacob's Island's cultural identity ever since the novel was published – even though it also contributed to arguments for its demolition, which effaced the conditions it describes. By the end of the nineteenth century, the built environment did not contain relics of the cityscape that had inspired Dickens's representation. Warehouses replaced the crazy dwellings and the ditches were filled up. Aleida Assmann has argued, however, that the passing on of stories is fundamental to the way we construct cultural memories and interpret our material world.

> The shattered fragments of a lost or destroyed way of life are used to authenticate stories that in turn become reference points for a new cultural memory. That places require explanation, and their relevance and meaning can only be maintained through stories that are continuously transmitted.[87]

Dickens's significance to cultural memories of Jacob's Island is thus reinforced by the reproducibility and apparent constancy of his description, in contrast to the non-presence of the built environment he describes. Such uses of Dickensian afterlives effect acts of violence, as they can manipulate how the site's previous residents are perceived, or erase them from cultural history. By contrast, literary tourism continues to reinforce Jacob's Island's association with Dickens to this day. Plaques erected in the area by Southwark Borough Council register its association with *Oliver Twist* and embed references to the novel in a heritage trail in the district. Tracing Dickensian afterlives about Jacob's Island thus enables us to perceive how literature still affects how we conceive and construct the past and, through this, London's contemporary built environment.

Notes

1. 'The boundaries of this district on the West and North are St. Saviour's Dock and the Thames bank, which here begins to be called "Bermondsey Wall". On the South it is bounded by Dockhead and the road towards Rotherhithe, whilst on the east it is encircled by a tidal stream called the Neckinger' (Lees Bell, p. 37).
2. Ibid., p. 36.
3. Tales of the area's history vary, highlighting the obscurity of its past. Angus B. Reach explains that monks worked an industry of water mills on the site, part of which was later transformed into a semi-rural place of retreat called Cupid's Gardens, probably in the early-modern period (p. 16). However, Rev. W. Lees Bell states that 'what history it may have commences with the reign of Queen Anne' (pp. 36–7).
4. *Hansard*, vol. 120 (29 Apr 1852), cc 1283–315 (c. 1292).
5. Mayhew, 'A Visit to the Cholera Districts of Bermondsey', p. 4.

6. Shepard, p. 21.
7. Reach, p. 14.
8. Archaeological research in Jacob's Island has also indicated that its sanitary condition 'certainly was as bad as [Dickens] described, and quite possibly worse' (Saxby, p. 15).
9. London, Southwark Local History Library and Archive, 1265. *Bermondsey Improvement Commission: Committee of Health Minute Book* (1853), p. 79.
10. Goodlad, p. 526.
11. SLHLA, *Bermondsey Improvement Commission: Committee of Health Minute Book*, p. 34. The first petition to the landlord was recorded on 15 October 1853, when he was asked to take action within forty-eight hours. The landlord evidently ignored their order, for a week later 'The Clerks reported that the Owner of the 7 Houses in Metcalf Court having neglected to comply with the Magistrates orders to cleanse the Cellars of those Houses, Mr Duckett had pursuant to the direction of the Committee been employed and had emptied and cleansed the same at an expense of £12.15.0. which the Committee recommended to be paid, and that the Clerks, should be authorised by the Guardians to make proceedings against the Owner to recover the amount, together with the Costs and expenses of the Summons Notice and ordered proceeding consequent thereon' (ibid., p. 42).
12. Wohl, p. 18.
13. Charles Dickens, 'Preface to the "Cheap Edition" (1850)', in Dickens, *Oliver Twist*, ed. Philip Horne, pp. 461–4, p. 461.
14. Dickens, *Speeches*, p. 130.
15. At least initially, the MBW gave higher priority to the preservation of expensive properties than to ensuring sufficient housing for the poor: 'the Metropolitan Board of Works' Superintending Architect [told the Select Committee], when examining the Bill for Southwark Street in 1857, that the course given to it enabled them to skirt *several* expensive properties (including Barclay Perkins's Brewery – "That was a property which it was desirable to avoid") and save £200,000, while displacing fourteen hundred people living in the slums of Christchurch and St Saviour's. "No inconvenience is anticipated and the Bill does not contain any provisions," ran the written statement' (Dyos and Reeder, 'Slums and Suburbs', p. 367). Centralisation, therefore, did not ensure encompassing social or environmental reform. Nevertheless, the MBW's projects were conceived for public benefit. Their protection of private interests was probably influenced by wider trends in urban planning, which conceived slum demolitions as socially ameliorative, as well as being directed by considerations of efficacy and expense.
16. London's administration remained multi-faceted; the MBW operated alongside other authorities, like the existing public health agency in Britain, the General Board of Health (GBH). The GBH was a centrally

administered body; however, it was different to the MBW because, although the improvements recommended by the GBH were decided by a central board of inspectors, these developments were still administered at a parochial level. The GBH had the power to set up local boards of health, which would oversee matters relating to water supply, house drainage, sewerage and sewage treatment, and would also maintain roads and regulate new construction (Hamlin, p. 276).

17. Dickens, 'To W. W. F. De Cerjat, 30 November 1865', *Letters, Vol. 11*, pp. 114–17, p. 116.
18. Dodd, 'Modern Bermondsey', p. 20.
19. Lees Bell, pp. 42–3. Reverend W. Lees Bell was vicar of the parish of Christ Church in Bermondsey. A huge increase in the population of Bermondsey in the nineteenth century necessitated the formation of several new parishes (Malden (para 14 of 48)). Although originally in the parish of St Mary Magdalen in Bermondsey, Jacob's Island was united with some other impoverished neighbouring areas in 1848 to make the new parish of Christ Church (Lees Bell, p. 43).
20. Timbs, *Curiosities of London*, p. 50. Another reason that Dickens's description may have been able to adopt such imaginative authority in the case of Jacob's Island was the discrepancies between other accounts. Reports detailing the area in the nineteenth century are generally uncertain about Jacob's Island's specific location, variously attributing it to the districts of Bermondsey or Rotherhithe.
21. *Report of the Metropolitan Sanitary Association* (1850).
22. Rigney, *The Afterlives of Walter Scott*, p. 19.
23. Dodd, 'Modern Bermondsey', p. 20.
24. Wilkinson, n.p.
25. Nead, *Victorian Babylon*, p. 31.
26. Dodd, 'Modern Bermondsey', p. 20.
27. Ibid., p. 21.
28. Reach, p. 14.
29. Dodd wrote extensively for high-quality and popular periodicals, including sixty-five pieces for *Household Words* (*Dickens Journals Online*).
30. Douglas-Fairhurst, p. 144.
31. Goodlad, p. 536.
32. Ibid., p. 536.
33. Ibid., p. 531.
34. Reach, p. 12.
35. In *Victorian Babylon*, Nead argues that nineteenth-century writers referred to statistical analysis in textual accounts of the city in attempts to understand and represent the rapidly expanding city. However, it remained difficult to comprehend the city's vastness: 'Rather than offering any numerical truth about the city, therefore, these statistics evoked a poetic image of London as an immense open-mouthed body,

consuming everything that comes within its grasp' (p. 15). Searching the records of trials at the Old Bailey also reveals no mention of Jacob's Island. However, specific streets in that area are named, usually in relation to crimes of theft. For instance, in March 1839 William Watson, a resident of the area, was found guilty of stealing shirts and imprisoned for six months (*Old Bailey Proceedings Online* (www.oldbaileyonline.org, version 7.2, 18 October 2015), March 1839, trial of WILLIAM WATSON (t18390304-966)). While *Oliver Twist* may have brought the name 'Jacob's Island' into common usage, then, the area was not as invisible to London's populace as Reach suggests.

36. *Oxford English Dictionary Online* (last accessed 25 May 2017).
37. Dodd, 'Modern Bermondsey', p. 20.
38. Mayhew does, however, quote Dickens elsewhere in *London Labour and the London Poor*. In 'Of Second-hand Store Shops', for instance, he refers to Dickens as 'one of the most minute and truthful of observers' (p. 24, vol. 2).
39. Intersections between Reach's and Mayhew's writing are somewhat to be expected. Mayhew's 'Visit to the Cholera Districts of Bermondsey' was written in his role as 'Metropolitan Correspondent' to the *Morning Chronicle*. Reach was Mayhew's colleague. The *Morning Chronicle* sent correspondents to enquire into the 'Condition of England' in diverse regions. Reach was correspondent for the manufacturing districts at the same time as Mayhew pursued his metropolitan investigations.
40. Anthony Ashley Cooper (1850), 'Report of the General Board of Health on the Epidemic Cholera of 1848 & 1849', on *British Parliamentary Papers* (last accessed 5 Jan. 2014), p. 24.
41. Mayhew, 'A Visit to the Cholera Districts of Bermondsey', p. 4.
42. See, for instance, *Hansard*, 3rd ser., vol. 117 (5 June 1851), c. 463.
43. Janis McLarren Caldwell's work supports this statement. She argues that '[e]specially in his later fiction and journalism, Dickens insistently prioritises sanitation above any other kind of reform' (Janis McLarren Caldwell, 'Illness, disease and social hygiene', in Ledger and Furneaux (eds), pp. 343–9, p. 346).
44. Dickens, *Speeches*, p. 107.
45. Ibid., p. 107.
46. Anita McConnell, 'Laurie, Sir Peter (1778–1861)', on *Oxford Dictionary of National Biography* (last accessed 18 May 2013) (paragraph 3 of 5).
47. Charles Dickens, 'The Chimes', in *Charles Dickens: The Christmas Books*, ed. Michael Slater, pp. 149–245, p. 170.
48. Slater, 'Carlyle and Jerrold into Dickens', p. 524, fn. 55.
49. K. J. Fielding, 'Metropolitan Sanitary Association, 6 February 1850 [Notes]', in Charles Dickens, *Speeches*, p. 109.
50. Pettitt, *Patent Inventionsi,* p. 157.
51. Ibid., p. 158.
52. Dickens, '*To* Henry Austin', *Letters, Vol.* 6, pp. 69–70.

53. Slater, *Charles Dickens*, p. 304.
54. Charles Dickens, 'Preface to the "Cheap Edition" (1850)', p. 463.
55. Ibid., p. 463.
56. Ibid., p. 462.
57. Charles Dickens, 'Preface to the Cheap Edition (1850)', in *Martin Chuzzlewit*, pp. 783–4, p. 784.
58. Philip Collins calls Dickens 'a conscious manipulator of his readers' and hearers' emotions (though not an insincere one)' (p. 30).
59. Anon. (1850), 'Mr. Charles Dickens and Sir Peter Laurie', *Observer*, 21 Apr., p. 6.
60. Dickens, *Speeches*, p. 130. Italics in original.
61. Dickens, '*To* Henry Austin, 29 January 1850*', p. 18.
62. Elaine Hadley explains: 'When a person requested relief, he or she was to be given a choice: either come live in the workhouse and live the life of a pauper divorced from the market, or live without relief under the terms of the marketplace. In theory, if a person entered the workhouse, he or she acknowledged destitution and accepted the identity of a true pauper. If one did not accept this definition, one proved to be an independent labourer only disguised as a pauper, a person who could in fact work, as demonstrated by the decision to go home' (p. 92).
63. Hamlin, *Public Health and Social Justice in the Age of Chadwick*, p. 4.
64. *Letters, Vol.* 6, p. 18, fn. 4.
65. Ibid., p. 51, fn. 4.
66. Dickens, '*To* Henry Austin, 15 July 1850*', *Letters, Vol.* 6, p. 132.
67. Dickens thanks Austin for sending him a 'Report' in '*To* Henry Austin, 29 January 1850*', p. 18. The editors conclude that this may refer to the 'Report of the Metropolitan Commission of Sewers on the prevention of cholera by sanitary improvements, which cited improvements to Jacob's Island as an example of the cheapness of taking action' (*Letters, Vol.* 6, p. 18, fn. 5).
68. Beames, p. 88.
69. Dickens, '*To* Miss Burdett Coutts, 7 January 1853', *Letters, Vol.* 7, pp. 2–4, p. 3.
70. Anon., 'Charles Booth and Jacobs Island', *infed* (para 1 of 3).
71. Charles Dickens, 'Author's Preface (1867)', in Dickens, *Oliver Twist*, Vintage, pp. xiii–xvi, p. xvi.
72. Anon. (1872), 'Jacob's Island Ragged School, Bermondsey', *Ragged School Union Magazine*, Feb., pp. 34–8, pp. 35–6.
73. Ibid., p. 34.
74. Ibid., p. 36.
75. Ibid., p. 35.
76. Forster, pp. 157–8.
77. Jackson, *Jacob's Island*, p. 1.
78. 'Bermondsey' (1851), in *England's Census*, *Ancestry* (last accessed 16 Feb. 2013).

79. Erll, *Memory in Culture*, p. 24.
80. Ibid., p. 9.
81. Benjamin, 'On the Concept of History' (thesis V).
82. Nead, *Victorian Babylon*, p. 32.
83. Macaulay, pp. 454–5.
84. London, Southwark Local History Library and Archive, PC942.16413. *Press Cuttings File: Bermondsey*, Anon., 'Lair is Doomed', in *Daily Mirror* (30 Apr. 1924), newspaper cutting; London, Southwark Local *History Library and Archive*, PC942.16413. *Press Cuttings File: Bermondsey*, Anon., 'Dickens's "Jacob's Island" To Go' (15 Feb. 1923), newspaper cutting; Anon. (1920), 'Where Bill Sikes Died', *The Times*, 42491, 17 Aug., p. 7.
85. Jackson, *Jacob's Island*, p. 1.
86. Anon., 'Where Bill Sikes Died', p. 7.
87. Aleida Assmann, p. 292.

Coda

> In former times great objects were attained by great work. When evils were to be reformed, reformers set about their heavy task with grave decorum and laborious argument. [. . .] We get on now with a lighter step, and quicker: ridicule is found to be more convincing than argument, imaginary agonies touch more than true sorrows, and monthly novels convince, when learned quartos fail to do so. If the world is to be set right, the work will be done by shilling numbers.
>
> Of all such reformers Mr Sentiment is the most powerful. It is incredible the number of evil practices he has put down: it is to be feared he will soon lack subjects, [. . .] Mr Sentiment is certainly a very powerful man, and perhaps not the less so that his good poor people are so very good; his hard rich people so very hard; and the genuinely honest so very honest. Namby-pamby in these days is not thrown away if it be introduced in the proper quarters [. . .][1]

Anthony Trollope's satirical portrait of Dickens as Mr Popular Sentiment in *The Warden* (1855) touches on many of the questions *Dickens and Demolition* has explored. In what ways do literary works intersect with contemporary improvements? How are such developments envisioned and implemented, and by whom? Can the impact of fictional texts be traced in material change? Trollope represents a society in which literary novelty is a more 'powerful' driver of reform than rigorous research. In so doing, *The Warden* registers a shift in how such interventions are planned and implemented from earlier periods of development. One major change is in the personnel involved. Aside from the intercessions of authors, Trollope notes that '[w]e get on now with a lighter step', and so implies that women are adopting a more formative role. The narrator's stance on women's and Mr Sentiment's involvement is ambivalent. There are misogynistic and homophobic overtones to his use of the word 'namby-pamby', which connotes an 'insipidly pretty, affectedly or childishly simple' and 'effeminate' lack of 'vigour or drive' among this class of reformers.[2] Nevertheless, the satire also emphasises the instrumentality of diverse, and previously unlikely, actors in pushing through material change 'quicker' than before.

The greater speed of recent improvements is certainly represented as a positive development from the 'grave decorum and laborious argument' of former times; however, Trollope's narrator indicates that rushing through reforms makes it unlikely that they will adequately address the problems they seek to amend. Trollope's major criticism is that Mr Sentiment rapidly adopts and discards pet causes, and so does not take the time to engage with any of them thoroughly. Recalling Dickens's well-publicised dispute with Sir Peter Laurie only five years before, discussed in Chapter 5, Trollope even likens Mr Sentiment's approach to Laurie's unfounded and bombastic treatment of social issues. Laurie's catch-phrase assertion that he will simply 'put down' the people or behaviours to which he objects is ironically associated with Mr Sentiment. Likewise, the mawkish characterisation in his novels is presented as superficial and oversimplified, and his transient and careless engagement with social problems is aligned with the cheap and hasty production and consumption of his 'shilling numbers'. Conversely, though his style is sugary and ill informed, his arguments are 'not thrown away'.

Trollope's narrator finds Mr Sentiment's didactic style and 'namby-pamby' abrasive, but notes that the accessibility of his novels allows his works to manipulate his readers' emotions effectively. Indeed, Mr Sentiment's style is identified as one of the reasons why his works are able to drive contemporary reforms:

> The artist who paints for the million must use glaring colours, as no one knew better than Mr Sentiment when he described the inhabitants of his almshouse; and the radical reform which has now swept over such establishments has owed more to the twenty numbers of Mr Sentiment's novel, than to all the true complaints which have escaped from the public for the last half-century.[3]

The novel inspires positive action but Mr Sentiment himself is portrayed as calculating. This implies that his interest in social issues is ultimately self-serving. Thus Trollope's characterisation makes the reforms encouraged by his novels feel grubby. It insinuates that these good works are driven by selfish, capitalist motivations, foolishly missed by the reading public. Mr Sentiment is at fault for exploiting the gullibility of his readers, yet society is equally to blame. Just as Mr Sentiment's engagement with complex societal issues is likened to the disposable materiality of his monthly numbers, so the public's social conscience is presented as equally ephemeral. Literary novelty provokes speedy responses, while 'true sorrows' and precise evidence fail to stimulate a reaction.

Drawing attention to both the popularity and the mass dissemination of his fiction, *The Warden* attributes Mr Sentiment's power to influence a large portion of the public to a combination of stylistic, material and social factors. Similarly, Dickens's potentially instrumental sway in public matters depended on the fact that his career and richly extractable style coincided with a period in which processes of metropolitan improvement were fragmented between multiple interested parties and diverse areas in the city. Chapter 1 identified Dickens's popular appeal, and the public's reception of his novels as both realistic and imaginatively engaging, as reasons why his works dovetailed generatively with the specific contexts in which London's cityscape was changed in his lifetime. Dialectical relations between his fiction and the social processes driving material change in the mid-nineteenth century were enabled equally by his unique representation of urban life in his novels, and the widespread circulation and remediation of his texts. However, *Dickens and Demolition* has suggested that the straightforward cause-and-effect narrative implied by Trollope does not reflect the unpredictable routes by which Dickens's works had a material impact on London's built environment. In fact, the contributions that Dickens's fiction made to driving metropolitan improvements were often indirect.

Dickens and Demolition has argued that Dickens's legacies can be traced in surprising, physical effects in London's built environment. By exploring diverse afterlives of his fiction, as well as his interventions in contemporary urban issues, the book has proposed that the impact of literary works lingers in the world around us in ways of which we may not always be conscious. Indeed, Dickensian afterlives are traceable in demolitions that have erased areas of Old London from the capital. Demolitions were conceived as a means of addressing environmentally determined social problems. Consequently, Dickens's characters and descriptions were particularly useful as rhetorical or representational tools to identify specific slums as problem areas, or to reinforce their already negatively perceived social identities. Dickensian tropes offered a legible vocabulary with which contemporaries with a public voice imaginatively localised large and complex social problems in certain sites. Investing real locales with imaginative associations thus permitted the demolition of these places to be conceived as attacks on urban 'nuisances'. At a time when reforms were mostly localised within parishes, Dickens's works were used to associate wider social problems with certain places. Therefore, building on the work of urban theorists and scholarship on literary afterlives, this book has contended that there are multiple intersections between imaginative writing and processes of spatial or material production and destruction.

Contrary to Trollope's portrayal, in which Mr Sentiment calculates what causes his fiction will serve, practices of mobilising Dickens's work to comment on contemporary London reveal that his texts had polymodal afterlives that were usually beyond his control. This is not to say that he did not try to influence how other people interpreted and used his fiction. As Chapters 4 and 5 explored, Dickens participated in producing Dickensian afterlives, and attempted to direct how the social roles of his novels were understood by other people. His efforts met with mixed success. Although certain campaigners were keen to align their opinions with those of a popular and influential cultural icon, many others selectively appropriated and reinterpreted his fiction to suit their own agendas. This has political and social implications, particularly given the impact that urban modernisations had on the poor. Despite Dickens's lifelong commitment to social reform, Chapters 3 and 5 contended that his works were brought into dialogue with processes that resulted in the displacement of slum communities, and in eschewing their living memories from public images and cultural memories of the demolished sites. The documents that survive in archives disclose that Dickens's descriptions of vanished areas were repeatedly presented as accounts of certain metropolitan districts, despite – or, perhaps, because of – the melodramatic, 'glaring colours' in which these places were depicted in his fiction. Meanwhile characters were repurposed as representatives of the area's residents, so enabling simplified portrayals of complexly differentiated social spaces, which often demonised these less affluent places and people by implying that they were largely criminal.

One similarity between Trollope's satire and how slum clearances were conceptualised in the mid-nineteenth century is that – even when the desire to implement altruistic reform was genuine – improvements did not have the ameliorative impact that their advocates hoped. Chapter 1 explained that demolitions were conceived as part of a process of creative destruction, which would ultimately lead to improved living conditions for both the poor and the wealthy. Conversely, the fragmented and overlapping processes spurring London's modernisation during Dickens's lifetime meant that this imagined progress was rarely achieved. *Dickens and Demolition* has argued that it was because Dickens's career was concurrent with this simultaneously interventionist and piecemeal approach to urban planning that Dickensian afterlives were able to be repurposed as effective representational or rhetorical devices, which ultimately contributed to driving material change in certain areas of London. Dickensian afterlives facilitated the communication of coherent and clear representations of a capital that was changing before the public's eyes, as demolitions reordered the built environment and the population boomed. However, Dickens's efficacy in improvement campaigns was short-lived.

The material legacies of his imaginative works always depended on, and were limited by, economic, spatial and societal considerations. The disjointed processes of urban development, in which Dickensian afterlives could have a 'power' to highlight specific areas in need of reform, changed in the same year that *The Warden* was published. When the Metropolitan Board of Works (MBW) was formed in 1855, previously disparate bodies and unconnected projects were consolidated by this one organisation. The transition from a localised to a far-reaching approach to modernisation in London was not immediate or straightforward; nevertheless, 1855 marks the beginning of a new phase of urban development. Dickensian afterlives were still used as rhetorical or representational tools after this date but were less likely to influence material alterations to London's built environment. Not only had the city moved on – it no longer resembled his descriptions and Dickens's London was reimagined as a representation of its past – but also the MBW were able to take a broader view when they planned new developments, which made the practice of identifying specific places as problem locales less pertinent. Today, Dickens's legacies in the built environment are generally perceived in the preservation of historic buildings. However, *Dickens and Demolition* has examined how the cultural shift that reconceived his fiction as a historical document, rather than an urgent call for reform, began in his lifetime. Indeed, as Chapter 5 discussed, the improvements that he had advocated, or that Dickensian afterlives had been used to support, were not complete by the time that Dickens's London began to be nostalgically reimagined. Even though Dickens continued to campaign on behalf of various causes during his career, opposing views of his fiction, as either relevant or outdated, coexisted and overlapped in the mid-nineteenth century.

The diverse afterlives that this study has investigated indicate that heterogeneous historical and social pressures contributed to cultural and spatial production in the nineteenth century, but this miscellany is also characteristic of archival research. Studies of Dickens are particularly suited to archival enquiries. Dickens was popular and prolific, as well as widely adapted and freely appropriated in his lifetime. This has left a vast repository of Dickensian, and Dickens-inspired, products and allusions in circulation. Add to this Dickens's uniquely enduring popularity and celebrity status, which has made these artefacts valuable to collectors, and it is easy to see why material and textual traces have survived in abundance. Gaps and mysteries remain but, in comparison to other popular nineteenth-century writers – G. W. M. Reynolds, for instance – the evidence on which my conclusions are based is more readily available because of my specific focus on Dickens. The proliferation of Dickensian afterlives in multiple fora and debates possibly suggests that his material legacies are unique. Nevertheless, further research is required to determine whether other writers' work also intersected dialectically with processes of material change. Although this book has argued that the material effects of Dickens's works were enabled by a combination of contextual and stylistic factors, I hope that other studies will develop and question these assertions by investigating how literature interconnects with the production of space in other cities, countries and eras.

Written at a moment when all intellectual production is increasingly interrogated for 'impact', this study investigates the sometimes unexpected material effects of Victorian fiction. The imaginative and the practical are interconnected. Fiction literally played a part in bringing down buildings and redeveloping slum areas. *Dickens and Demolition* thus contends that literary work does not occupy a separate creative sphere, but intersects dialectically with capitalist and social pressures that shape the built environment. This has an impact on people as well as on places. We must recognise and appreciate how literary and popular culture is used to shape the world we live in, in both real and perceptual ways, so that we can identify occasions when it is mobilised to advocate potentially damaging change. Dickensian afterlives carry multiple agendas, and convey diverse connotations, which are based on the original texts in varying degrees. Rather than offering a stable symbolic vocabulary, appropriations of his works, and other popular culture, are porous and mobile. In seeing this, we can resist being led by the appeal of apparently recognisable imagery.

Notes

1. Trollope, pp. 153–4.
2. *Oxford English Dictionary* online (last accessed 6 Oct. 2015).
3. Trollope, p. 156.

Archival Sources and a Note on Method

Dickens and Demolition analyses an evidence base drawn from both material and digital collections. Alongside online newspaper, periodical and parliamentary archives such as *Newsvault*, *Hansard* and the *Old Bailey Online*, investigation of holdings in museums and libraries has revealed substantial stores of Dickensian afterlives. These have included: paintings and ephemera at the Museum of London; rare books and letters at the Huntington Library; plans, government acts and minute books at the Camden Local Research Library, Guildhall Library Archives, London Metropolitan Archives, Southwark Local History Library and Archive, and Westminster City Archives; and theatrical playbills, images and scripts at the Islington Local History Centre and the Victoria and Albert Theatre Archive. In juxtaposing these diverse findings, this study exposes interrelations between fictional and non-fictional representations of London and its modernisation.

It was necessary to examine both material and digital resources whilst researching this project because an over-reliance on any one collection would have probably skewed my findings. As Michael Foucault and Jacques Derrida long since argued, archives are ideologically loaded spaces, vulnerable to manipulation. The histories we construct from the artefacts they preserve can never be wholly objective or complete. In Walter Benjamin's words, 'any order is a balancing act of extreme precariousness'.[1] Searching archives held by a variety of different institutions, and in different media, thus allowed me to test my findings through comparison. Nevertheless, it is fair to say that this project would have been near impossible without the digitisation of press and periodical runs over recent years.

Digital tools such as keyword and date searches, cross-searching across different collections, and opportunities to visualise data in new ways – such as graphs that plot the frequency of search terms – enable users to navigate terrifyingly vast collections in accessible formats. Digitisation considerably expanded the scope of available resources, while the ability to search for keywords allowed me to identify, examine and trace the dissemination of Dickensian afterlives. Keyword searches return quantitative results, which have been helpful in identifying repetitive or cumulative reoccurrences of my search terms. However, the view is limited by the fact that this mode of investigation fails to pick up subtle or allusive intertexts, and so it was necessary to balance and interrogate these findings with wider browsing in both online and material collections. Moreover, even when keyword searches appeared to have uncovered a pattern, it was necessary to examine each appropriation of Dickens individually, as different users mobilised the same image or character for multiple purposes. Therefore, while my analysis certainly historicises textual encounters between Dickens's fiction and new contexts, and foregrounds 'sociopolitical and economic meanings', following Isobel Armstrong's recommendation in *Victorian Glassworlds*, these were questioned and problematised by 'semiological analysis'.[2]

What follows are lists of: (1) the newspapers and periodicals that I have searched using digital platforms; (2) websites and online archives that have extended the remit of this study to include official and legal arenas, as well as giving me further contextual information. Full references to each article quoted, as well as the sources I have drawn on directly from material archives, are included in the notes.

Newspapers and Periodicals Consulted

Aberdeen Journal
Age
All the Year Round
Athenaeum
Belfast News-Letter
Bentley's Miscellany
Blackburn Standard
Bradford Observer
Bristol Mercury
British Quarterly Review
Builder
Caledonian Mercury
Chambers's Journal of Popular Literature, Science and Arts

Citizen
Cleave's Gazette of Variety
Court Magazine and Monthly Critic
Daily Graphic
Daily Mirror
Daily News
Daily South Carolinian
Dundee Courier and Argus
Edinburgh Evening News
English Illustrated Magazine
Englishwoman's Domestic Magazine
Era
Evening Telegraph Star and Sheffield Daily Times
Examiner
Figaro in London
Frank Leslie's Illustrated Newspaper
Fraser's Magazine for Town and Country
Friend of India
Gentleman's Magazine
Glasgow Herald
Good Words
Hampshire Advertiser
Hampshire Telegraph
Harper's Magazine
Household Words
Hull Daily Mail
Illustrated London News
Illustrated Magazine of Art
Illustrated Review
Independent Statesman
Inter Ocean
Jackson's Oxford Journal
John Bull
Leeds Mercury
Leicester Chronicle
Leisure Hour
Literary Gazette: A Weekly Journal of Literature, Science, and the Fine Arts
Liverpool Mercury
Lloyd's Sunday News
London Journal
London Saturday Journal
London Society

Ludgate Monthly
Manchester Times
Methodist
Morning Chronicle
Morning Oregonian
Morning Post
Northern Star and National Trades' Journal
Observer
Once a Week
Pennsylvania Inquirer and Daily Courier
Penny Magazine
Punch
Quarterly Review
Ragged School Union Magazine
Reynolds's Miscellany of Romance, General Literature, Science, and Art
Reynolds's Newspaper
Royal Cornwall Gazette, Falmouth Packet & Plymouth Journal
Satirist; or, the True Censor of the Times
St. James's Magazine
Standard
Strand Magazine
Sussex Chronicle
Tatler
Temple Bar
Theatrical Journal
The Economist
The Times
Time
Tinsleys' Magazine
Tomahawk: A Saturday Journal of Satire
Trewman's Exeter Flying Post or Plymouth and Cornish Advertiser
Universal Review
Watchman
Woman's Signal

Websites Consulted

Ancestry <http://www.ancestry.co.uk/>
arthurlloyd.co.uk <http://www.arthurlloyd.co.uk/Theatreland/Theatreland.htm#18001870>
British History Online <http://www.british-history.ac.uk/>

British Library Website <http://www.bl.uk/>
British Parliamentary Papers <http://parlipapers.chadwyck.co.uk/>
Charles Booth Online Archive <http://booth.lse.ac.uk>
David Perdue's Charles Dickens Page <http://charlesdickenspage.com/>
Dickens 2012 <http://www.dickens2012.org/>
Dickens Journals Online <http://www.djo.org.uk/>
Dickens Our Mutual Friend Reading Project <https://dickensourmutualfriend.wordpress.com/>
Dictionary of Victorian London <http://www.victorianlondon.org/>
Field Lane <http://www.fieldlane.org.uk/heritage.php>
Hansard <http://hansard.millbanksystems.com/>
infed <http://www.infed.org/>
Jewish Virtual Library <http://www.jewishvirtuallibrary.org>
Kent University Library Website <http://www.kent.ac.uk/library/>
Map and Plan Collection Online <http://mapco.net/>
Museum of London Collections Online <http://collections.museumoflondon.org.uk/online/object/721431.html>
Old Bailey Proceedings Online <http://www.oldbaileyonline.org/>
Open University Website <http://www.open.ac.uk/>
Oxford Dictionary of National Biography <http://www.oxforddnb.com/>
Oxford English Dictionary <http://www.oed.com/>
Southwark Bridge Website <http://www.southwarkbridge.co.uk/history/old-southwark-bridge.htm>
UCL Bloomsbury Project <http://www.ucl.ac.uk/bloomsbury-project/streets/middle_row_holborn.htm>
Victorian Web <http://www.victorianweb.org/>
Wellcome Collection <http://www.wellcomecollection.org/>
World Cat <http://www.worldcat.org/>

Notes

1. Benjamin, 'Unpacking My Library', p. 60.
2. Armstrong, p. 15.

Select Bibliography

Primary Sources

Acton, William (1857), *Prostitution, Considered in its Moral, Social, and Sanitary Aspects, In London and Other Large Cities. With Proposals for the Mitigation and Prevention of its Attendant Evils*, London: John Churchill.

Ainsworth, William Harrison ([1839] 2010), *Jack Sheppard*, London: Penguin Books.

Almar, George ([1840]), *Olivier Twist. A Serio-Comic Burletta, In Three Acts. As Performed at the Royal Surrey Theatre Nov. 19th 1838*, London: Chapman and Hall.

Anon. (1893), *Baroness Burdett-Coutts: A Sketch of Her Public Life and Work Prepared for the Lady Managers of the World's Columbian Exposition by Command of Her Royal Highness, Princess Mary Adelaide, Duchess of Teck*, London: Unwin Brothers; Chicago: A. C. McClurg and Company.

Anon. (1867), *The Charles Dickens Dinner. An Authentic Record of The Public Banquet Given to Mr. Charles Dickens, at the Freemasons' Hall, London, On Saturday, November 2, 1867, Prior to his Departure for the United States. With a Report of the Speeches from Special Shorthand Notes*, London: Chapman and Hall.

Ashton, John (1888), *The Fleet: Its River, Prison and Marriages*, New York: Scribner and Welford.

Bagehot, Walter (1909), *Estimations in Criticism*, vol. II, London: Andrew Melrose.

Barnett, C. Z. ([1838]), *Oliver Twist, or, The Parish Boy's Progress. A Domestic Drama, in Three Acts*, London: J. Duncombe and Co.

Beames, Thomas (1852), *The Rookeries of London: Past Present and Prospective*, 2nd edn, London: Thomas Bosworth.

Burdett Coutts, Angela ([1865]), *The Ambulatory Schoolmaster. Miss Burdett-Coutt's* [*sic*] *Letter on the Extension of National Education. With Extract from "The Times" of January 19, 1865*, London: Strangeways and Walden.

— ([1865]), *A Summary Account of Prizes for Common Things Offered and Awarded by Miss Burdett Coutts at the Whitelands Training Institution. In Three Parts,* new edn, London: Hatchard and Co.

— (ed.) (1893), *Woman's Mission: A Series of Congress Papers on the Philanthropic Work of Women by Eminent Writers*, London: Sampson Low, Marston and Company.

Carpenter, Mary (1851), *Reformatory Schools, for the Children of the Perishing and Dangerous Classes, and for Juvenile Offenders*, London: C. Gilpin; Edinburgh: Adam and Charles Black; Dublin: J. and B. Gilpin.

Chadwick, Edwin (1843), *Report of the Sanitary Condition of the Labouring Population of Great Britain. A Supplementary Report on the Results of a Spiecal* [sic] *Inquiry into the Practice of Internment in Towns. Made at the Request of Her Majesty's Principal Secretary of State for the Home Department*, London: W. Clowes and Sons.

Chappell, Jennie ([1900]), *Noble Work by Noble Women: Sketches of the Lives of Baroness Burdett-Coutts, Lady Henry Somerset, Miss Sarah Robinson, Mrs. Fawcett, and Mrs. Gladstone*, London: S. W. Partridge and Co.

Collins, Wilkie (1873), *The New Magdalen: A Dramatic Story, In a Prologue and Three Acts*, London: published by the author.

Cunningham, Peter, F.S.A. (1850), *Hand-Book of London. Past and Present. New Edition Corrected and Enlarged*, London: John Murray.

Dickens, Charles ([1841] 2003), *Barnaby Rudge: A Tale of the Riots of 'Eighty*, ed. John Bowen, London: Penguin Books.

— ([1853] 2012), *Bleak House*, ed. Nicola Bradbury, London: Penguin Books.

— (1982), *Charles Dickens: The Christmas Books, Volume 1*, ed. Michael Slater, Harmondsworth: Penguin Books, 1982.

— ([1843] 2003), *A Christmas Carol and Other Christmas Writings*, ed. Michael Slater, London: Penguin Books.

— ([1850] 2004), *David Copperfield*, ed. Jeremy Tambling, London: Penguin Books.

— (2000), *The Dent Uniform Edition of Dickens' Journalism, Volume 4. The Uncommercial Traveller and Other Papers, 1859–70*, ed. Michael Slater and John Drew, London: J. M. Dent.

— ([1833–9] 1996), *Dickens' Journalism. Sketches by Boz and Other Early Papers, 1833–39*, ed. Michael Slater, London: Phoenix.

— ([1848] 2008), *Dombey and Son*, ed. Alan Horsman, Oxford: Oxford University Press.

— ([1861] 1993), *Great Expectations*, ed. Margaret Cardwell, Oxford: Clarendon Press.

— ([1854] 2003), *Hard Times*, ed. Kate Flint, London: Penguin Books.

— (1853), 'A Home for Homeless Women', *Household Words*, 7: 161, 23 Apr. 1853, 169–75.

— ([1837]), *Is She His Wife? or, Something Singular. A Comic Burletta, in One Act. No. 470. Dicks' Standard Plays*, London: John Dicks.

— (1965), *The Letters of Charles Dickens, The Pilgrim Edition, Volume One 1820–1839*, ed. Madeline House and Graham Storey, Oxford: Clarendon Press.
— (1969), *The Letters of Charles Dickens, The Pilgrim Edition, Volume Two 1840–1841*, ed. Madeline House and Graham Storey, Oxford: Clarendon Press.
— (1974), *The Letters of Charles Dickens, The Pilgrim Edition, Volume Three 1842–1843*, ed. Madeline House and Graham Storey, Oxford: Clarendon Press.
— (1977), *The Letters of Charles Dickens, The Pilgrim Edition, Volume Four 1844–1846*, ed. Kathleen Tillotson, Oxford: Clarendon Press.
— (1981), *The Letters of Charles Dickens, The Pilgrim Edition, Volume Five 1847–1849*, ed. Graham Storey and K. J. Fielding, Oxford: Clarendon Press.
— (1988), *The Letters of Charles Dickens, The Pilgrim Edition, Volume Six 1850–1852*, ed. Graham Storey and Kathleen Tillotson, Oxford: Clarendon Press.
— (1996), *The Letters of Charles Dickens, The Pilgrim Edition, Volume Seven 1853–1855*, ed. Graham Storey, Kathleen Tillotson and Angus Easson, Oxford: Clarendon Press.
— (1995), *The Letters of Charles Dickens, The Pilgrim Edition, Volume Eight 1856–1858*, ed. Graham Storey and Kathleen Tillotson, Oxford: Clarendon Press.
— (1997), *The Letters of Charles Dickens, The British Academy Pilgrim Edition, Volume Nine 1859–1861*, ed. Graham Storey, Oxford: Clarendon Press.
— (1998), *The Letters of Charles Dickens, The British Academy Pilgrim Edition, Volume Ten 1862–1864*, ed. Graham Storey, Oxford: Clarendon Press.
— ([1857] 2003), *Little Dorrit*, ed. Stephen Wall and Helen Small, London: Penguin Books.
— ([1844] 2004), *Martin Chuzzlewit*, ed. Patricia Ingham, London: Penguin Books.
— (1838), *Memoirs of Joseph Grimaldi. Edited by 'Boz.' With Illustrations by George Cruikshank. Vol. I*, 2 vols, London: Richard Bentley.
— (1838), *Memoirs of Joseph Grimaldi. Edited by 'Boz.' With Illustrations by George Cruikshank. Vol. II*, 2 vols, London: Richard Bentley.
— ([1870] 1972), *The Mystery of Edwin Drood*, ed. Margaret Cardwell, Oxford: Clarendon Press.
— ([1839] 2003), *Nicholas Nickleby*, ed. Mark Ford, London: Penguin Books.
— ([1841] 2008), *The Old Curiosity Shop*, ed. Elizabeth M. Brennan, Oxford: Oxford University Press.
— ([1838] 2007), *Oliver Twist*, London: Vintage Books.
— ([1838] 2009), *Oliver Twist*, ed. Philip Horne, London: Penguin Books.

— ([1838] 1993), *Oliver Twist: Norton Critical Edition*, ed. Fred Kaplan, New York and London: W. W. Norton and Company.

— (1851), 'On Duty with Inspector Field', *Household Words*, 3: 64, 14 Jun., 265–70.

— ([1865] 2008), *Our Mutual Friend*, ed. Michael Cotsell, Oxford: Oxford University Press.

— (1850), 'A Preliminary Word', *Household Words*, 1: 1, 30 Mar., 1–2.

— (1852), 'A Sleep to Startle Us', *Household Words*, 4: 103, 13 Mar., 577–80.

— (1983), *Sikes and Nancy and Other Public Readings*, ed. Philip Collins, Oxford and New York: Oxford University Press.

— ([1836] 1995), *Sketches by Boz*, ed. Dennis Walder, Harmondsworth: Penguin Books.

— (1960), *The Speeches of Charles Dickens*, ed. K. J. Fielding, Oxford: Clarendon Press.

— ([1859] 2003), *A Tale of Two Cities*, ed. Richard Maxwell, London: Penguin Books.

—, and Richard H. Horne, (1851), 'Shakespeare and Newgate', *Household Words*, 4: 80, 4 Oct., 25–7.

—, and W. H. Wills (1850), 'The Doom of English Wills', *Household Words*, 2: 27, 28 Sep., 1–4.

Dodd, George (1842), 'Modern Bermondsey', *London*, London: Charles Knight, 17–32, vol. 3.

— (1853), 'Overland Tour to Bermondsey', *Household Words*, 6: 149, 29 Jan., 462–6.

Edwards, Percy J. (1898), *History of London Street Improvements, 1855–1897*, London: P. S. King and Son.

Emson, Frank E. ([1881?]), *Bumble's Courtship. From Dickens's 'Oliver Twist.' A Comic Interlude, in One Act*. London and New York: S. French.

Forster, John ([1876] 1911), *The Life of Charles Dickens, With 500 Portraits, Facsimiles and Other Illustrations,* ed. B. W. Matz, London: Chapman and Hall, vol. 1.

Gavin, Hector (1848), *Sanitary Ramblings, Being Sketches and Illustrations of Bethnal Green*, London: John Churchill.

Godwin, George (1854), *London Shadows: A Glance at the 'Homes' of the Thousands*, London: George Routledge and Co.

— ([1859] 1972), *Town Swamps and Social Bridges*, New York: Humanities Press and Leicester University Press.

Gomme, G. Laurence, F.S.A. etc. (1898), *London in the Reign of Victoria (1837–1897)*, London: Blackie and Son.

Hill, Octavia (1875), *Homes of the London Poor*, London: Macmillan and Co.

— (1877), *Our Common Land (And Other Short Essays)*, London: Macmillan and Co.

Hindley, Charles (1881), *A History of the Cries of London, Ancient and Modern*, London: Reeves and Turner.

Hogg, John (1837), *London As It Is: Being a Series of Observations on the Health, Habits, and Amusements of the People*, London: John Macrone.

Hollingshead, John (1861), *Ragged London in 1861*, London: Smith, Elder and Co.

Hotton, John Camden, George Augustus Sala and Arthur Penrhyn Stanley (1870), *Charles Dickens: The Story of His Life*, New York: Harper and Brothers.

Jerome, Jerome K. ([1885] 2011), *On the Stage – And Off & Stage-Land*, Whiskey Priest.

Lees Bell, Rev. W., M.A. (1880), *The History of Bermondsey*, London: Shaw and Sparks.

Lewes, George Henry (1847), 'The Condition of Authors in England, Germany, and France', *Fraser's Magazine for Town and Country*, 35: 207, Mar., 285–95.

Macaulay, Thomas Babington (1849), *The History of England from the Accession of James II*, London: Longman, Brown, Green, and Longmans; Reprinted in Philadelphia: E. H. Butler and Co.

Martineau, Harriet (1855), *The Factory Controversy; A Warning Against Meddling Legislation, Issued by the National Association of Factory Occupiers*, London: Ireland and Co.

Mayhew, Henry (1861), *London Labour and the London Poor. The London Street-Folk*, London: Griffin, Bohn, and Company, vol. 2.

— (1849), 'A Visit to the Cholera Districts of Bermondsey', *Morning Chronicle*, 24939, 24 Sep., p. 4

Mayhew, Henry, and John Binny (1862), *The Criminal Prisons of London and Scenes of London*, London: Griffin, Bohn and Co.

Metropolitan Sanitary Association (1850), *Report of the Metropolitan Sanitary Association, British Library Website* <http://www.bl.uk/learning/images/makeanimpact/publichealth/large12722.html> (last accessed 19 Oct. 2015).

Morley, Henry (1852), 'Another Lung for London', *Household Words*, 6: 141, 4 Dec., 275–7.

Partington, C. F. (ed.) (1834), *Views of London and its Environs; Embracing their Antiques Modern Improvements, andc. andc. From Original Drawings by Eminent Artists. Vol. I*, London: Allan Bell and Co, 1834.

— (ed.) (1834), *Views of London and its Environs; Embracing their Antiques Modern Improvements, andc. andc. From Original Drawings by Eminent Artists. Vol. II*, London: Simpkin and Marshall.

Pemberton, Thomas Edgar (1888), *Charles Dickens and the Stage: A Record of His Connection with the Drama as Playwright, Actor and Critic*, London: George Redway.

Porter, G. R. (1836), *The Progress of the Nation, In Its Various Social and Economical Relations, from the Beginning of the Nineteenth Century to the Present Time, Sections I. and II. Population and Production*, London: Charles Knight and Co.

Reach, Angus B. (1846), *London Penetralia*, London: Bradbury and Evans.

Reynolds, G. W. M. ([1845] 1996), *The Mysteries of London*, ed. Trefor Thomas, Keele: Keele University Press.

Siddons, Henry, after Engle (1822), *Practical Illustrations of Rhetorical Gesture and Action*, London: Sherwood, Neely and Jones.

Thornbury, Walter (1872), *Old and New London: A Narrative of its History, Its People, and Its Places, Volume II. Illustrated with Numerous Engravings from the Most Authentic Sources*, 6 vols, London, Paris and New York: Cassell, Petter and Galpin.

Timbs, John (1867), *Curiosities of London: Exhibiting the Most Rare and Remarkable Objects of Interest in the Metropolis; with nearly Sixty Years Personal Recollections. New Edition, Corrected and Enlarged*, London: John Camden Hotten.

— ([between 1868 and 1889]), *The Romance of London. Historic Sketches, Remarkable Duels, Notorious Highwaymen, Rogueries, Crimes, and Punishments, and Love and Marriage*, London: Frederick Warne and Co.

Tristan, Flora ([1842] 1982), *The London Journal of Flora Tristan 1842; or, The Aristocracy and the Working Class of England*, trans. Jean Hawkes, London: Virago Press.

Trollope, Anthony ([1855] 2015), *The Warden*, Harmondsworth: Penguin.

Wilkinson, Robert (1819), *Londina Illustrata. Graphic and Historic Memorials of Monasteries, Churches, Chapels, Schools, Charitable Foundations, Palaces, Halls, Courts, Processions, Places of Early Amusement and Modern and Present Theatres, in the Cities and Suburbs of London and Westminster*, London: Robert Wilkinson.

Secondary Literature

Ackroyd, Peter (2002), *Dickens: Abridged Edition*, London: Vintage Books.

Adachi, Paul J. C., and Teena Willoughby (2011), 'The Effect of Video Game Competition and Violence on Aggressive Behavior: Which Characteristic Has the Greatest Influence?', *Psychology of Violence*, 1: 4, 259–74.

Agathocleous, Tanya (2011), *Urban Realism and the Cosmopolitan Imagination in the Nineteenth Century: Visible City, Invisible World*, Cambridge: Cambridge University Press.

Allen, Michael (2011), *Charles Dickens and the Blacking Factory*, St Leonards: Oxford-Stockley Publications.

Allen, Richard (2012), '*Oliver Twist*: The Late-Victorian Legacy', *Anglia Ruskin University Website*, Dickens' Legacy Conference, Anglia Ruskin University, Cambridge, 14 April 2012 <http://www.anglia.ac.uk/ruskin/en/home/faculties/alss/deps/english_media/research/research_activities/dickens_legacy.Maincontent.0007.file.tmp/oliver_twist_the_late_victorian_legacy.pdf> (last accessed 22 Jun. 2013).

Altick, Richard D. (1978), *The Shows of London*, Cambridge, MA, and London: The Belknap Press of Harvard University Press.

— (1980), 'Varieties of Readers' Response: The Case of *Dombey and Son*', *Yearbook of English Studies*, 10, 70–94.

Anderson, Benedict (2006), *Imagined Communities: Reflections on the Origin and Spread of Nationalism*, London: Verso.

Arac, Jonathan (1979), *Commissioned Spirits: The Shaping of Social Motion in Dickens, Carlyle, Melville, and Hawthorne*, New Brunswick, NJ: Rutgers University Press.

Armstrong, Isobel (2008), *Victorian Glassworlds: Glass Culture and the Imagination, 1830–1880*, Oxford and New York: Oxford University Press.

Arnold, Dana (ed.) (1999), *The Metropolis and its Image: Constructing Identities for London c. 1750–1950*, Oxford: Blackwell.

Aronofsky Weltman, Sharon (2011), '"Can a Fellow Be a Villain All His Life?": *Oliver!*, Fagin, and Performing Jewishness', *Nineteenth-Century Contexts*, 33: 4, 371–88.

Arundell, Dennis (1978), *The Story of Sadler's Wells 1683–1977*, Newton Abbot: David and Charles.

Assmann, Aleida (2011), *Cultural Memory and Western Civilization: Functions, Media, Archives*, Cambridge: Cambridge University Press.

Assmann, Jan (1995), 'Collective Memory and Cultural Identity', *New German Critique*, 65, Spring/Summer, trans. John Czaplicka, 125–33. [Originally published: Assmann, Jan, and Tonio Hölscher (eds) (1988), *Kultur und Gedächtnis*, Frankfurt/Main: Suhrkamp, pp. 9–19.]

Auslander, Leora (2005), 'Beyond Words', *The American Historical Review*, 110: 4, Oct., 961–1326.

Austin, J. L. (1962), *How to Do Things with Words: The William James Lectures Delivered at Harvard University in 1955*, Oxford: Clarendon Press.

Austin, Linda M. (2007), *Nostalgia in Transition, 1780–1917*, Charlottesville and London: University of Virginia Press.

Aycock Metz, Nancy (1979), 'The Artistic Reclamation of Waste in *Our Mutual Friend*', *Nineteenth-Century Fiction*, 34: 1, Jun., 59–72.

Bann, Stephen (1984), *The Clothing of Clio: A Study of the Representation of History in Nineteenth-century Britain and France*, Cambridge: Cambridge University Press.

Barrow, Rosemary (2010), 'Toga Plays and *Tableaux Vivants*: Theatre and Painting on London's Late-Victorian and Edwardian Popular Stage', *Theatre Journal*, 62: 2, May, 209–26.

Barthes, Roland (1989), 'The Reality Effect', in *The Rustle of Language*, trans. Richard Howard, Berkeley and Los Angeles: University of California Press, pp. 141–8.

Baucom, Ian (1999), *Out of Place: Englishness, Empire, and the Locations of Identity*, Princeton, NJ: Princeton University Press.

Baudrillard, Jean ([1981] 1994), *Simulacra and Simulation*, trans. Sheila Faria Glaser, Ann Arbor: University of Michigan Press.

Benjamin, Walter ([1982] 2002), *The Arcades Project*, trans. Howard Eiland and Kevin McLaughlin, prepared on the basis of the German volume edn by Rolf Tiedmann, Cambridge, MA, and London: The Belknap Press of Harvard University Press.

— ([1940] 2005), 'On the Concept of History', trans. Dennis Redmond, *Marxists Internet Archive* <https://www.marxists.org/reference/archive/benjamin/1940/history.htm> (last accessed 4 Apr. 2015).

— (1969), 'Unpacking My Library: A Talk about Book Collecting', *Illuminations*, ed. Hannah Arendt, trans. Harry Zohn, New York: Schocken Books, pp. 59–67.

Bennett, Tony ([1986] 1988), 'Media, "Reality", Signification', in Michael Gurevitch, Tony Bennett, James Curran and Janet Woollacott (eds) *Culture, Society and the Media*, London and New York: Routledge, pp. 287–308.

Berman, Marshall (1983), *All That Is Solid Melts Into Air: The Experience of Modernity*, London and New York: Verso.

Blake, Kathleen (1997), '"Bleak House", Political Economy, Victorian Studies', *Victorian Literature and Culture*, 25: 1, 1–21.

— (2009), *Pleasures of Benthamism: Victorian Literature, Utility, Political Economy*, Oxford and New York: Oxford University Press.

Blake Oleksijczuk, Denise (2011), *The First Panoramas: Visions of British Imperialism*, Minneapolis and London: University of Minnesota Press.

Bolter, Jay David, and Richard Grusin (2000), *Remediation: Understanding New Media*, Cambridge, MA, and London: MIT Press.

Bolton, H. Philip (1987), *Dickens Dramatized*, London: Mansell Publishing.

Booth, Michael R. (1991), *Theatre in the Victorian Age*, Cambridge: Cambridge University Press.

— (1981), *Victorian Spectacular Theatre 1850–1910*, Boston, London and Henley: Routledge and Kegan Paul.

Bowen, John (2000), *Other Dickens: Pickwick to Chuzzlewit*, Oxford: Oxford University Press.

Bowen, John, and Robert L. Patten (eds) (2006), *Palgrave Advances in Charles Dickens Studies*, Basingstoke and New York: Palgrave Macmillan.

Bowler, Peter J. (1989), *The Invention of Progress: The Victorians and the Past*, Oxford: Basil Blackwell.

Boym, Svetlana (2001), *The Future of Nostalgia*, New York: Basic Books.

Bradby, David, Louis James, and Bernard Sharratt (eds), *Performance and Politics in Popular Drama: Aspects of Popular Entertainment in Theatre, Film and Television 1800–1976*, Cambridge: Cambridge University Press.

Brake, Laurel (2015), 'Looking Back', *Victorian Periodicals Review* 48: 3, Fall, 312–22.

— (2011), '"Time's Turbulence": Mapping Journalism Networks', *Victorian Periodicals Review*, 44: 2, 115–27.

Brake, Laurel, Bill Bell and David Finkelstein (eds) (2000), *Nineteenth-century Media and the Construction of Identities*, Basingstoke: Palgrave.

Brake, Laurel, and Julie Codell (2005), 'Introduction: Encountering the Press', in Laurel Brake and Julie F. Codell (eds), *Encounters in the Victorian Press: Editors, Authors, Readers*, Basingstoke: Palgrave Macmillan, pp. 1–7.

Brantlinger, Patrick (1977), *The Spirit of Reform: British Literature and Politics, 1832–1867*, Cambridge, MA, and London: Harvard University Press.

Bratton, Jacky (2003), *New Readings in Theatre History*, Cambridge: Cambridge University Press.

Brewer, David A. (2005), *The Afterlife of Character, 1726–1825*, Philadelphia: University of Pennsylvania Press.

Briggs, Asa (1963), *The Age of Improvement 1783–1867*, London: Longmans, Green and Co.

Brodie, Marc (2003), 'Free Trade and Cheap Theatre: Sources of Politics for the Nineteenth-century London Poor', *Social History*, 28: 3, Oct., 346–60.

Brooks, Peter (1995), *The Melodramatic Imagination: Balzac, Henry James, Melodrama, and the Mode of Excess*, New Haven, CT, and London: Yale University Press.

Broughton, T. (2015), 'The Life and Afterlives of Captain Hedley Vicars: Evangelical Biography and the Crimean War', *19: Interdisciplinary Studies in the Long Nineteenth Century*, 20.

Buck-Morss, Susan (1989), *The Dialectics of Seeing: Walter Benjamin and the Arcades Project*, Cambridge, MA, and London: MIT Press.

Buckley, Matthew (2002), 'Sensations of Celebrity: Jack Sheppard and the Mass Audience', *Victorian Studies*, 44: 3, Spring, 423–63.

Burn, W. L. (1964), *The Age of Equipoise: A Study of the Mid-Victorian Generation*, London: George Allen and Unwin.

Butler, Judith (1999), *Gender Trouble: Feminism and the Subversion of Identity*, New York and London: Routledge.

Butt, John, and Kathleen Tillotson (1957), *Dickens at Work*, London: Methuen and Co.

Carey, John (1973), *The Violent Effigy: A Study of Dickens' Imagination*, London: Faber and Faber.

Chase, Karen, and Michael Levenson (2000), *The Spectacle of Intimacy: A Public Life for the Victorian Family*, Princeton and Oxford: Princeton University Press.

Chittick, Kathryn (1990), *Dickens and the 1830s*, Cambridge: Cambridge University Press.

Clark, T. J. (2004), 'The View From Notre-Dame', in Vanessa R. Schwartz and Jeannene M. Przyblyski (eds), *The Nineteenth-century Visual Culture Reader*, New York and London: Routledge, pp. 178–93.

Clark Hillard, Molly (2009), 'Dickens's Little Red Riding Hood and Other Waterside Characters', *SEL Studies in English Literature 1500–1900*, 49: 4, Autumn, 945–73.

Claybaugh, Amanda (2007), *The Novel of Purpose: Literature and Social Reform in the Anglo-American World*, Ithaca, NY, and London: Cornell University Press.

Clayton, Jay (2009), *Charles Dickens in Cyberspace: The Afterlife of the Nineteenth Century in Postmodern Culture*, Oxford: Oxford University Press.

Clemm, Sabine (2009), *Dickens, Journalism, and Nationhood: Mapping the World in Household Words*, New York and London: Routledge.

Cohen, Marc D. (2012), 'How Dickens Co-opted the British Theatrical Adaptation Industry in 1844: Part I', *Dickensian*, 108(2): 487, Summer, 126–40.

— (2012), 'How Dickens Co-opted the British Theatrical Adaptation Industry in 1844: Part II', *Dickensian*, 108(3): 488, Winter, 231–47.

Collins, K. K., and Alan M. Cohn (1982), 'Charles Dickens, Harriet Martineau, and Angela Burdett Coutts's "Common Things"', *Modern Philology*, 79: 4, May, 407–13.

Collins, Philip (1994), *Dickens and Crime*, 3rd edn, Basingstoke: Macmillan Press.

Connor, Steven (ed.) (1996), *Charles Dickens*, London and New York: Longman.

Cotsell, Michael A. (ed.) (1998), *Critical Essays on Charles Dickens's A Tale of Two Cities*, New York: G. K. Hall and Co.

Crary, Jonathan (2002), 'Gricault, the Panorama, and Sites of Reality in the Early Nineteenth Century', *Grey Room*, 9, Autumn, 5–25.

Cuming, Emily (2013), '"Home is home be it never so homely": Reading Mid-Victorian Slum Interiors', *Journal of Victorian Culture*, 18: 3, October, 368–86.

Daly, Nicholas (2015), *The Demographic Imagination and the Nineteenth-century City: Paris, London, New York*, Cambridge: Cambridge University Press.

— (2004), *Literature, Technology, and Modernity, 1860–2000*, Cambridge: Cambridge University Press.

— (1999), 'Railway Novels: Sensation Fiction and the Modernization of the Senses', *ELH*, 66: 2, Summer, 461–87.

Dames, Nicholas (2001), *Amnesiac Selves: Nostalgia, Forgetting, and British Fiction, 1810–1870*, Oxford: Oxford University Press.

Darling, Elizabeth, and Lesley Whitworth (eds) (2007), *Women and the Making of Built Space in England, 1870–1950*, Aldershot and Burlington, VT: Ashgate.

Daunton, M. J. (1990), 'Housing', in F. M. L. Thompson (ed.) *The Cambridge Social History of Britain 1750–1950, Volume 2 People and Their Environment*, Cambridge: Cambridge University Press, pp. 195–250.

Davis, Jim, and Victor Emeljanow (2001), *Reflecting the Audience: London Theatregoing, 1840–1880*, Iowa City: University of Iowa Press.

Davis, Paul (1990), *The Lives and Times of Ebenezer Scrooge*, New Haven, CT, and London: Yale University Press.

Davis, Tracy C., and Peter Holland (eds) (2007), *The Performing Century: Nineteenth-century Theatre's History*, Basingstoke and New York: Palgrave Macmillan.

De Certeau, Michel (1984), *The Practice of Everyday Life*, trans. Steven F. Rendail, Berkeley: University of California Press.

De Cesari, Chiara, and Ann Rigney (eds) (2014), *Transnational Memory: Circulation, Articulation, Scales*, Berlin and Boston: Walter de Gruyter.

De Maré, Eric (1973), *Victorian London Revealed: Gustave Doré's Metropolis*, Harmondsworth: Penguin Books.

Dennis, Richard (2008), *Cities in Modernity: Representations and Productions of Metropolitan Space, 1840–1930*, Cambridge: Cambridge University Press.

Derrida, Jacques, and Eric Prenowitz (1995), 'Archive Fever: A Freudian Impression', *Diacritics*, 25: 2, Summer, 9–63.

Dickens Fellowship, 'History of the Fellowship', on *Dickens Fellowship Website* <http://www.dickensfellowship.org/history-fellowship> (last accessed 3 Jun. 2017).

Dillon, Brian (2005), *In the Dark Room: A Journey in Memory*, Dublin: Penguin Ireland.

Dobraszczyk, Paul (2005), 'Sewers, Wood Engraving and the Sublime: Picturing London's Main Drainage System in the *Illustrated London News*, 1859–62', *Victorian Periodicals Review*, 38: 4, 349–78.

Donald, James (1992), 'Metropolis: The City as Text', in Robert Bocock and Kenneth Thompson (eds), *Social and Cultural Forms of Modernity*, Cambridge: Polity Press in Association with Blackwell Publishers and The Open University, pp. 417–71.

Douglas-Fairhurst, Robert (2011), *Becoming Dickens: The Invention of a Novelist*, Cambridge, MA, and London: The Belknap Press of Harvard University Press.

— (2002), *Victorian Afterlives: The Shaping of Influence in Nineteenth-century Literature*, Oxford and New York: Oxford University Press.

Drew, John M. L. (2003), *Dickens the Journalist*, Basingstoke: Palgrave Macmillan.

Dyos, H. J., and Michael Wolff (eds) (1973), *The Victorian City: Images and Realities*, vol. 1, London and New York: Routledge.

Easley, A. (2011), 'Introduction to the Special Issue: Victorian Networks and the Periodical Press', *Victorian Periodicals Review*, 44: 2, 111–14.

Eisenstein, Sergei (1977), 'Dickens, Griffith, and the Film Today', in *Film Form: Essays in Film Theory*, ed. and trans. Jay Leyda, San Diego, New York and London: Harcourt, pp. 195–255.

Elliott, Larry (2016), 'Dhaka's Dickensian Workhouses Should Shame Us All', *Guardian*, 18 Dec. <https://www.theguardian.com/business/2016/dec/18/dhaka-dickensian-workhouses-should-shame-us-all> (last accessed 3 Apr. 2016).

Eltis, Sos (2013), *Acts of Desire: Women and Sex on Stage, 1800–1930*, Oxford: Oxford University Press.

Erll, Astrid (2011), *Memory in Culture*, trans. Sara B. Young, Basingstoke: Palgrave Macmillan. [Original German language edn: Erll, Astrid (2005), *Kollektives Gedächtnis und Erinnerungskulturen. Eine Einführung*, Stuttgart: J. B. Metzlersche Verlagsbuchhandlung und Carl Ernst Poeschel Verlag.]

— (2006), 'Re-writing as Re-visioning', *European Journal of English Studies*, 10: 2, 163–85.

— (2011), 'Traumatic Pasts, Literary Afterlives, and Transcultural Memory: New Directions of Literary and Media Memory Studies', *Journal of Aesthetics and Culture*, 3: 1, 7186.

— (2011), 'Travelling Memory', *Parallax*, 17: 4, 4–18.

—, and Ann Rigney (2006), 'Literature and the Production of Cultural Memory: Introduction', *European Journal of English Studies*, 10: 2, 111–15.

—, and Ann Rigney (eds) (2009), *Mediation, Remediation, and the Dynamics of Cultural Memory*, Berlin and New York: Walter de Gruyter.

Fairclough, Mary (2013), *The Romantic Crowd: Sympathy, Controversy and Print Culture*, Cambridge and New York: Cambridge University Press.

Feldman, David (2013), 'Conceiving Difference: Religion, Race and the Jews in Britain, c. 1750–1900', *History Workshop Journal*, 76, Autumn, 160–86.

— (1994), *Englishmen and Jews: Social Relations and Political Culture, 1840–1914*, New Haven, CT, and London: Yale University Press.

— (2011), 'Jews in the East End, Jews in the Polity, "The Jew" in the Text', *19: Interdisciplinary Studies in the Long Nineteenth Century*, 13, 1–25.

Field Lane Foundation (1972), *The Field Lane Story*, London: Field Lane Foundation.

Fielding, K. J. (1951), 'Sir Francis Burdett and Oliver Twist', *The Review of English Studies*, 2: 6, Apr., 154–7.

Fitz-Gerald, S. J. Adair (1910), *Dickens and the Drama: Being an Account of Charles Dickens's Connection with the Stage and the Stage's Connection with Him*, London: Chapman and Hall.

Flanders, Judith (2012), *The Victorian City: Everyday Life in Dickens' London*, London: Atlantic Books.

Foote Whyte, William (1974), 'Social Organisation in the Slums', in Scott Greer and Ann Lennarson Greer (eds), *Neighborhood and Ghetto: The Local Area in Large-scale Society*, New York: Basic Books, pp. 37–45.

Foucault, Michel ([1975] 1995), *Discipline and Punish: The Birth of the Prison*, trans. Alan Sheridan, New York: Vintage Books.

— ([1967] 1984), 'Of Other Spaces, Heterotopias', *Architecture, Mouvement, Continuité*, trans. Jay Miskowiec, *MIT Website*, <http://web.mit.edu/allanmc/www/foucault1.pdf> (last accessed 26 Feb. 2014), pp. 1–9.

— ([1976] 1980), 'Questions on Geography', trans. Colin Gordon, *NYIT Website* <http://iris.nyit.edu/~rcody/Thesis/Readings/Foucault%20-%20Geography.pdf> (last accessed 26 Feb. 2014), pp. 173–82.

— 'What is an Author?', *Aesthetics, Method, and Epistemology: Essential Works of Foucault 1954–1984, Vol.* 2, ed. James D. Faubion, trans. Robert Hurley and Others, New York: New Press.

Francis, Emma, and Nadia Valman (2011), 'Introduction: Revisiting the Victorian East End', *19: Interdisciplinary Studies in the Long Nineteenth Century*, 13, 1–7.

Freedgood, Elaine (2006), *The Ideas in Things: Fugitive Meaning in the Victorian Novel*, Chicago and London: University of Chicago Press.

Freeman, Michael (1999), *Railways and the Victorian Imagination*, New Haven, CT, and London: Yale University Press.

Freud, Sigmund (1919), 'The Uncanny', *MIT Website* <http://web.mit.edu/allanmc/www/freud1.pdf> (last accessed 10 Jan. 2010), pp. 1–21.

Frisby, David (2001), *Cityscapes of Modernity: Critical Explorations*, Cambridge: Polity Press.

— (2002), *Fragments of Modernity: Theories of Modernity in the Work of Simmel, Kracauer and Benjamin*, Cambridge, MA: MIT Press.

Furneaux, Holly (2009), *Queer Dickens: Erotics, Families, Masculinities*, Oxford: Oxford University Press.

Gallagher, Catherine (2006), *The Body Economic: Life, Death, and Sensation in Political Economy and the Victorian Novel*, Princeton and Oxford: Princeton University Press.

— (1985), *The Industrial Reformation of English Fiction: Social Discourse and Narrative Form 1832–1867*, Chicago and London: University of Chicago Press.

Garrett, Peter K. (1980), *The Victorian Multiplot Novel: Studies in Dialogical Form*, New Haven, CT, and London: Yale University Press.

Garrod Bush, Nicole (2015), 'Kaleidoscopism: The Circulation of a Mid-century Metaphor and Motif', *Journal of Victorian Culture*, 20: 4, 509–30.

Gieseking, Jen Jack (2015), 'Useful In/stability: The Queer Social and Spatial Production of the Lesbian Herstory Archives', *Radical History Review* ,122, 25–37.

Gilroy, Paul (1999), *The Black Atlantic: Modernity and the Double Consciousness*, London and New York: Verso.

Gleadle, Kathryn (2001), *British Woman in the Nineteenth Century*, Basingstoke: Palgrave.

Goldberg, Michael (1972), 'From Bentham to Carlyle: Dickens' Political Development', *Journal of the History of Ideas*, 33: 1, Jan.–Mar., 61–76.

Goodlad, Lauren M. E. (2003), 'Is There a Pastor in the "House"?: Sanitary Reform, Professionalism, and Philanthropy in Dickens's Mid-century Fiction', *Victorian Literature and Culture*, 31: 2, 525–53.

Gordon, John (2011), *Sensation and Sublimation in Charles Dickens*, New York: Palgrave Macmillan.

Griffith, Ben W., Jr (1957), 'Dickens the Philanthropist: An Unpublished Letter', *Nineteenth-century Fiction*, 12: 2, Sep., 160–3.

Guéry, François, and Didier Deleule ([1972] 2014), *The Productive Body*, trans. Philip Barnard and Stephen Shapiro, Winchester and Washington: Zero Books.

Hadley, Elaine (1995), *Melodramatic Tactics: Theatricalized Dissent in the English Marketplace, 1800–1885*, Stanford, CA: Stanford University Press.

Hall, Thomas (2010), *Planning Europe's Capital Cities: Aspects of Nineteenth-century Urban Development*, Oxford and New York: Routledge.

Hamlin, Christopher (1998), *Public Health and Social Justice in the Age of Chadwick: Britain 1800–1854*, Cambridge: Cambridge University Press.

Hammond, Mary (2015), *Charles Dickens's Great Expectations: A Cultural Life, 1860–2012*, Farnham: Ashgate.

Hanbery MacKay, Carol (ed.) (1989), *Dramatic Dickens*, New York: St Martin's Press.

Harben, Henry A. (1918), *A Dictionary of London, Being Notes Topographical and Historical Relating to the Streets and Principal Buildings in the City of London*, London: Robert Jenkins.

Hardy, Barbara (2008), *Dickens and Creativity*, London and New York: Continuum.

— (1970), *The Moral Art of Dickens*, London and Dover, NH: Athlone Press.

Hartley, Jenny (2008), *Charles Dickens and the House of Fallen Women*, London: Methuen.

Harvey, David C. (2003), '"National" Identities and the Politics of Ancient Heritage: Continuity and Change at Ancient Monuments in Britain and Ireland, c.1675–1850', *Transactions of the Institute of British Geographers, New Series*, 28: 4, Dec., 473–87.

Hell, Julia, and Andreas Schonle (eds) (2010), *Ruins of Modernity*, Durham, NC, and London: Duke University Press.

Hibbert, Christopher, Ben Weinreb, Julia Keay, John Keay and Matthew Weinreb (1983), *The London Encyclopaedia*, 3rd edn, London: Macmillan.

Hill, Nancy K. (1981), *A Reformer's Art: Dickens' Picturesque and Grotesque Imagery*, Athens, OH, and London: Ohio University Press.

Hofer-Robinson, Joanna (2018), '"Kaleidoscopes of Changing Pictures": Representing Nations in Toy Theatre', *Journal of Victorian Culture*, 23: 1 Jan., 45–83.

Holder, Heidi J. (2003), 'Outcast London on the Victorian and Edwardian Stage', *Theatre History Studies*, 23, Jun., 49–64.

Hollington, Michael (1984), *Dickens and the Grotesque*, London and Sydney: Croom Helm.

Horne, Philip (2009), 'Introduction', in Charles Dickens, *Oliver Twist*, ed. Philip Horne, London: Penguin Books, pp. xiii–xliv.

House, Humphrey (1950), *The Dickens World*, 2nd edn, London, Oxford and New York: Oxford University Press.

Huguet, Christine (ed.) (2011), *Charles Dickens L'Inimitable/The Inimitable*, Paris: Democratic Books.

Huhtamo, Erkki (2013), *Illusions in Motion: Media Archaeology of the Moving Panorama and Related Spectacles*, Cambridge, MA: MIT Press.

Humphries, Steve, and Gavin Weightman (1983), *The Making of Modern London 1815–1914*, London: Sidgwick and Jackson.

Hunt, Tristram (2004), *Building Jerusalem: The Rise and Fall of the Victorian City*, London: Weidenfeld and Nicolson.

Hutcheon, Linda, with Siobhan O'Flynn (2013), *A Theory of Adaptation*, 2nd edn, Abingdon: Routledge.

Hyde, Ralph (1988), *Panoramania! The Art and Entertainment of the 'All-embracing' View*, London: Trefoil Publications in association with Barbican Art Gallery.

Inwood, Stephen (2005), *City of Cities: The Birth of Modern London*, London: Macmillan.

Jackson, H. W. (1948), *Jacob's Island*, London: Bermondsey Central Library. [First published in *Southwark and Bermondsey Recorder* (24 Aug. 1917 to 25 Jan. 1918).]

James, Russell D., MA (2004), 'All Holdings are Local: Archivists and Local Government Archives', *Journal of Archival Organization*, 2: 3, 75–82.

Jarvie, Paul A. (2005), *Ready to Trample on All Human Law: Financial Capitalism in the Fiction of Charles Dickens*, New York and London: Routledge.

John, Juliet (ed.) (2006), *Charles Dickens's Oliver Twist: A Sourcebook*, London and New York: Routledge.

— (2010), *Dickens and Mass Culture*, Oxford and New York: Oxford University Press.

— (2012), 'Global Dickens: A Response to John Jordan', *Literature Compass*, 9: 7, 10 Jul., 502–7.

— (ed.) (2012), *Dickens and Modernity*, Cambridge: D. S. Brewer.

Jones, Colin (2006), *Paris: Biography of a City*, London: Penguin Books, 2006.

—, Josephine McDonagh and Jon Mee (eds), (2009) *Charles Dickens, A Tale of Two Cities and the French Revolution*, Basingstoke: Palgrave Macmillan.

Jordan, John O. (ed.) (2001), *The Cambridge Companion to Charles Dickens*, Cambridge: Cambridge University Press.

— (2009), 'Global Dickens', *Literature Compass*, 6: 6, 16 Oct., 1211–23.

—, and Robert L. Patten (eds) (1995), *Literature in the Marketplace: Nineteenth-century British Publishing and Reading Practices*, Cambridge: Cambridge University Press.

Jordanova, Ludmilla (2000), *History in Practice*, London: Arnold.

Kafka, Ben (2012), *The Demon of Writing: Powers and Failures of Paperwork*, New York: Zone Books.

Keating, Peter (ed.) (1976), *Into Unknown England 1866–1913: Selections from the Social Explorers*, Manchester: Manchester University Press.

Kirkland, Richard (2012), 'Reading the Rookery: The Social Meaning of an Irish Slum in Nineteenth-century London', *New Hibernia Review*, 16: 1, Spring, 16–30.

Koven, Seth (2004), *Slumming: Sexual and Social Politics in Victorian London*, Princeton and Oxford: Princeton University Press.

Kucich, John (1987), *Repression in Victorian Fiction: Charlotte Brontë, George Eliot, and Charles Dickens*, Berkeley, Los Angeles and London: University of California Press.

Kukathas, Chandran (1998), 'Liberalism and Multiculturalism: The Politics of Indifference', *Political Theory*, 26: 5, Oct., 686–99.

Lane, Lauriat, Jr (1958), 'Dickens' Archetypal Jew', *PLA*, 73: 1, 94–100.

Ledger, Sally (2007), *Dickens and the Popular Radical Imagination*, Cambridge: Cambridge University Press.

—, and Holly Furneaux (eds) (2011), *Charles Dickens in Context*, Cambridge: Cambridge University Press.

Lefebvre, Henri (1991), *The Production of Space*, trans. Donald Nicholson-Smith, Oxford and Cambridge, MA: Blackwell.

Leitch, Thomas (2007), *Film Adaptation and its Discontents: From Gone with the Wind to The Passion of the Christ*, Baltimore: John Hopkins University Press.

Lewis, Susan S. ([2012]), 'The Artistic and Architectural Patronage of Angela Burdett Coutts', unpublished doctoral thesis, Royal Holloway.

Litvak, Joseph (1992), *Caught in the Act: Theatricality in the Nineteenth-century English Novel*, Berkeley, Los Angeles and Oxford: University of California Press.

London Topographical Society (1982), *The A to Z of Georgian London*, London: London Topographical Society.

Lowenthal, David (1985), *The Past is a Foreign Country*, Cambridge: Cambridge University Press.

Lucas, John (1980), *The Melancholy Man: A Study of Dickens's Novels*, Brighton: Harvester Press.

Lynch, Kevin (1960), *The Image of the City*, Cambridge, MA: Technology Press and Harvard University Press.

Macaulay, Rose (1966), *Pleasure of Ruins*, London: Thames and Hudson.

McCann, Andrew (2011), 'Ruins, Refuse, and the Politics of Allegory in The Old Curiosity Shop', *Nineteenth-century Literature*, 66: 2, Sep., 170–94.

McDonagh, Josephine (2003), *Child Murder and British Culture 1720–1900*, Cambridge: Cambridge University Press.

— (2010), 'On Settling and Being Unsettled: Legitimate Settlement around 1850', in Margot Finn, Michael Lobban and Jenny Bourne Taylor (eds), *Legitimacy and Illegitimacy in Nineteenth-century Law, Literature and History*, Houndsmill: Palgrave Macmillan, pp. 48–66.

McKee, Patricia (2014), *Reading Constellations: Urban Modernity in Victorian Fiction*, Oxford: Oxford University Press.

Mackenzie, Hazel, and Ben Winyard (eds) (2013), *Charles Dickens and the Mid-Victorian Press, 1850–1870*, Buckingham: University of Buckingham Press.

McMaster, Juliet (1987), *Dickens the Designer*, Totowa, NJ: Barnes and Noble Books.

Magnet, Myron (1985), *Dickens and the Social Order*, Philadelphia: University of Pennsylvania Press.

Maguire, Hugh (2000), 'The Victorian Theatre as a Home from Home', *Journal of Design History*, 13: 2, 107–21.

Malden, H. E. (ed.) (1912), '"Parishes: Bermondsey", in *A History of the County of Surrey, 4* (1912), 17–24', *British History Online* <http://www.british-history.ac.uk> (last accessed 13 Dec. 2013).

Malik, Rachel (2012), 'Stories Many, Fast and Slow: *Great Expectations* and the Mid-Victorian Horizon of the Publishable', *English Literary History*, 79: 2, Summer, 477–500.

Mancoff, Debra N., and D. J. Trela (eds) (1996), *Victorian Urban Settings: Essays on the Nineteenth-century City and its Contexts*, New York and London: Garland Publishing.

Mandler, Peter, 'Demolition', *Inventing Urban Modernity: Building the Present by Constructing the Past, City-centric Symposium,* King's College London, London, 23 Jun. 2014, unpublished keynote address.

— (2002), *History and National Life*, London: Profile Books.

Margary, Harry (1987), *The A to Z of Victorian London*, Lympne Castle, Kent: Harry Margary, in association with Guildhall Library, London.

Martínez Alfaro, María Jesús (1996), 'Intertextuality: Origins and Development of the Concept', *Atlantis*, 18: 1/2, Jun.–Dec., pp. 268–85.

Matus, Jill L. (2009), *Shock, Memory and the Unconscious in Victorian Fiction*, Cambridge: Cambridge University Press.

Mays, Kelly J. (2011), 'Looking Backward, Looking Forward: The Victorians in the Rearview Mirror of Future History', *Victorian Studies*, 53: 3, Spring, 445–56.

Mazzeno, Laurence W. (2008), *The Dickens Industry: Critical Perspectives 1836–2005*, Rochester, NY: Camden House.

Meisel, Martin (1983), *Realizations: Narrative, Pictorial, and Theatrical Arts in Nineteenth-century England*, Princeton, NJ: Princeton University Press.

Mellor, Leo (2011), *Reading the Ruins: Modernism, Bombsites and British Culture*, Cambridge: Cambridge University Press.

Melman, Billie (2006), *The Culture of History: English Uses of the Past 1800–1953*, Oxford: Oxford University Press.
Miller, D. A. (1988), *The Novel and the Police*, Berkeley, Los Angeles and London: University of California Press.
Miller, Henry J. (2009), 'John Leech and the Shaping of the Victorian Cartoon: The Context of Respectability', *Victorian Periodicals Review*, 42: 3, Fall, 267–91.
Miller, J. Hillis (1958), *Charles Dickens: The World of His Novels*, Cambridge, MA: Harvard University Press; London: Oxford University Press.
— (1977), 'The Critic as Host', *Critical Inquiry*, 3: 3, Spring, 439–47.
— (1990), *Victorian Subjects*, Hemel Hempstead: Harvester Wheatsheaf.
Moody, Jane (2000), *Illegitimate Theatre in London, 1770–1840*, Cambridge: Cambridge University Press.
Moore, Grace (2004), *Dickens and Empire: Discourses of Class, Race and Colonialism in the Works of Charles Dickens*, Aldershot: Ashgate.
Morley, Malcolm (1947), 'Early Dramas of Oliver Twist', *Dickensian*, 43: 282, Spring, 74–9.
Morton, Timothy (2009), *Ecology Without Nature: Rethinking Environmental Aesthetics*, Cambridge, MA, and London: Harvard University Press.
Mowry Roberts, Vera (1966), 'New Viewpoints on Nineteenth Century Scene Design', *Educational Theatre Journal*, 18: 1, Mar., 41–6.
Mukherji, Sajni (1981), 'Telescopic Philanthropy: Attitudes to Charity and the Empire in Charles Dickens', *Economic and Political Weekly*, 16: 42/43, Oct., 9–18.
Mussell, James, 'Cohering Knowledge in the Nineteenth Century: Form, Genre and Periodical Studies', *Victorian Periodicals Review*, 42: 1, Spring, 93–103.
— (2014), 'Elemental Forms: The Newspaper as Popular Genre in the Nineteenth Century', *Media History*, 20: 1, 4–20.
— (2012), *The Nineteenth-century Press in the Digital Age*, Basingstoke: Palgrave Macmillan.
— (2015), 'Repetition: Or, "In Our Last"', *Victorian Periodicals Review*, 48: 3, Fall, 343–58.
Nead, Lynda (1990), *Myths of Sexuality: Representations of Women in Victorian Britain*, Oxford: Basil Blackwell.
— (2000), *Victorian Babylon: People, Streets and Images in Nineteenth-century London*, New Haven, CT, and London: Yale University Press.
Newsom, Robert (1977), *Dickens on the Romantic Side of Familiar Things: Bleak House and the Novel Tradition*, New York: Columbia University Press.
Nisbet, Ada, and Blake Nevius (eds) (1971), *Dickens Centennial Essays*, Berkeley, Los Angeles and London: University of California Press.
Nora, Pierre (1989), 'Between Memory and History: *Les Lieux de Mémoire*', trans. Marc Roudebush, *Representations*, 26, Spring, 7–24.

Nord, Deborah Epstein (1995), *Walking the Victorian Streets: Women, Representation, and the City*, Ithaca, NY, and London: Cornell University Press.

Novak, Daniel A. (2008), *Realism, Photography, and Nineteenth-century Fiction*, Cambridge: Cambridge University Press.

O'Neill, Brendan (2017), 'The Grenfell Tower Inferno Shames London', *Spectator*, 15 Jun., <https://blogs.spectator.co.uk/2017/06/grenfell-tower-inferno-shames-london/#> (last accessed 26 Jun. 2017).

Orlando, Francesco (2006), *Obsolete Objects in the Literary Imagination: Ruins, Relics, Rarities, Rubbish, Uninhabited Places, and Hidden Treasures*, trans. Gabriel Pihas and Daniel Seidel, with the collaboration of Alessandra Grego, New Haven, CT, and London: Yale University Press.

Orton, Diana (1980), *Made of Gold: A Biography of Angela Burdett Coutts*, London: Hamish Hamilton.

Orwell, George ([1940] 2012), *Charles Dickens*, eBooks@Adelaide, University of Adelaide Library <http://ebooks.adelaide.edu.au/o/orwell/george/charles-dickens/> (last accessed 27 Feb. 2014).

Palmer, William J. (1974), 'The Movement of History in *Our Mutual Friend*', *PMLA*, 89: 3, May, 487–95.

Palmeri, Frank (2004), 'Cruikshank, Thackeray, and the Victorian Eclipse of Satire', *SEL Studies in English Literature 1500–1900*, 44: 4, Fall, 753–77.

Parker, Andrew, and Eve Kosofsky Sedgwick (eds) (1995), *Performativity and Performance*, London and New York: Routledge.

Parody, Clare (2011), 'Franchising/Adaptation', *Adaptation*, 4: 2, Jul., 210–18.

Paroissien, David (ed.) (2008), *A Companion to Charles Dickens*, Malden, Oxford and Victoria: Blackwell.

Patten, Robert L. (2012), *Charles Dickens and 'Boz': The Birth of the Industrial-Age Author*, Cambridge: Cambridge University Press.

Pearce, Susan M. (ed.) (1994), *Interpreting Objects and Collections*, London and New York: Routledge.

Penner, Louise, and Tabitha Sparks (eds) (2016), *Victorian Medicine and Popular Culture*, Abingdon and New York: Routledge.

Pettitt, Clare (2004), *Patent Inventions – Intellectual Property and the Victorian Novel*, Oxford: Oxford University Press.

— (2009), 'Peggotty's Work-box: Victorian Souvenirs and Material Memory', *Romanticism and Victorianism on the Net*, 53, Feb., <http://www.erudit.org/revue/ravon/2009/v/n53/029896ar.html> (last accessed 4 Apr. 2013).

Philpott, Thomas Lee (1978), *The Slum and the Ghetto: Neighbourhood Deterioration and Middle-class Reform, Chicago, 1880–1930*, New York: Oxford University Press.

Philpotts, Trey (2014), *The Companion to Dombey and Son*, Liverpool: Liverpool University Press.

— (2014), 'Dickens, the Metropolis and the Railway: Displacement or Progress?', *Dickens Quarterly*, 31: 4, Dec., 334–42.

Picard, Liza (2005), *Victorian London: The Life of a City 1840–1870*, London: Weidenfeld and Nicolson.

Piggott, Gillian (2012), *Dickens and Benjamin: Moments of Revelation, Fragments of Modernity*, Farnham: Ashgate.

Plotz, John (2000), *The Crowd: British Literature and Public Politics*, Berkeley, Los Angeles and London: University of California Press.

Poovey, Mary (1995), *Making a Social Body: British Cultural Formation, 1830–1864*, Chicago and London: University of Chicago Press.

Porter, Roy (2000), *London: A Social History*, London: Penguin Books.

Prochaska, F. K. (1980), *Women and Philanthropy in Nineteenth-century England*, Oxford: Clarendon Press.

Pykett, Lyn (2002), *Charles Dickens*, Basingstoke: Palgrave.

Radcliffe, Caroline, and Kate Mattacks (2009), 'From Analogues to Digital: New Resources in Nineteenth-century Theatre', *19: Interdisciplinary Studies in the Long Nineteenth Century*, 8.

Ragussis, Michael (2010), *Theatrical Nation: Jews and Other Outlandish Englishmen in Georgian Britain*, Philadelphia: University of Pennsylvania Press.

Reed, John R. (1999), 'Dickens on Jacob's Island and the Functions of Literary Description', *Narrative*, 7: 1, Jan., 22–36.

Richardson, Ruth (2013), 'At the Workhouse on Cleveland St', *Spitalfields Life*, 12 Oct. <http://spitalfieldslife.com/2013/10/12/at-the-workhouse-on-cleveland-st/> (last accessed 13 Aug 2015).

— (2012), *Dickens and the Workhouse: Oliver Twist and the London Poor*, Oxford: Oxford University Press.

—, and Robert Thorne (1994), *The Builder: Illustrations Index 1843–1883*, London: Builder Group and Hutton and Rostron.

Rigney, Ann (2012), *The Afterlives of Walter Scott*, Oxford: Oxford University Press.

Robbins, Bruce (1990), 'Telescopic Philanthropy: Professionalism and Responsibility in *Bleak House*', Homi K. Bhabha (ed.), *Nation and Narration*, London and New York: Routledge, pp. 213–30.

Roberts, Doreen (1993), 'Introduction', in Charles Dickens, *Bleak House*, ed. Doreen Roberts, Ware: Wordsworth Editions, pp. v–xix.

Robinson, Alan (2004), *Imagining London, 1770–1900*, Basingstoke: Palgrave Macmillan.

Robinson, Brian (1996), 'Charles Dickens and London: The Visible and the Opaque', *GeoJournal*, 38: 1 (*Geography and Literature*), Jan., 59–74.

Romano, John (1978), *Dickens and Reality*, New York: Columbia University Press.

Rosenberg, John D. (2005), *Elegy for an Age: The Presence of the Past in Victorian Literature*, London: Anthem Press.

Samuel, Raphael (1994), *Theatres of Memory Volume 1: Past and Present in Contemporary Culture*, London and New York: Verso.

Sanders, Andrew (2003), *Charles Dickens*, Oxford and New York: Oxford University Press.

— (2001), *Dickens and the Spirit of the Age*, Oxford: Clarendon Press.

Sanders, Julie (2006), *Adaptation and Appropriation*, London and New York: Routledge.

Saxby, David (2012), 'Digging Jacob's Island: A New Chapter for *Oliver Twist*', *Current Archaeology*, 22: 12, Mar., 12–17.

Schlicke, Paul (1985), *Dickens and Popular Entertainment*, London, Boston and Sydney: Allen and Unwin.

Schwarzbach, F. S. (1979), *Dickens and the City*, London: Athlone Press.

Seaman, L. C. B. (1973), *Life in Victorian London*, London: B. T. Batsford.

Seed, David (2004), 'Touring the Metropolis: The Shifting Subjects of Dickens's London Sketches', *The Yearbook of English Studies*, 34, 155–70.

Sen, Sambudha (2008), 'Hogarth, Egan, Dickens, and the Making of an Urban Aesthetic', *Representations*, 103: 1, Summer, 84–106.

— (2009), 'Radical Satire and Respectability: Comic Imagination in Hone, Jerrold and Dickens', in Aruna Krishnamurthy (ed.), *The Working-Class Intellectual in Eighteenth- and Nineteenth-century Britain*, Farnham: Ashgate, pp. 143–65.

Shannon, Mary L. (2015), *Dickens, Reynolds, and Mayhew on Wellington Street: The Print Culture of a Victorian Street*, Farnham: Ashgate.

Shattock, Joanne (2011), 'Professional Networking, Masculine and Feminine', *Victorian Periodicals Review*, 44: 2, 128–40.

Shepard, Will ([1977]), 'The Administration and Financing of Sewer Construction in Bermondsey, 1851–1860', unpublished doctoral thesis, London School of Economics.

Sheppard, Francis (1971), *London 1808–1870: The Infernal Wen*, London: Secker and Warburg.

— (1988), *London: A History*, Oxford: Oxford University Press.

Sicher, Efraim (2003), *Rereading the City Rereading Dickens: Representation, the Novel, and Urban Realism*, New York: AMS Press.

Skilton, David (2007), 'Tourists at the Ruin of London: The Metropolis and the Struggle for Empire', *Cercles*, 17, 93–119.

Slater, Michael (1970), 'Carlyle and Jerrold into Dickens: A Study of The Chimes', *Nineteenth-Century Fiction*, 24: 4, Charles Dickens Centennial, Mar., 506–26.

— (2009), *Charles Dickens*, New Haven, CT, and London: Yale University Press.

— (1983), *Dickens and Women*, London, Melbourne and Toronto: J. M. Dent and Sons.

Smith, Grahame (1968), *Dickens, Money, and Society*, Berkeley and Los Angeles: University of California Press.

Smith, Neil (1990), *Uneven Development: Nature, Capital and the Production of Space*, Oxford: Basil Blackwell.

—, and Peter Williams (eds) (1986), *Gentrification of the City*, Boston: Allen and Unwin.

Stallybrass, Peter, and Allon White (1986), *The Politics and Poetics of Transgression*, London: Methuen.

Stam, Robert (2005), 'Introduction: The Theory and Practice of Adaptation', in Robert Stam and Alessandra Raengo (eds), *Literature and Film: A Guide to the Theory and Practice of Film Adaptation*, Malden, Oxford and Victoria: Blackwell Publishing, pp. 1–52.

Stamp, Gavin (1986), *The Changing Metropolis: Earliest Photographs of London 1839–1879*, Harmondsworth: Penguin Books.

Stedman Jones, Gareth (1983), *Languages of Class: Studies in English Working Class History*, Cambridge: Cambridge University Press.

— (1971), *Outcast London: A Study in the Relationship Between Classes in Victorian Society*, Oxford: Clarendon Press.

Stoneman, Patsy (1996), *Brontë Transformations: The Cultural Dissemination of Jane Eyre and Wuthering Heights*, London: Prentice Hall/ Harvester Wheatsheaf.

Stuchebrukhov, Olga (2005), 'The "Nation-less" State of Great Britain and the Nation-State of France in *Household Words*', *Victorian Periodicals Review,* 38: 4, 392–413.

Swift, Roger, and Sheridan Gilley (eds) (2011), *Irish Identities in Victorian Britain*, London and New York: Routledge.

— (eds) (1985), *The Irish in the Victorian City*, London, Sydney and Dover, NH: Croom Helm.

Tambling, Jeremy (2012), 'Dickens, Benjamin and the City: The "Object Riddled with Error"', *Dickens Quarterly*, 29: 3, Sep., 197–213.

— (1995), *Dickens, Violence and the Modern State: Dreams of the Scaffold*, Basingstoke: Macmillan Press.

— (2009), *Going Astray: Dickens and London*, Harlow: Pearson Education.

Thacker, Andrew (2003), *Moving Through Modernity: Space and Geography in Modernism*, Manchester and New York: Manchester University Press.

Tholfsen, Trygve R. (1977), *Working Class Radicalism in Mid-Victorian England*, New York: Columbia University Press.

Thompson, E. P. (1991), *Customs in Common*, London: Merlin Press.

Thompson, James (2013), *British Political Culture and the Idea of "Public Opinion", 1867–1914*, Cambridge: Cambridge University Press.

Tilley, Heather (2011), 'The Sentimental Touch: Dickens's *Old Curiosity Shop* and the Feeling Reader', *Journal of Victorian Culture*, 16: 2, Aug., 226–41.

Tindall, Gillian (1991), *Countries of The Mind: The Meaning of Place to Writers*, London: Hogarth Press.

Tomalin, Claire (2011), *Charles Dickens: A Life*, London: Viking.

Tucker, Pilgrim (2017), 'The Grenfell Tower Fire was the End Result of a Disdainful Housing Policy', *Guardian*, 20 Jun. <https://www.theguardian.com/commentisfree/2017/jun/20/grenfell-fire-housing-policy-social-housing-tenants> (last accessed 26 Jun. 2017).

Tunbridge, Laura (2006), 'From Count to Chimney Sweep: Byron's "Manfred" in London Theatres', *Music and Letters*, 87: 2, May, 212–36.

Turner, Mark W. (2010), 'Companions, Supplements, and the Proliferation of Print in the 1830s', *Victorian Periodicals Review*, 43: 2, Summer, 119–32.

— (2002), 'Periodical Time in the Nineteenth Century', *Media History*, 8: 2, 183–96.

Tyler, Daniel (ed.) (2013), *Dickens's Style*, Cambridge: Cambridge University Press.

Van Ghent, Dorothy (1950), 'The Dickens World: A View from Todgers's', *The Sewanee Review*, 58, 419–38.

Vernon, James (2014), *Distant Strangers: How Britain Became Modern*, Berkeley and Los Angeles: University of California Press.

Vlock, Deborah (1998), *Dickens, Novel Reading, and the Victorian Popular Theatre*, Cambridge: Cambridge University Press.

Walder, Dennis (2008), 'Introduction', in Charles Dickens, *Dombey and Son*, ed. Alan Horsman, Oxford: Oxford University Press, pp. vii–xxiv.

Watson, Nicola J. (ed.) (2009), *Literary Tourism and Nineteenth-century Culture*, Basingstoke: Palgrave Macmillan.

Weiner, Deborah E. B. (1994), *Architecture and Social Reform in Late-Victorian London*, Manchester and New York: Manchester University Press.

Weinstein, Benjamin (2011), *Liberalism and Local Government in Early Victorian London*, Woodbridge: Royal Historical Society/Boydell Press.

Welsh, Alexander (1986), *The City of Dickens*, Cambridge, MA, and London: Harvard University Press.

— (1977), 'Time and the City in *The Chimes*', *Dickensian*, 73(1): 381, Jan., 8–17.

Werner, Alex, and Tony Williams (2011), *Dickens's Victorian London, 1839–1901*, London: Ebury Press.

White, Jerry (2007), *London in the Nineteenth Century: 'A Human Awful Wonder of God'*, London: Jonathan Cape.

Wilcox, Scott B. (1988), 'Unlimiting the Bounds of Painting', in Ralph Hyde, *Panoramania! The Art and Entertainment of the 'All-Embracing' View*, London: Trefoil Publications in association with Barbican Art Gallery, pp. 13–44.

Williams, Raymond (1973), *The English Novel from Dickens to Lawrence*, London: Chatto and Windus.

Williams Elliott, Dorice (2002), *The Angel out of the House: Philanthropy and Gender in Nineteenth-century England*, Charlottesville and London: University Press of Virginia.

Wilstach, Paul (1902), 'Dramatisations of Dickens', *The Bookman*, 14, Sep. 1901 to Feb. 1902, 52–62.

Wohl, Anthony S. (2002), *The Eternal Slum: Housing and Social Policy in Victorian London*, New Brunswick, NJ, and London: Transaction Publishers.

Wolff, Larry (1996), '"The Boys are Pickpockets, and the Girl is a Prostitute": Gender and Juvenile Criminality in Early Victorian England from *Oliver Twist* to *London Labour*', *New Literary History*, 27: 2, 227–49.

Wolfreys, Julian (2012), *Dickens's London: Perception, Subjectivity and Phenomenal Urban Multiplicity*, Edinburgh: Edinburgh University Press.

— (2006), *The Old Story, With a Difference: Pickwick's Vision*, Columbus: Ohio State University Press.

— (1998), *Writing London: The Trace of the Urban Text from Blake to Dickens*, Basingstoke: Macmillan Press.

Woloch, Alex (2003), *The One Vs. The Many: Minor Characters and the Space of the Protagonist in the Novel*, Princeton and Oxford: Princeton University Press.

Wood, Gillen D'Arcy (2001), *The Shock of the Real: Romanticism and Visual Culture, 1760–1860*, New York and Basingstoke: Palgrave.

Wright, Patrick (2009), *On Living in an Old Country: The National Past in Contemporary Britain*, Oxford: Oxford University Press.

Yelling, J. A. (1986), *Slums and Slum Clearance in Victorian London*, London: Allen and Unwin.

Ziter, Edward (2003), *The Orient on the Victorian Stage*, Cambridge: Cambridge University Press.

Index

CPSIA information can be obtained
at www.ICGtesting.com
Printed in the USA
BVHW061554300620
582685BV00002B/17

9 781474 462730